JONATHAN SWIFT AND IRELAND

OLIVER W. FERGUSON is assistant professor of English at Duke University. He previously taught at the University of Arkansas and The Ohio State University.

Jonathan Swift
AND IRELAND

———————◆———————

OLIVER W. FERGUSON

University of Illinois Press, Urbana, 1962

in memory of my father

ACKNOWLEDGMENTS

———————•◆•———————

I should like, first of all, to acknowledge my obligation to the late Arthur W. Secord, Professor of English at the University of Illinois, who directed my doctoral dissertation on Swift's Irish writings. For his kindness, patience, and guidance, I am in his debt. Much of the research for the dissertation was made possible by the generosity of Rotary International, which awarded me a Foundation Fellowship in 1953-54, for study at University College, London. In England I received valuable suggestions from Professor James A. Sutherland, of University College, London, and Professor Herbert Davis, of Oxford University. During the summer of 1955, I was able, with a postdoctoral fellowship from The Ohio State University, to undertake further research in England and in Ireland. To the donors of these fellowships — and to the Duke University Council on Research — I am grateful.

My indebtedness to various libraries and institutions is also great: the University of Illinois Library; The Ohio State University Library; the Duke University Library; the British Museum; the Goldsmiths' Library of Economic Literature (University of London Library); the Victoria and Albert Museum; the Public Record Office, London; the University Library, Cambridge; the Bodleian Library; the Library of Trinity College, Dublin; the Pearse Street Library, Dublin; the Royal Irish Academy, Dublin; the Royal Dublin Society; Marsh's Library, Dublin; and the National Library of Ireland. It is a pleasure here to acknowledge my debt to the staff of all of these institutions, especially to Mr. William O'Sullivan, Keeper of Manuscripts at Trinity College, Dublin, and to Dr. Richard J. Hayes, Director of the National Library of Ireland. For permission to quote from manuscripts in their respective institutions, I wish to thank the Board of Trinity College, Dublin; the Keeper of Manuscripts at the British Museum; the City Librarian of the Pearse Street Library; and the Controller of H. M. Stationery

Office, for permission to reproduce unpublished Crown copyright material in the Public Record Office, London.

I am grateful to several former and present colleagues for advice and services always willingly rendered: Professor John Harold Wilson, of The Ohio State University; Professor John H. Fisher, of Indiana University; Mr. George E. Dorris, of Rutgers University; Professor Richard W. Van Fossen, of Cornell College; and Professors Carl L. Anderson and George W. Williams, of Duke University. From the beginnings of this study to its completion, I have profited from the counsel of Professors Louis A. Landa, of Princeton University, and Robert W. Rogers, of the University of Illinois. My interest in Swift's Irish career grew out of discussions with Professor Landa eight years ago in London; and he never failed to respond to my frequent demands on his knowledge of Swift and eighteenth-century Ireland. Professor Rogers has read this book in more stages of development than he probably cares to remember; his criticisms and suggestions have been of immeasurable benefit. Two equally long-suffering friends have been Professors Irvin Ehrenpreis, of Indiana University, and Charles B. Wheeler, of The Ohio State University, both of whom have given me more time, aid, and comfort than I had a right to ask.

Finally, I owe a very special debt to Joanne and John and Charles, who also served.

Durham, North Carolina
August, 1961

CONTENTS

ABBREVIATIONS USED IN THE NOTES

Boulter	*Letters Written by His Excellency Hugh Boulter . . . to Several Ministers of State in England* (Dublin, 1770).
Corr	*The Correspondence of Jonathan Swift,* ed. F. Elrington Ball (London, 1910-14).
Coxe	William Coxe, *Memoirs of the Life and Administration of Sir Robert Walpole, Earl of Orford* (London, 1798).
Drapier's Letters	*The Drapier's Letters to the People of Ireland,* ed. Herbert Davis (Oxford, 1935).
Gilbert Collection	Letters (holographs and transcripts) of Irish clergymen in the Gilbert Collection, Pearse Street Library, Dublin (MSS 27 and 28).
Journal to Stella	*Journal to Stella,* ed. Harold Williams (Oxford, 1948).
King Corr	The correspondence of Archbishop William King, at Trinity College, Dublin. Holograph, contemporary copies and transcriptions (by T. Fisher).
Letters to Ford	*The Letters of Jonathan Swift to Charles Ford,* ed. David Nichol Smith (Oxford, 1935).
Poems	*The Poems of Jonathan Swift,* ed. Harold Williams. Second Edition (Oxford, 1958).
Prose Works	*The Prose Works of Jonathan Swift,* ed. Herbert Davis (Oxford, 1939———).
Southwell Papers, B.M., Add. MSS	Correspondence of Edward Southwell in the British Museum.
S.P.D. (P.R.O.)	State Papers Domestic (Public Record Office, London).
T. Scott	*The Prose Works of Jonathan Swift,* ed. Temple Scott (London, 1897-1908).
Teerink	H. Teerink, *A Bibliography of the Writings in Prose and Verse of Jonathan Swift* (The Hague, 1937).

Let Ireland tell, how Wit upheld her cause

(*POPE*, EPISTLE TO AUGUSTUS)

Introduction

A plaque fixed to the south wall of St. Patrick's Cathedral, Dublin, displays — "in large letters, deeply cut, and strongly gilded" — the epitaph which Yeats called the greatest in history:

Hic depositum est Corpus
JONATHAN SWIFT S. T. D.
Hujus Ecclesiæ Cathedralis
Decani,
Ubi sæva Indignatio
Ulterius
Cor lacerare nequit.
Abi Viator
Et imitare, si poteris,
Strenuum pro virili
Libertatis Vindicatorem.

The epitaph, which was written by Swift himself, is best remembered for the lines, "Ubi sæva Indignatio Ulterius Cor lacerare nequit"; Swift's "fierce indignation" has fascinated readers from his day to our own. The concluding statement in the epitaph, however, is of more significance. The way to understanding much of the

I

man, the priest, and the writer lies in the recognition that Swift regarded his life as dedicated to the cause of liberty.

It is probably true, as Maurice Johnson has argued, that the term *libertatis* in the epitaph is intended in a sense that includes, but goes far beyond, political liberty; that Swift saw his career as a long struggle "to free the world from ignorance and error," to liberate man "from the darkness that dwells within."[1] Such an interpretation is perfectly in accord with Swift's conception of his duty as Christian moralist — a duty which he met not only as an Anglican priest but also as the author of *A Tale of a Tub* and *Gulliver's Travels*. Swift did, nevertheless, devote much of his time and his passion to the more limited cause of political liberty; and nowhere did he do so more intensely or more dramatically than in — and in behalf of — his native Ireland.

In this study of Swift's Irish writings, I have tried to show why and how circumstances in the country in which Swift was for so long an unwilling resident compelled him to undertake the cause of Ireland's liberty. His involvement was gradual and reluctant, but it was inevitable; and once he committed himself, he remained for the rest of his life "the Irish Patriot." A part of my purpose has been to justify his right to this title, which was bestowed on him by the Irish of his time but which has been questioned more than once in the two hundred years following his death. Although it was the rights of the Anglo-Irish minority that Swift most often championed, the force, the clarity, and the courage with which he resisted England's Irish policy — and the earnestness with which he tried to alleviate Ireland's domestic problems — amply atone for his limited conception of Irish liberty.

Finally, I have tried to demonstrate that Swift's "fierce indignation" in the end extended to the very people whose rights he so vehemently affirmed. The numerous tracts which Swift addressed to the Irish contain proposals ranging from boycott to bog drainage, but all of them are grounded on his conviction that patriotism is a virtue and a duty. He attempted much for Ireland, but he also demanded much; and he never forgave the nation for failing to respond adequately to his call. Swift himself reviewed his Irish career in his "Verses on the Death of Dr. Swift"; and through a

---

[1] "Swift and 'The Greatest Epitaph in History,'" *Publications of the Modern Language Association*, LXVIII (1953), 824.

persona ("One quite indiff'rent to the Cause") he evaluated his efforts to free the "servile Race in Folly nurs'd":

> He gave the little Wealth he had,
> To build a House for Fools and Mad:
> And shew'd by one satyric Touch,
> No Nation wanted it so much:
> That Kingdom he hath left his Debtor,
> I wish it soon may have a Better.[2]

This epitaph, in both its indignation and its challenge to future patriots to emulate Swift's services for Ireland, anticipated the more profound one in St. Patrick's Cathedral.

---

[2] *Poems,* II, 572.

———•———

CHAPTER I

The "Singular Condition" of Eighteenth-Century Ireland

[1]

Although Jonathan Swift was born in Dublin, his earliest memories must have been associated with England, according to a strange story which he related in his fragmentary autobiography. When he was a year old, his nurse was suddenly called to her home in Whitehaven, and, "being . . . extremely fond of the infant, she stole him on shipboard unknown to his mother . . . and carried him with her to Whitehaven, where he continued for almost three years."[1] A year or so before he wrote the autobiography, Swift had referred to this story in a letter; and he lamented that he had not died, at the age of three, in England.[2]

Swift never hid his feelings about the country of his birth. When he was in London during the four last years of Anne's reign, he protested almost too much his indifference to Irish affairs; and he was equally outspoken about the reward he desired for his activities as apologist for the Tories: "My ambition is to live in England,

---

[1] T. Scott, XI, 376.

[2] *Corr*, VI, 21-22. The exact date of the composition of the autobiography is not known, but a letter from Swift to Pope written in 1739 suggests that the autobiography had been written not long before (see *ibid.*, VI, 126-127, and especially p. 127, n. 2).

and with a competency to support me with honor."[3] Without question, the cruelest disappointment of his life was the reward which, in 1713, the ministry gave him, the deanery of St. Patrick's Cathedral. Before the news of his appointment was confirmed, he wrote to Stella that he could find no joy at the prospect of passing his days in Ireland, and his correspondence after 1714 is filled with complaints of his having been condemned to lifelong exile — "Wretched Dublin, in miserable Ireland" is the heading of one of the letters. After almost a quarter of a century as Dean of St. Patrick's, he was still protesting the accident of birth that had made him (at least in the popular sense) an Irishman: "I happened to be dropped here."[4]

Swift's attitude toward the nation whose history has been called "a mournful series of calamities"[5] is understandable. In seventeenth- and eighteenth-century political allegories, Ireland often appears as England's younger brother or sister; a more accurate designation would have been "unwanted stepchild." In the sixth *Drapier's Letter* Swift described, with only slight exaggeration, "the grossest Suppositions" that the English entertained of the lesser nation: "As to *Ireland,* they know little more than they do of *Mexico;* further than that it is a Country subject to the King of *England,* full of Boggs, inhabited by wild *Irish Papists;* who are kept in Awe by mercenary Troops sent from thence: And their general Opinion is, that it were better for *England* if this whole Island were sunk into the Sea."[6]

But no matter how understandable his reluctance to accept his bitter heritage, Swift was linked by birth, education, and profession to Ireland. He was born in Dublin in 1667. From 1673 until 1682, he attended Kilkenny School, and in 1686 he was awarded the B.A. degree from Trinity College, Dublin. In 1695 he was ordained a priest in the Church of Ireland and given the living of Kilroot, near Belfast. Five years later he received the benefice of Laracor, in the diocese of Meath. His subsequent tenure as Dean of St. Patrick's extended from 1713 to his death in 1745. Swift's

---

[3] *Letters to Ford,* p. 7 (see also *Journal to Stella,* II, 405 and *Corr,* I, 288); *Corr,* I, 254.

[4] *Journal to Stella,* II, 662; *Corr,* III, 287; VI, 21.

[5] Thomas Newenham, *A View of the Natural, Political, and Commercial Circumstances of Ireland* (London, 1809), p. 164.

[6] *Drapier's Letters,* p. 128.

career began and ended in Ireland, and his involvement with that nation's problems was inevitable. It could not have been otherwise with a man of his temperament and convictions. He might detest the country, but he could not ignore it.

[II]

As a Protestant Anglo-Irishman, Swift was a member of a privileged class. The outbreak of the Revolution of 1689 in Ireland had seriously jeopardized the supremacy of the Anglo-Irish (Swift was one of many who fled to England at the beginning of the war), but the collapse of James's cause and the surrender at Limerick in 1691 left them more completely in power than they had ever been. During the Protestant Ascendancy — the period from 1691 to 1800 — the Irish Catholics, who made up the great bulk of the population, were under the absolute control of the Protestant minority.[7] The position occupied by this minority, however, was strong only in comparison with that of the Catholics whom they suppressed, for they were themselves subjected to England's domination.

Though in title a kingdom, eighteenth-century Ireland was in fact virtually an English colony. Almost all important government and ecclesiastical positions were held by English appointees. In addition, a number of minor posts, pensions, and sinecures held by nonresident Englishmen were a constant drain on the nation's economy.[8] The country had its own parliament, but its powers were so curtailed as to make it little more than a rubber stamp for measures enacted in England.[9] Under the terms of Poynings' Law,

---

[7] It is impossible to be certain of the exact proportion of Catholics to Protestants during the Protestant Ascendancy. Estimates vary from 2 to 1 up to 5 to 1 (see W. E. H. Lecky, *A History of Ireland in the Eighteenth Century* [London, 1892], I, 239-240). In *A Modest Proposal*, Swift computed the ratio at 3 to 1 (*Prose Works*, XII, 112).

[8] In 1729, Thomas Prior computed the money sent annually to England in salaries and pensions at £300,000 in *A List of the Absentees of Ireland, and the Yearly Value of Their Estates and Incomes Spent Abroad. With Observations on the Present State and Condition of that Kingdom* (Dublin, 1729). Absentee officials included the lord treasurer, the commissioners of revenue, the auditor-general, the secretary to the lord lieutenant, and the secretary of state. In addition, £40,000 a year was paid to two-thirds of the general officers and one-fourth of the commissioned officers of the army, who resided in England.

[9] T. Scott, I, lxi. For a more detailed treatment of the historical material covered in this chapter, see the following: Lecky; Robert Dunlop, *Ireland from the Earliest Times to the Present Day* (Oxford, 1922); George

an act passed during the reign of Henry VII, the Irish Parliament could not convene without the consent of the King, and it could pass no laws without the approval of the King and the English Privy Council. It was convened and prorogued by the lord lieutenant, acting on orders from England. In session it could submit "Heads of Bills" to England for approval. There the Privy Council could delete, add, or reject as it saw fit. When — and if — the bill was returned to the Irish Parliament, it had to be passed with whatever alterations it had met with in England, or be rejected *in toto*.

Parliament had been infrequently called during the seventeenth century, but after the Revolution of 1689 it was customarily convened every other year — not in the interest of legislation for Ireland, but to pass on money bills to cover the expenses of administration. Government was nominally administered by the lord lieutenant, who was almost always an English nobleman[10] and who was responsible to the executive in London and not the legislature in Dublin. Actually the lords lieutenant did little, for they usually resided in England except when the Irish Parliament was in session. "We know very well," wrote the Drapier, in his fourth *Letter*, "that the Lords Lieutenants for several Years past, have not thought this Kingdom *Worthy the Honour of their Residence,* longer than was absolutely necessary for the King's Business; which consequently *wanted no Speed in the Dispatch.*"[11] During the lord lieutenant's absence, the country's affairs were in the hands of the lords justice, who were appointed with a strict regard for their adherence to England's interests. In 1719, for example, William King, Archbishop of Dublin and a loyal Whig of long standing, was not reappointed a lord justice because of his opposition to the English-inspired Toleration Act of that year.[12]

Although England had thus secured political control of Ireland,

O'Brien, *The Economic History of Ireland in the Eighteenth Century* (Dublin and London, 1918); Alice E. Murray, *A History of the Commercial and Financial Relations Between England and Ireland from the Period of the Restoration* (London, 1903).

[10] Robert Dunlop, "Ireland in the Eighteenth Century," *The Cambridge Modern History* (New York, 1925), VI, 486. The Duke of Ormonde was the only Irish-born vice-regent during the first half of the eighteenth century. He held office in 1703-07 and 1711-12.

[11] *Drapier's Letters*, p. 71.

[12] Sir Charles Simeon King, ed., *A Great Archbishop of Dublin* (London, New York, and Bombay, 1906), p. 218.

she made no serious attempt to interfere in the nation's commercial affairs before the Navigation Acts of the Restoration. The Act of 1660 had accorded Ireland the same status as England by stipulating that goods from America or from outside the British colonial system be imported in either English or Irish ships. It was in 1663 that the first distinction between the colonial trade of England and Ireland was made. The Navigation Act of that year prohibited the exportation of goods to any English colony unless they were loaded in English ships at English ports. This act did not injure Ireland immediately, because horses and victuals from Ireland were excepted from the prohibition, and at the time Ireland had practically no manufactured goods to export. The real threat of the act lay in the conception of Ireland as a colony, a threat that was realized in subsequent Navigation Acts during Charles II's reign which were specifically aimed at Ireland and which added the earlier exceptions to the prohibited list. An even more serious blow to Ireland's economy was the legislation in 1666 which laid prohibitory duties on Irish livestock imported into England. This act destroyed the market which had accounted for three-fourths of the whole trade of Ireland.[13]

This measure, however prejudicial to Ireland's interests, was entirely in England's right; she could legitimately levy duties on her imports as she pleased. After the Revolution of 1689, however, England determined to keep Ireland in a position where she could be no threat to the mother country, politically or economically. In 1691 the English Parliament passed a measure which required all members of the Parliament of Ireland to take an oath disavowing the Doctrine of Transubstantiation, thus barring Catholics from taking seats in Parliament. Because such a design suited its own purposes, the Irish Parliament — made up mostly of Protestant landowners — acquiesced without protesting England's interference in Ireland's internal affairs.

The full effect of this voluntary submission was not felt until 1699. In that year, to protect her own manufacture from Irish competition, England passed an act which absolutely prohibited Ireland from exporting her woolen goods to any country and which permitted the exportation of unworked wool to only a few specified English ports, under conditions which gave England a virtual

[13] Murray, p. 31.

monopoly in Irish raw wool.[14] This act was passed directly by the English Parliament and was the full expression of England's conception of Ireland as a subject colony. It set the pattern of England's exploitation of Ireland for the next hundred years — a pattern broad in its application but simple in its object: the maximum utilization of Ireland's resources for England's profit. Thus an English parliament in 1699 could cripple the Irish woolen industry to benefit English weavers; and thus an English king in 1722 could sacrifice a whole nation "meerly to put an Hundred thousand Pounds into the Pocket of a *Sharper.*"[15]

The Woolen Act practically destroyed Ireland's most flourishing industry. Thousands of weavers left the country, and thousands more remained to starve in Ireland. The only uses to which Ireland could put her abundant wool were to turn it into home markets and to smuggle it to the Continent. The first of these outlets was impeded by English competition: By the unscrupulous use of Poynings' Law, England prevented Ireland from levying protective duties on English goods. The second did yield some profit (in 1720 Swift credited the illegal trade as being Ireland's "only Support

---

[14] For a recent discussion of the events leading to the passing of the Woolen Act, see H. F. Kearney, "The Political Background to English Mercantilism, 1695-1700," *The Economic History Review* (second ser.), XI (1959), 484-496. Mr. Kearney is concerned chiefly with showing the political, as distinct from the economic, motives behind the act. The Tories, under the leadership of Sir Edward Seymour, backed the demands of English woolen interests to restrict the woolen industry in Ireland to domestic consumption. The Tory strategy was to use this issue to embarrass William III by forcing him to choose between his interests in England and in Ireland. This purely political motive, Kearney concludes, makes the Irish Woolen Act "mercantilist with a difference" — that is, commercial interests were determining national policy, and not vice versa (pp. 495-496). This is quite correct, if one remembers (as does Kearney) that the motivation was not exclusively political and that the jealousy of English woolen producers was an important, indeed the initiating, factor in the act. The fact of the matter is that eighteenth-century Ireland was a political and an economic pawn for English statesmen and businessmen. As for Kearney's statement that the Woolen Act was "unwelcome to the English government [that is, the executive as distinct from the legislative branch] and so far from being an example of the way in which the state controlled commerce it showed how commercial interests control state policy" (p. 495), the circumstances of its passage illustrate the growing power of Parliament over the Crown in the eighteenth century. The Irish were quick to recognize that the real threat to their prosperity was from the English ministry and not the Crown.

[15] *Drapier's Letters*, p. 72.

for several Years past"),[16] but it was undistributed, the bulk of the peasantry having been displaced so that their farms could be turned into grazing lands; and before the middle of the eighteenth century, France, the chief customer in the clandestine trade, was paying Ireland in claret, brandy, and silks instead of in badly needed specie.[17] This precarious commerce, the provision trade with the Continent, and a linen industry in its infancy,[18] were almost the only sources of Ireland's income during the first half of the eighteenth century.

Such interference with Ireland's economy was in accord with accepted mercantilist theory of the time. England presumed the right to advance her own interest at the expense of her colonies by a thorough control of imports and exports to maintain a balance of trade favorable to herself. "[Where] the Trade of *Ireland* comes to interfere with any main branches of the Trade of *England* . . . the encouragement of such Trade ought to . . . give way to the Interest of Trade in *England*." So wrote Sir William Temple in his *Essay upon the Advancement of Trade in Ireland* (1673). He felt no awkwardness, apparently, in applying mercantilist colonial policy to a kingdom. His *Essay* shows that he recognized the dangers of an utterly impoverished Ireland; as such, she was England's "weak side." But her prosperity should be carefully regulated: "Some branches of Trade ought not wholly to be supprest, but rather so far admitted as may serve the general consumption of this Kingdom, lest by too great an importation of Commodities, though out of *England* it self, the Money of this Kingdom happen to be drawn away in such a degree, as not to leave a stock sufficient for turning the Trade at home."[19]

Temple did not approve of the Cattle Act of 1666, but his opposition was owing primarily to his concern for England. The Irish trade with the Continent in beef, hides, and butter had risen sharply with the closing of English ports to Irish livestock. This hurt England not only by the direct competition with the English cattle

---

[16] *Prose Works,* IX, 15.

[17] O'Brien, p. 187; and see T. Scott, VII, 161-162.

[18] Although England had agreed to encourage the linen industry to recompense Ireland for the loss of the woolen trade, she did little enough to keep her bargain (see O'Brien, pp. 193ff.). Swift called the industry "casual, corrupted, and at Mercy" (*Prose Works,* XII, 10).

[19] Sir William Temple, *An Essay upon the Advancement of Trade in Ireland,* from *Miscellanea,* second ed. (London, 1681), pp. 111-112.

trade on the Continent, but also by causing Ireland to buy more manufactured goods from her new continental markets than from England.[20] In his zeal to regulate Ireland's trade to England's advantage, Temple came close to anticipating the Woolen Act of 1699. Noting with concern the flourishing state of the Irish woolen industry, he warned against giving it further encouragement. His reasons for fearing any further developments in the industry are typical of the English attitude toward Ireland that was to be responsible for so much of the repressive legislation during the succeeding century. First, following accepted mercantilist doctrine, he opposed a free market for Irish wool because it would "give so great a damp to the Trade of *England*." Second, he feared a prosperous woolen trade for Ireland because "thereby the present Riches of this Kingdom would be mightily encreased, and great advantages might be made by the connivance of Governours."[21] In other words, a too prosperous Ireland might be dangerous to England.

It would have been difficult enough for Ireland to maintain a stable economy under these external restraints; as it was, internal conditions — partly the fault of England's interference, partly the fault of the Irish themselves — weakened the country even further. In the face of the restrictions on their wool and cattle, Irish landowners still turned the largest part of their lands into grazing. Swift labelled this policy "an Absurdity, that a *wild Indian* would be ashamed of,"[22] but the landlords' motives were selfish rather than absurd. In addition to the illegal wool trade with France, there was the lucrative — and legal — trade in cattle with every country in the world except Great Britain. Also, it was less expensive to manage grazing lands than to operate tillage on a comparable scale. Enclosures and drainage were unnecessary; a grazier's hut was cheaper to build and maintain than a good farmhouse; fewer tenants were needed to manage pasture lands than to cultivate large farms — a point Swift noted when he ironically proposed that the whole of Ireland be depopulated and turned into one vast grazing land for England's benefit.[23] As a result of the landlords' policy, the bulk of the people were not only deprived of any adequate share of the country's income, but also, as more and more land

---

[20] *Ibid.*, pp. 128-130.   [21] *Ibid.*, p. 113.   [22] *Prose Works*, XII, 18.
[23] *Ibid.*, XII, 173-178.

was turned from tillage to pasture, many tenants were dispossessed.[24]
And because of the scarcity of arable land, it was necessary to
import grain from England, an added burden because of Ireland's
dwindling stock of money.

 One of the most serious evils that plagued Ireland's agriculture
was absenteeism. In 1725, Swift computed that absentees drew off
annually one-third of the rents yielded by Irish lands.[25] Many of
the landowners were Englishmen who had been given their estates
out of confiscations following the Civil War or the Revolution;
others were English speculators who had bought Irish land during
the sales of forfeited estates. Neither group was likely to reside
in Ireland. And during the early decades of the eighteenth century,
an increasing number of landlords from older Anglo-Irish families
deserted their country for London, lured there by the higher standard of living and the attractions of the capital. In addition to
draining Ireland's money into England, this widespread absenteeism
led to a system of land tenure that was ruinous to the peasantry.
To avoid the responsibilities of managing their estates from England, many of the absentees let large tracts of land for life or for
a term of nine hundred and ninety-nine years. In time, as the value
of land rose, the original tenants became landlords themselves —
"middlemen," as they were called — and sublet at a profit. The
lands were usually extensive enough for the sublessees to continue
the process with each increase in the value of the land. The Irish
tenant at the bottom of this descending scale of middlemen, the
laborer who actually lived on the land, felt the accumulated weight
of as many as three or four intervening transactions, and in consequence he paid, or contracted to pay, exorbitant rents. To realize
the last penny of profit, the middleman let small tracts of land at

[24] Archbishop King wrote to Swift in 1712, "I doubt not, but you hear of
[the] vile practice of houghing and destroying cattle, that is spread in
several counties: several thousand sheep and bullocks have been thus
destroyed. . . . The pretence is this; lands of late have been raised mightily
in their rates, and the poor people not being able to pay when demanded
are turned out of their farms, and one man stocks as many as ten, twenty,
or perhaps a hundred inhabited. . . . The land will yield a great deal
more when there is found only a shepherd or cowherd to pay out of it,
than it can yield when some inhabitants are first to be fed out of it. This
turning the poor people to grazing has made them desperate, and they
everywhere endeavour to destroy whole stocks of cattle, that they may get
land to plough at the former rate" (*Corr,* I, 318).
[25] *Drapier's Letters,* p. 156.

very short terms and when the leases expired, auctioned them to the highest bidder. The tenant thus had no assurance of continuing on the land and consequently felt no obligation to improve it during his residence; indeed, any improvements he made would raise the value of the farm and practically insure his not being able to renew his lease at the higher rent.

This system was ultimately injurious to the landlord as well as to the tenant, for it encouraged irresponsibility in the men who farmed his land. By getting a lease at extravagant terms that he never intended to fulfill, the impecunious laborer could always compete successfully at an auction with an honest, relatively solvent farmer. And since the terms he entered into to get his lease were so high that they could never be discharged, he produced only enough to allow him to pay his landlord the pittance that would maintain his uncertain tenure; the more he produced, the more would be liable to seizure by the landlord. At the expiration of his lease, he would either be outbid by someone who offered terms more outrageously high than his own, or he would be given a renewed tenure because his debt was so large that his landlord could not afford to let him go.[26] Thus the very class of workers who could have effected a real agricultural reform were for the most part never given the chance to do so; and the men who were given the leases deliberately debased agricultural standards. The indifference of the landlords to the whole system of land rentals was probably a more damaging effect of absenteeism, in the long run, than the immediate and obvious ones; for the absentee landlord deprived Ireland not only of the income so desperately needed, but also of the guidance and stability of an educated, wealthy class residing on the land and overseeing its development and improvement.

As long as Ireland remained under the political control of England, her natural economic development was certain to be restricted. She could, however, have mitigated some of her internal problems. Residence of landlords would have been one way. Another would have been for the Irish people to present a common front of unity and coöperation. Such a common front, however, was impossible. "We have just Religion enough," Swift once wrote, among other "moral and diverting" sententiae, "to make us *hate*, but not enough

---

[26] M. Longfield, "The Tenure of Land in Ireland," *Systems of Land Tenure in Various Countries,* ed. J. W. Probyn (London, 1881), pp. 16-17.

to make us *love* one another."[27] The truth of this aphorism is woefully demonstrated in Ireland's history. ⋌

Ireland was divided into three bitterly opposed religious factions. The major cleavage found Protestant dissenters and members of the established church on one side and the Catholics on the other. After the surrender of Limerick, the Protestant landowners pushed through Parliament a set of vicious penal laws to keep the Catholics disorganized and dispirited. There was religious hatred enough in the spirit that produced these laws, but the dominant motives behind them were economic and political. The Attainder Act passed by James's Irish Parliament in 1689 provided for an almost complete resettlement of Ireland in favor of the Catholics.[28] All acts of this Parliament were of course declared void after the defeat of James's army, but the Irish Protestants remembered their narrow escape and were determined that the Catholics would never again be a threat to their security. William III was not eager to penalize the Catholics merely because of their religion; consequently, the Treaty of Limerick, drawn up largely under his direction, was not unduly severe. The civil articles of the treaty would have allowed the Catholics to retain the religious and civil rights they had enjoyed under Charles II. The idea of anything more than a bare toleration, however, was repugnant to the Irish Protestants whose estates had been endangered during the Revolution. For this reason, the Irish Parliament refused, in 1697, to confirm this part of the treaty. In order to gain permission from England to pass the anti-Catholic legislation that they desired, they surrendered their hitherto tenaciously held right to originate money bills. The result of this barter was the penal laws. Their object was not simply to suppress a religion; it was to obliterate an entire culture. Every facet of this culture—economic, religious, humanistic, social—was affected. ⋋ Under the penal laws, Catholics were forbidden to hold Crown offices or to practice law; if engaged in trade, they could hire only two apprentices, and they were excluded from the guilds. They could not purchase land or take a lease for longer than thirty-one years. The few who had kept their estates after the Revolution could not bequeath them to the eldest sons, but instead had to

---

[27] *Prose Works*, I, 241.

[28] J. G. Simms, *The Williamite Confiscation in Ireland, 1690-1703* (London, 1956), p. 22.

divide the lands into small farms among all their children; and they were at the mercy of any member of their families, who, by joining the established church, could deprive the Catholic head of the house of all but a life interest in his estate. They could not send their children to a seminary, either at home or abroad, but had to entrust their education to the care of Protestant schools. They could not possess or carry arms — either the squire's fowling piece or the gentleman's small sword. They could not own a horse valued at over £5 (a Protestant, seeing a horse he liked, could give its Catholic owner £5 and take it for his own). In 1691 the English Parliament had deprived them of the right to sit in Parliament; in 1727 the Irish Parliament took away the elective franchise.

There were strict regulations against the priesthood. All archbishops, bishops, deans, and vicars-general were ordered to leave the country; any remaining or returning were subject to the penalties of high treason — hanging and quartering. The inferior clergy could celebrate mass only if they were registered with the government. Unregistered priests faced transportation; if they returned to Ireland, they could be hanged. And to register, a priest was obliged to take the Oath of Abjuration, declaring that James II had "no right or title whatsoever" to the crown — not a sentiment for a sincere Catholic to profess easily. The record of the nonjurors in England shows that even some Protestants had difficulty in reconciling the oath with their convictions.

The penal laws actually on the statute books bordered on the grotesque, but a projected measure of 1719 went beyond all bounds. The House of Commons passed an act providing that all unregistered priests who were first offenders be branded on the cheek ("with a large P") ; the Irish Privy Council submitted it to England, with the refinement that instead of branding, the penalty be castration. This was too much even for English apathy, and for probably the only time since the seventeenth century, Poynings' Law was put to good use. The English Privy Council — with a show of mercy much like that of the King of Lilliput to Gulliver — rejected the substituted penalty in favor of branding. On its return to Ireland for final passage, the bill was thrown out altogether by the Lords, not because of any humanitarian promptings, but because of a technicality involving Catholic leases.[29]

---

[29] The foregoing discussion of the penal laws is based on Lecky, I, 136-163.

Those laws threatening the Catholic clergy with banishment or death were probably rarely applied during the eighteenth century; but — contrary to some later apologists — the disabling statutes were enforced as rigidly as possible,[30] and the system which Burke described as "a machine of wise and elaborate contrivance; and as well fitted for the oppression, impoverishment, and degradation of a people, and the debasement, in them, of human nature itself, as ever proceeded from the perverted ingenuity of man," accomplished its purpose with a terrible thoroughness.[31] It did not take very long. By 1703, Catholics owned only 14 per cent of the land, as contrasted to the 59 per cent in their possession in 1641. Their legal status was succinctly defined by John Bowes, Lord Chancellor of Ireland around the middle of the century: "The law does not suppose," he declared, "any such person to exist as an Irish Roman Catholic." In 1709, Swift could write of them with an easy callousness, "We look upon them to be altogether as inconsiderable as the Women and Children."[32]

In the oppression of the Catholics, the members of the established church and the Protestant dissenters were in full agreement, but in all else they were divided. The most important group of Irish dissenters, in number and influence, were the Ulster Presbyterians. Although they were too well established to be denied a practical toleration, they were not legally granted the same status with dissenters in England until the Toleration Act of 1719; and the Sacramental Test Act (passed in 1704 and not repealed until 1780) excluded them from civil and military posts.[33] The attitude of the Presbyterians toward this act was characteristic of the benighted policy of vindictiveness and fear that made Ireland such an easy prey to English exploitation during the Protestant Ascendancy. The Test clause was tacked to a new set of disabling laws against the

---

[30] Edmund Curtis, *A History of Ireland* (London, 1957), pp. 285-287.

[31] The quotation is from Burke's *Letter to Sir Hercules Langrishe* (see *The Works of Edmund Burke* [Bohn's Standard Library, London, 1896], III, 343).

[32] Simms, p. 195; quoted by Lecky, I, 146; *Prose Works*, II, 120.

[33] The terms of the Irish Test Act were almost identical with those imposed on English dissenters; but, as J. C. Beckett argues, the Test could not have affected all, or even most, of those Presbyterians who held minor posts. It disabled the dissenters most seriously in barring them from the municipal corporations (see *Protestant Dissent in Ireland, 1687-1780* [London, 1948], pp. 48-49).

Catholics, and although the Presbyterians were naturally opposed to the rider, they were willing to submit to it in order more thoroughly to suppress the Catholics.[34]

A great many members of the established church disapproved of the dissenters on doctrinal grounds, but the deeper reason for the church's inveterate hostility to them was fear. The Irish Presbyterians were on a different footing from dissenters in England, who were divided into various splinter sects and scattered throughout the kingdom. Because of the Scottish migration to Ulster in the seventeenth century, the Presbyterians were settled in one part of the country. Their common origin, doctrine, and locale gave them a position much stronger than that of dissenters in England. In total number the Ulster Presbyterians almost equalled conforming communicants throughout Ireland, and in their stronghold of Londonderry they greatly outnumbered them. Here they were in effect the "national church," and they met in open assembly and built new chapels in defiance of the Church of Ireland. The established clergy quite naturally took every means to check this threat to their privileged status, and they were supported by most of the lay members of Parliament, whose opposition to dissenters was largely dictated by economic motives. The majority of the landlords had been harmed by the effects of the Woolen Act, and they feared and envied the growing financial power of the Ulster Presbyterians, whose linen industry was developing, however slowly, unchecked by England.[35]

This combination of secular and ecclesiastical opposition was sufficient to deprive Protestant dissenters of rights enjoyed by members of the Church of Ireland. What few benefits the dissenters received during the first half of the eighteenth century were initiated by the English Whigs, who felt that the only division in

---

[34] On February 19, 1704, Edward Southwell, Secretary of State, wrote to the Earl of Nottingham, who had tacked the Test Clause to the Popery Bill: "The R. Catholicks have desired to be heard agst. the Popery Bill. . . . When first the newes came of the Sacramental Test being added, there was some noise made by the Dissenters: and som . . . endeavour'd to try what strength there might be in the House to favour the taking it out: But they mett so little encouragement, and even those gentlemen were so sensible of the great advantages occuring by the Bill for suppressing the Popish Interest, that they have almost declined any farther talk about it" (*S.P.D.* [P.R.O.] 63/364).

[35] Beckett, pp. 14-17, 38.

Ireland should be between Protestant and Catholic and that a common accord should exist among all Irish Protestants. The leaders of the Church of Ireland, however, knew that in the event of any conflict with the Catholics, self-preservation would compel the Presbyterians to support the Protestant interest, as they had done in 1689. As practical politicians, therefore, the established clergy were unwilling to pay for services that could be freely secured, and they were strong enough in the Irish Lords to block any English maneuvers to relieve dissenters. The English ministry could have acted directly by exercising England's claim to legislate for Ireland, but they were not willing to arouse the Irish Parliament and thereby endanger more important bills — especially the voting of supplies for the civil establishment. Consequently, they had to be content with the small gains they could achieve indirectly, by influencing members of the Irish Parliament to pass measures that would make the condition of the dissenters somewhat easier (bills such as the Toleration Act) and by trying to mitigate the execution of the disabling acts already passed.[36]

Coöperation in Ireland's common cause was made virtually impossible not only by religious differences but also by the conflicting attitudes toward England of three distinct groups, termed by contemporaries and later historians the native interest, the English interest, and the Irish interest. The native interest was made up of the Gaelic Catholic population. They were, as Swift described them, "Hewers of Wood and Drawers of Water," without leaders or discipline.[37] They were, of course, opposed to the English government which maintained the minority that victimized them. The English interest — the most powerful of the three groups — was represented by Dublin officialdom, mostly English appointees and the Anglo-Irish supporters of England's policies. The native and the English interests had completely opposite attitudes toward England. To the native interest, England was the conqueror and the despoiler; to the English interest, she was the mother country to whom they owed their security and their power. A position somewhere between these extremes was maintained by the Irish interest, a group of Anglo-Irish Protestants who acknowledged England's sovereignty over Ireland but who refused to submit without protest to the economic and legislative restrictions imposed on them

---

[36] *Ibid.*, pp. 18-19.   [37] *Prose Works*, II, 120.

by the English Parliament. In their struggle against these restrictions, the Irish interest became the only organized opposition to England's Irish policy during the Protestant Ascendancy.

This opposition was founded on the theory that Ireland was dependent on the Crown of England, but not the Parliament, and that the descendants of the original English settlers of Ireland had equal rights with their fellow subjects in England. Hence, the interference of the English Parliament in Irish affairs was an encroachment not only on the King's prerogative but also upon the rights of Englishmen in Ireland. The *locus classicus* for this conception of the status of the Anglo-Irish is William Molyneux's *The Case of Ireland's Being Bound by Acts of Parliament in England*, published in 1698.[38] Molyneux, already an eminent figure in Dublin as a philosopher, mathematician, and member of Parliament for the university, was moved to determine *"how far the Parliament of* England *may think it Reasonable to intermeddle with the Affairs of* Ireland" by two events, both affecting the jurisdiction of the Irish Parliament. In 1692, William King, Bishop of Derry (later Archbishop of Dublin), brought suit against the Irish Society, the proprietors of large holdings in his diocese, to prevent their leasing

---

[38] Molyneux was not the first statesman to claim legislative independence for Ireland, but he was easily the best known before Grattan. *The Case of Ireland* was the first and most outspoken expression of the concept during the Protestant Ascendancy, when the status of the Irish Parliament was under severe attack. In the reigns of Henry IV, Henry V, and Henry VI, the question of legislative jurisdiction in Ireland was disputed by the Parliaments of England and Ireland, and in 1641 the Irish Commons asserted their independence of the English Parliament, a claim that was reaffirmed the following year by the Confederate Catholics of Ireland (see J. T. Ball, *Historical Review of the Legislative Systems Operative in Ireland, from the Invasion of Henry the Second to the Union* [London and Dublin, 1888], pp. 16-17; and Charles H. McIlwain, *The American Revolution* [New York, 1923], pp. 29-45, *passim*). An important precursor of *The Case of Ireland* (and one which Molyneux almost certainly made use of) was *A Declaration Setting Forth How, and by What Means, the Laws and Statutes of England, from Time to Time, Came to Be of Force in Ireland*, an anonymous treatise that circulated widely in manuscript during the 1640's. It claimed that *"Ireland* is a free and distinct kingdom of itself . . . and the King's Majesty, is supreme head of the body politick of *Ireland*, and . . . the Parliament of *England* hath no more jurisdiction in *Ireland*, than it hath in *Scotland"* (quoted by McIlwaine, pp. 36-37). Molyneux was also indebted to the work of Sir William Domville, who in 1660 wrote a treatise asserting Ireland's legislative independence (see Caroline Robbins, *The Eighteenth-Century Commonwealthman* [Cambridge, Mass., 1959], p. 140).

land to Presbyterians. The Irish Lords found in favor of the bishop, but in 1698 their decision was overruled by the House of Lords in England.[39] In the same year, the proposed Woolen Act was in debate in the English Commons. This "present Juncture of Affairs, when the Business of *Ireland* . . . [was] under the Consideration of both Houses of the English Parliament," occasioned *The Case of Ireland*.[40]

The Case of Ireland is an answer to England's claim of legislative supremacy over Ireland. It is a dispassionate examination of Ireland's status during five hundred years of relations with England; its argument is largely historical, based on scores of precedents. Beginning with Henry II's expedition to Ireland in 1171, Molyneux showed that it could not properly be termed a conquest because Henry was met with "an Intire and Voluntary Submission of all the Ecclesiastical and Civil States of *Ireland*. . . . Where there is no Opposition, *such a Conquest* can take no place."[41] Nor was Ireland an English colony, for in his donation of Ireland to John, Henry proclaimed the country a *"Separate* and *Distinct Kingdom";* only after John became King of England and Ireland was it annexed to England under the same ruler. Ireland's constitution, acts of the English Parliament, the English monarch's title as King of England and Ireland, all refuted the current claim of colonial status.[42] On the question of the Anglo-Irish, Molyneux argued that the first English settlers had been regarded as English subjects, their rights guaranteed by Henry II.[43] Consequently, their descendants had the same rights, as had Englishmen of subsequent migrations. The constitutional validity of Molyneux's argument is debatable.[44] Its real strength is the unequivocal assertion of the rights of the subject under a constitutional monarchy. Molyneux was a friend of Locke, whose influence on *The Case of Ireland* is apparent. "How justly," Molyneux wrote to him, "England can

---

[39] *A Great Archbishop*, pp. 35-36.

[40] William Molyneux, *The Case of Ireland's Being Bound by Acts of Parliament in England* (Dublin, 1698), pp. 2-3; and see also Robbins, p. 139.

[41] Molyneux, p. 13.　　[42] *Ibid.*, pp. 39-41, 148-149.　　[43] *Ibid.*, pp. 37-38.

[44] G. M. Trevelyan argues that Ireland was actually conquered by England in 1689 and that her constitution was based on that conquest (*England Under Queen Anne* [London, 1936], III, 170). Murray, O'Brien, and Lecky all deny the constitutionality of England's claim to legislate for Ireland.

bind us without our *consent* and *representatives,* I leave to the author of the two treatises of government to consider."[45]

Molyneux's protest failed in its purpose. The English Parliament declared *The Case of Ireland* seditious (legend has it that it was burned by the common hangman)[46] and the year after its publication passed the act restricting Irish wool. But Molyneux had begun a protest that the Irish interest was to echo throughout the century. His book had a persistent hold on the Irish for a hundred years after it was written. It had many reprintings during the eighteenth century (one at the time of Wood's halfpence); it supplied the major theme of the *Drapier's Letters;* Swift and Grattan made it the foundation of their argument for Ireland's legislative independence.

During the stormy years of Swift's intervention in Irish politics, the Irish interest had capable leaders in Parliament. One of the most outspoken was Robert Molesworth, created Viscount Molesworth in 1719. A member of the Parliaments of England and Ireland for some thirty years, Molesworth was extremely influential among the liberal Whigs. He had been a friend of Molyneux, and his reputation as a defender of Ireland's rights is attested by the fact that Swift dedicated the fifth *Drapier's Letter* to him.[47] Among the spiritual peers, William King, "the most famous archbishop Dublin has ever possessed,"[48] was the acknowledged leader of the Irish interest; he was aided by his brother prelates Edward Synge, Archbishop of Tuam; John Stearne, Bishop of Clogher; and Theophilus Bolton, Bishop of Clonfert. After 1720, the unofficial spokesman for the Irish interest was Swift. As this roster indicates, allegiance to Ireland's cause cut across the party lines of Whig and Tory. It is true that during Oxford's ministry of 1710-14 the fear of Jacobitism had made Ireland violently anti-Tory,[49] but as the

---

[45] *Some Familiar Letters Between Mr. Locke, and Several of His Friends* (London, 1708), p. 263. The letter was written in March, after Molyneux had finished *The Case of Ireland.*

[46] See the article on Molyneux in the *Dictionary of National Biography.*

[47] For an account of Molesworth's career, see Robbins, pp. 91-133.

[48] G. T. Stokes, *Some Worthies of the Irish Church* (quoted in *A Great Archbishop,* p. vii).

[49] Archbishop King wrote to Swift in 1711, "I believe the generality of the citizens and gentlemen of Ireland are looked on as friends to the Whiggish interest. But it is only so far as to keep out the Pretender, whom

threat of the Pretender lessened and the new Whig ministry showed an increasing indifference to Ireland's welfare, supporters of the Irish interest forgot party distinctions. The group became increasingly articulate during the 1720's, and, if not a deterrent, was at least an almost constant embarrassment to the ministry's Irish policy.

The effectiveness of the Irish interest, however, was seriously impaired by their inability and their unwillingness to speak for all of Ireland. A minority whose very existence depended upon English power, they upheld through necessity and conviction the *de facto* rule of the Protestant Ascendancy. Most of them regarded the Irish Catholics — the "mere Irish," as they were called — as a conquered people and approved of the penal laws; and most of them, as members of the established church, were uncompromising in their attitude toward the Protestant dissenters (Molesworth was a notable exception).[50] It is ironic that the Irish interest were in a very real sense trapped by their loyalty to the established ecclesiastical and secular order, for that order made possible, if not inevitable, many of the ills which they sought to redress.

[III]

The compound of self-interest and folly, bigotry and conflicting alliances in the Ireland that Swift knew created a combination of conditions and problems unparalleled in any other country. As Swift became more and more involved in Irish affairs, the theme of Ireland's uniqueness among nations recurred with almost predictable regularity in his writings: Ireland was "the only Kingdom I ever heard or read of, either in ancient or modern Story, which was denied the Liberty of exporting their native Commodities and Manufactures, wherever they pleased." It was "the first imperial

---

they mortally fear . . . and so many . . . papers have been spread here . . . to persuade them that the Tories design to bring him in, that it is no wonder they are afraid of them" (*Corr*, I, 261-262).

[50] As a friend of such men as Toland, Wharton, and Godolphin, Molesworth had no sympathy with high church attitudes toward dissenters. In 1713, he became involved in a quarrel with the Irish Lords and the lower house of Convocation which cost him his place on the Privy Council. Swift may have influenced Oxford's decision to remove Molesworth from the Council. He was certainly interested in the controversy, and he made it a part of his own quarrel with Richard Steele. *The Public Spirit of the Whigs* contains an attack on Steele for his *Englishman* of Jan. 19, 1714, written in support of Molesworth (see *Prose Works*, IV, xxiv-xxviii).

Kingdom, since *Nimrod*, which ever wanted Power, to *Coin* their own *Money.*" The Irish farmers were more wretched "than the *Peasants* in *France*, or the *Vassals* in *Germany* and *Poland.*" The "singular condition" of Ireland, "different from all others upon the face of the Earth," could not be remedied by conventional methods — and one of the last "remedies" that Swift ever proposed was calculated, as he was careful to make clear, *"for this one individual Kingdom of Ireland, and for no other that ever was, is, or I think ever can be upon Earth."*[51]

Swift was not in these passages guilty of hyperbole. The unique dilemma of eighteenth-century Ireland is an incontrovertible fact. Other peoples had been — indeed, were at this time — subjected to political, economic, or religious persecution; but, as a modern historian has expressed it, "In the case of Ireland everything was exaggerated."[52]

For example, although England's restrictions on Irish trade and industry were in accordance with mercantilist principles that were being practiced throughout Europe, these principles operated in Ireland with a difference. For one thing, England's policy was motivated not merely by economic considerations, but also by fear that the Catholics would defect to the Pretender's cause and that the Anglo-Irish, if allowed to prosper, would grow too powerful to control. Hence Ireland was not merely to be treated like a colony whose interests were secondary to the mother country; she was also to be kept poor for political reasons: During the debate on the Woolen Act, a member of the English Commons declared, "It is the interest of . . . this country, that Ireland should be humbled."[53] Furthermore, Ireland had the misfortune to be particularly suited to produce those commodities which most excited the jealousy of English competitors, and her proximity to England insured a more rigid enforcement of commercial restrictions than was possible, for example, in the American colonies. Most important, Ireland's dependent Parliament left her entirely at the mercy of English legislation. An independent nation could defend its markets by levying protective duties and by regulating its own exports. The Irish Parliament, stripped of all real authority by Poynings' Law, could do nothing to protect the country's trade. The restrictive legislation

---

[51] *Ibid.*, XII, 8, 57; IX, 21; XII, 65, 116.
[52] Murray, p. 13.   [53] Quoted by Kearney, p. 490.

of the seventeenth and eighteenth centuries made Ireland in effect a colony; yet she was not accorded the privileges that England gave the American colonies. "Ireland had," in the words of a modern economic historian, "all the disadvantages of both a colony and a foreign country without any of the advantages of either."[54]

Add to her indeterminate constitutional status the conflicting pulls of Catholic, Church of Ireland, and dissenting interests, and the case for Ireland's uniqueness is complete. Religious persecution existed in England and on the Continent, but not as it did in Ireland. Catholics and dissenters in England and Protestants on the Continent were minority groups. In Ireland, a majority was persecuted by a divided minority that was itself persecuted from across St. George's Channel.

In a paper he wrote after some fourteen years of residence in Ireland, Swift conceived a bizarre image to illustrate the basic fallacy in most of the current attempts to improve the country's condition: "Imagine a legislator forming a system for the government of Bedlam, and, proceeding upon the maxim that man is a sociable animal, should draw them out of their cells, and form them into corporations or general assemblies; the consequence might probably be, that they would fall foul on each other, or burn the house over their own heads."[55] Because Ireland was unique among all civilized nations of the world, her desperate malady could not be remedied by the systems of government and economy practiced by other countries. Such systems would be as inappropriate for Ireland as a parliament would be for Bedlam.

---

[54] O'Brien, p. 387.   [55] *Prose Works*, XII, 131.

CHAPTER II

The Injured Lady
and Her Champion

[1]

Swift was almost forty when he wrote his first extant analysis of
Ireland's plight. He had probably been exposed to the principles
of the Irish interest during his years at Trinity College, where
Molyneux's name was still honored,[1] but he left Trinity in 1689 to
become a member of Sir William Temple's household at Moor
Park, and until Temple's death in 1699, Swift spent all but about
three years in England. During this period his own career was too
uncertain to afford him the leisure to speculate on the problems of
Ireland. He had resigned his benefice at Kilroot in 1698, but after
Temple's death, Swift's hopes for preferment in England were at
an end; and he returned to Ireland in 1699 as chaplain to the new
lord justice, the Earl of Berkeley. Through the earl's influence,
he was appointed in 1700 to the vicarage of Laracor (with the
livings of Rathbeggan and Agher attached), and later the same year

---

[1] Swift's tutor at Trinity College was St. George Ashe, who had been a
friend of Molyneux's and with him, in 1683, was one of the founders of the
old Dublin Philosophical Society. Other founding members known to Swift
were William King and Narcissus Marsh, King's predecessor as Archbishop
of Dublin and the founder of Marsh's Library (see George T. Stokes,
Some Worthies of the Irish Church [London, 1900], p. 138).

he was made a prebendary of St. Patrick's Cathedral.[2] In 1701 he returned to England with Berkeley, but from June, 1704, until November, 1707, he was back in Ireland. It was in 1707 that he wrote his first Irish tract, *The Story of the Injured Lady*.

There can be no doubt that Swift's three-year residence in Ireland — his longest uninterrupted stay in the country since his departure from Dublin at the outbreak of the Revolution — was partly responsible for his writing *The Injured Lady*. His intimacy with the Earl of Pembroke, lord lieutenant in 1707, and with Thomas Molyneux, William's brother, may have increased his awareness of Irish politics, although the existing records indicate that this association was rather frivolous than otherwise.[3] A much more likely influence was William King, with whom, as prebendary of St. Patrick's, Swift was closely associated after 1700. The full history of the relationship of Swift and his archbishop is a checkered affair: English politics were to alienate them before they were ultimately reconciled by their common concern for Ireland. At the beginning of Swift's career in the church, the two were on friendly terms, and King must have stimulated Swift's interest in Ireland's problems — both secular and ecclesiastical. Few men in Dublin at the time were better qualified to do so. King was one of the leaders of the Irish interest; his suit against the Irish Society had raised the issue of Ireland's legislative jurisdiction; and he had helped bring Molyneux's *Case of Ireland* to the attention of William III.[4]

---

[2] Louis Landa, *Swift and the Church of Ireland* (Oxford, 1954), p. 27.

[3] John Forster, *The Life of Jonathan Swift* (London, 1875), pp. 191-196. In 1712, Swift wrote to Stella of his acquaintance with Samuel Molyneux, William's son: "His father wrote a book; I suppose you know it" (*Journal to Stella*, II, 567-568).

[4] King Corr, to Francis Annesley, April 16, 1698: "I have at the request of Mr. Molyneux desired you to assist Mr. Tollet . . . to present a book written by him to the King. . . . It concerns the present debates about the Subordination of Ireland to England in point of being obliged by English acts. I did not see it till it was printed off." Although he was willing to oblige Molyneux, in this same letter King expressed his doubts "whether anything of this nature may be seasonable at this time and whether it will not exasperate rather than prevent the mischief that is coming to us." Annesley was King's lawyer and a life-long friend and correspondent. He was a member of both the English and Irish Commons and in 1700 was elected one of the trustees for the sale of Irish estates forfeited by the Act of Resumption (see *A Great Archbishop*, p. 118, n. 1). An account of George Tollet, another of King's regular correspondents, is also in *A Great Archbishop*, pp. 26, 30-31.

Swift's first Irish tract was the slowly maturing result of this association with King and of several years of firsthand observation of Ireland's problems. His immediate incentive to write *The Injured Lady* was the pending legislative union of England and Scotland, which was being negotiated in 1706-07 and was finally effected on May 1, 1707.[5] The union was distasteful to Swift not only because he associated Scotland with dissenters and regicides, but also because it emphasized the unhappy status of Ireland. The Irish Commons had requested a union with England as recently as 1703, but their address had been ignored. England's contrasting attitude toward union with Scotland was a bitter reminder of her intention to keep Ireland in the position of a dependent colony.

The Story of the Injured Lady, in a Letter to Her Friend, with His Answer is an allegory. Swift may have chosen this device because he had used it with such felicity in *A Tale of a Tub,* published three years earlier; at any rate, *The Injured Lady* offers the only example of allegory in all of Swift's Irish tracts, with the exception of a brief passage in the fifth *Drapier's Letter.* In terms of the allegory, the Lady (Ireland) has been ruined and cast off by a Gentleman (England), who is now on the point of marrying the Lady's Rival (Scotland). The Gentleman's behavior puzzles the Lady because her appearance, condition, and fidelity are in every way superior to those of her Rival. Despite her insistence that she is giving "a very just impartial Character" of her Rival and herself, the comparison is obviously invidious.[6] The worst fault to which the Lady admits is the precipitous and warmhearted trust in her lover that led to her ruin; her appearance is "still fair enough," and whatever decline her beauty has suffered has been the result of "Grief and ill Usage." The Rival, on the other hand, has "bad Features, and a worse Complexion"; she is devoid of "Virtue, Honesty, Truth, or Manners"; and her past treatment of the Gen-

---

[5] In his *An Essay upon the Life, Writings, and Character of Dr. Jonathan Swift* (London, 1755), Deane Swift says that the tract "seems to have been written about seven or eight and forty years ago" (p. 205). An article by Godfrey Davies establishes beyond question that *The Injured Lady* was written with reference to the events immediately preceding the union, in May, 1707 (see "Swift's *The Story of the Injured Lady*," *Huntington Library Quarterly,* VI [1943], 473-489). Although written at this time, the tract was not published until 1746.

[6] All quotations from *The Injured Lady* and the *Answer* are from *Prose Works,* IX, 3-12.

tleman has been abominable, at one time leading to a dispute which resulted in his "poor Steward" being "knocked on the Head."

The Lady begins her story by telling how she had become the Gentleman's mistress, "half by Force, and half by Consent." This is probably a more realistic description of Ireland's acquiescence to Henry II than Molyneux's "Intire and Voluntary Submission." Even so, Swift and Molyneux alike regard England's subsequent treatment of Ireland as arbitrary and unconstitutional. Once the Gentleman had won her, the Lady continues, he followed the familiar pattern of successful seducers, "affecting on all Occasions to shew his Authority, and to act like a Conqueror." The Lady bore all his demands with patience: she supplanted her old servants with his favorites and continued to pay the usurpers when, as was generally the case, they quitted her estate to reside with their former master; and she agreed to have the Gentleman's steward manage her estate. With every concession, the Gentleman became more demanding. He ordered the Lady to have her tenants carry their goods "cross the River to his Town-market" (paying toll on both sides), where they sold them at half value. And because they were "a nasty Sort of People, and he could not endure to touch any Thing . . . [they] had a Hand in," they had to send all their products to him "in their Naturals." If a tenant carried "but a Piece of Bread and Cheese to eat by the Way, or an Inch of Worsted to mend his Stockings," his consignment was seized as contraband. The injustice of the economic restraints that England imposed upon Ireland is emphasized by the simplicity of Swift's homely analogy.

The allegory passes from economic to political grievances. The Gentleman has perverted into an instrument of exploitation the old agreement that he and the Lady have the same steward. Poynings' Law was originally conceived as a legislative safeguard to limit the power of ambitious lords lieutenant; it was enacted in 1487 after the Earl of Kildare, who sought to make himself *de facto* ruler of Ireland, forced a subservient Parliament to acknowledge the imposter Simnel King of England.[7] But English legislators of the seventeenth century saw Poynings' Law as a convenient means of furthering their raids on Ireland's resources. To let the Lady continue the story — "Now, the Turn he thinks fit to give this Compact of ours is very extraordinary; for he pretends that what-

---

[7] Dunlop, pp. 57-58.

ever Orders he shall think fit to prescribe for the future in his Family, he may, if he will, compel mine to observe them, without asking my Advice or hearing my Reasons."[8]

With his marriage to the Rival only a few days distant, the Gentleman's rejection of the Lady is complete. Her loyalty has been rewarded with abuse and contempt; she is to be "Semptress to his Grooms and Footmen" (Swift's angry reference to the half-hearted encouragement England was giving Ireland's infant linen industry, as a sop for the loss of her flourishing market in wool). But the Lady still remains loyal. She will have none of the blandishments of other "Offers" (from France and the Pretender); all she asks is "to enjoy a little Quiet, to be free from the Persecutions of this unreasonable Man . . . [to] manage my own little Fortune to the best Advantage."

The *Answer* to the Lady is brief. There is no point in reproaching her with past mistakes; the thing to be settled now is how she can best obtain the "little Quiet" she seeks. Her Friend advises her to call her tenants (the Irish Parliament) together and with them to make the following resolutions:

First. That your Family and Tenants have no Dependence upon the said Gentleman, further than by the old Agreement, which obligeth you to have the same Steward, and to regulate your Household by such Methods as you shall both agree to.

Secondly. That you will not carry your Goods to the Market of his Town, unless you please, nor be hindered from carrying them any where else.

Thirdly. That the Servants you pay Wages to shall live at Home, or forfeit their Places.

Fourthly. That whatever Lease you make to a Tenant, it shall not be in his Power to break it.[9]

The Injured Lady was not published in Swift's lifetime. Just why Swift withheld his tract is impossible to determine. It may be — as one scholar has suggested[10] — that he decided against publishing it because its forthright indictment of England might prejudice

---

[8] Herbert Davis (*Prose Works,* IX, x-xi) thinks this sentence may have been added in 1720, in reference to the Declaratory Act of 1719. However, England's actions in and prior to 1707 were sufficient examples of her arbitrary proceedings in Ireland (see Molyneux, pp. 2-3, 18). It is difficult to believe that Swift would have revised the tract as late as 1720 and still not have printed it.

[9] *Prose Works,* IX, 11.   [10] Davies, p. 484.

the success of negotiations which the Church of Ireland was on the point of opening with England to obtain Queen Anne's Bounty, the remission of the Crown taxes known as the "First Fruits and Twentieth Parts." This favor had been granted the Church of England in 1704, and at the time the Irish clergy had petitioned unsuccessfully for the same benefits. In 1707 they renewed their efforts, and Swift was sent to London to forward the church's application for the Queen's Bounty. The difficulty with this explanation for the suppression of *The Injured Lady* is that the tract was almost certainly written fully six months before the matter of the First Fruits was revived by the church, during the Convocation of which Swift was a member from July to October, 1707.[11] A statement in *The Injured Lady* dates its composition as some time between February and April of that year. Referring to the approaching nuptials of the Gentleman and her Rival, the Lady says, "there is now a Treaty of Marriage concluded between them, the Wedding Cloaths are bought, and nothing remaineth but to perform the Ceremony, which is put off for some Days, because they design it to be a publick Wedding."[12] The Scottish Parliament had agreed to the Articles of Union on January 16, 1707, and the English followed suit the next month; the articles were to go into effect on May 1. The union, therefore, had already become fact before Swift's election to the Irish convocation in July and long before he knew that he would be the church's agent in the business of the First Fruits. His fear of giving offense to the English government at the time he was asking favors of it would explain why *The Injured Lady* was not published after his arrival in London in November, but it does not explain his reluctance to publish it just after it was written. Perhaps Swift was following the advice he had given a friend in 1704: "Choose any subject you please, and write for your private diversion, or by way of trial; but be not hasty to write for the world. Besides, who that has a spirit would write in such a scene as Ireland?"[13]

Although Swift (for whatever reasons) did not publish his first Irish tract, *The Injured Lady* is of value in dating his interest in Irish affairs and in revealing — if only sketchily — the indispensable condition on which were based all the remedies he was later to offer for Ireland's improvement: the moral duty of the Irish people

---

[11] Landa, pp. 50-52.   [12] *Prose Works,* IX, 7.   [13] *Corr,* I, 44.

to do what they could to alleviate their sufferings. The *Answer* to the Lady's grievances is more than a protest. Instead of merely sympathizing with the Lady, the Friend places before her a responsibility: "Get your Tenants together as soon as you can, and make them agree to the following Resolutions." Though greatly wronged, the Lady must act, must help herself to the "little Quiet" she needs to survive ("a small prolongation of life," as Swift later defines this goal). Determined action would certainly mitigate the more pressing of Ireland's ills. It might possibly accomplish even more: If the resolutions of the Lady and her tenants fail to impress the Gentleman, the Friend promises to "think of something else that will be more effectual."[14] Through her common resolve for self-improvement, Ireland would achieve unity — a unity that might insure effective resistance to England's policies in the future.

Finally, *The Injured Lady* is important as evidence of Swift's familiarity, early in his career, with the principles advanced by William Molyneux in 1698. The first of the resolutions which the Friend urges the Lady to adopt is an allegorical statement of Molyneux's conception of Ireland's status as a nation. And one of the Lady's complaints suggests verbal as well as thematic similarities between Swift's tract and *The Case of Ireland*. Speaking of the Gentleman's assumed right to give orders to her people, the Lady says, "This leaveth me at such Confusion and Uncertainty, that my Servants know not when to obey me, and my Tenants, although many of them be very well inclined, seem quite at a Loss." Molyneux makes the same point toward the conclusion of his book: "The People of *Ireland* are left by this Doctrine in the Greatest *Confusion* and *Uncertainty* Imaginable. We are certainly bound to Obey the *Supream Authority* over us; and yet hereby we are not permitted to know *Who* or *What* the same is; whether the *Parliament of England*, or *that of Ireland*, or *Both;* And in what Cases the *One*, and in what the *Other*."[15] Swift probably never knew Molyneux, who died shortly after *The Case of Ireland* was published; but he knew his book and he made use of it in the earliest of his Irish tracts.

A few months after he wrote *The Injured Lady*, Swift was in London negotiating for the remission of the First Fruits. While he was there, an issue arose which not only threatened the success of

---

[14] *Prose Works*, IX, 12.   [15] *Ibid.*, IX, 8-9; Molyneux, p. 171.

his undertaking but also provided another instance of England's unwarranted interference in Ireland's domestic affairs. Toward the end of 1707 the Irish Presbyterians renewed their efforts to have the Sacramental Test Act repealed, and the Irish clergy were especially alarmed because the Whig ministry in England was supporting the dissenters. It soon became evident that the ministry intended to strike a bargain with the Church of Ireland, whose bishops in the Irish Lords could defeat any effort to remove the Test Act: the First Fruits in exchange for votes. In January, 1708, Swift wrote Archbishop King of hints of "a new difficulty" in his mission. In June these hints were confirmed when Godolphin, the Lord Treasurer, told Swift that the Queen's Bounty would be granted only if the Irish bishops made sufficient "acknowledgments."[16]

Even before his interview with Godolphin, Swift had complained to correspondents of the activities of Alan Brodrick, Speaker of the Irish Commons, who was then in London soliciting on behalf of the dissenters. Swift was outraged at Brodrick's suggestion that the ministry could relieve the dissenters by having the Test Act repealed by the English Parliament.[17] In a letter to King, he appeared ready to oppose this move publicly: "unless your Grace would send me your absolute commands to the contrary . . . I should hardly forbear publishing some paper in opposition to it."[18] It was two months before King answered this letter, and his reply made it obvious that he was unwilling to sanction Swift's proposed pamphlet. He did not refer directly to the veiled request for his approval, but his warning that letters were being intercepted at the post office in Dublin and his expressions of confusion as to the proper steps to take next in the matter of the First Fruits ("I find myself in a wood, and do not know but in such a case it is best to stand still till the mist clear") were sufficient indication that he would not give a direct answer to Swift's proposal.[19] Swift accordingly deferred his plans to write against the ministry's designs, for he was reluctant to do anything without his archbishop's permission at this critical juncture in his negotiations for the First Fruits.

For the remainder of the summer and into the fall of 1708, Swift continued his solicitations for the Queen's Bounty. Although his goal seemed more remote daily and although the ministry showed

---

[16] *Corr,* I, 67, 93. [17] *Ibid.,* I, 83. [18] *Ibid.,* I, 88. [19] *Ibid.,* I, 96.

no signs of abandoning their attack on the Test Act, Swift made no
further offers to write a pamphlet. Then, at the end of November,
he was told that his mission had been successful. The Earl of Pembroke was on the point of being replaced as lord lieutenant of
Ireland, but he assured Swift that the order for the remission of
the First Fruits had already been given. Pembroke's tidings were
premature by some two years. The earl had indeed been promised
the grant; but as Swift later wrote to King, there is a "difference
between a grant and the promise of a grant."[20] Swift had begun
to have some uneasy doubts in February; it was not, however,
until March that Pembroke's lame explanation made it perfectly
clear that the First Fruits had not in fact been granted. By that
time, Swift's long-promised pamphlet on the Sacramental Test Act
had been on sale in London for over a month. The erroneous report
that the Irish church had secured the Queen's Bounty removed any
need for reticence on the issue of the Sacramental Test Act, and
Swift was especially eager to enter the controversy at this time,
when it became known that Pembroke's successor as lord lieutenant
was the Earl of Wharton. Wharton's appointment was proof that
the ministry was as determined as ever in its opposition to the Test.
The new lord lieutenant had been one of the strongest advocates
for repeal, and among the many things for which he was notorious
was his ability to persuade, bribe, or intimidate to get what he
wanted.

Wharton made his attitude toward the dissenters and the Test
Act clear when, shortly after his appointment, he named as his
chaplain Ralph Lambert, a Whig clergyman who had recently
preached a violent sermon in support of the Irish dissenters. This
choice was particularly galling to Swift because he had had hopes of
becoming Wharton's chaplain, a position that would greatly enhance his opportunities for advancement in the church. King had
urged him to apply for the post, but he had declined to do so on
the grounds that any direct application would commit him to support — or at least not oppose — the ministry's campaign to repeal
the Test Act.[21] When, therefore, he was passed over and the
chaplaincy was given to a man of Lambert's known sentiments,
Swift's personal disappointment must have been tempered with
relief: With a major assault on the Test Act imminent and (as he

---

[20] *Ibid.*, I, 149.　　[21] *Ibid.*, I, 124, n. 3.

supposed) the First Fruits secured for his church, Swift could at last speak out. On November 30, 1708, he wrote to King and to John Stearne, Dean of St. Patrick's, that the Queen's Bounty had been granted and that Wharton had selected Lambert as his chaplain.[22] Early in January, 1709, there appeared in London *A Letter from a Member of the House of Commons of Ireland to a Member of the House of Commons in England, Concerning the Sacramental Test*. It was dated "Dublin, December the 4th, 1708"; its ostensible author was a member of the Irish Parliament. Swift adopted this persona not merely to protect himself (simple anonymity would have accomplished this), but, more important, to give the *Letter* authority. The argument that both the Commons and the Lords in Dublin were almost unanimously in favor of the Test Act carried conviction when made by a member of the Irish Commons.[23]

A Letter . . . Concerning the Sacramental Test is as much a protest against England's interference in the affairs of Ireland as it is a defense of the Test Act. Almost a year before he wrote the tract, Swift was alarmed that the ministry would follow Brodrick's suggestion to go over the head of the Irish Parliament to repeal the act. Such an action, he wrote, would be of "terrible consequence, both as to the thing and the manner, by the Parliament here interfering in things purely of Ireland, that have no relation to any interest of theirs." This statement is echoed in the *Letter:* The Sacramental Test Act, the Member of Parliament asserts, is "a Matter purely national, that cannot possibly interfere with the Trade and Interest of *England*."[24] After this positive declaration (the word "national" could not have gone unnoticed by English readers), the "author" adopts a tone of heavy irony. The people of Ireland are surprised at England's "wonderful kindness" in working for their interests — so surprised, in fact, that their wonder has got the better of their gratitude.

This shift in tone is inconsistent, but for Swift's purposes the author of the *Letter* need be consistent only in opposing the repeal of the Test Act, especially a repeal passed by the English Parliament. Swift did not want a consistently developed persona; indeed, the less developed the Member of Parliament, the more adaptable he is in Swift's hands. Thus in the short space of four paragraphs

---

[22] *Ibid.,* I, 123-126.   [23] *Prose Works,* II, 118-119.
[24] *Corr,* I, 84; *Prose Works,* II, 112.

the Member of Parliament passes from the angry Irish nationalist, to the disingenuous admirer of England, and finally to the clear-sighted polemicist who perceives that the ministry's real motives for supporting the Irish dissenters are to reward the politically faithful and to prepare the way for "the like *good Work* in *England*." It is in this last pose that he writes with the greatest intensity. The ministry is wrong, he sardonically advises, to be reticent in admitting that England's interests — and not Ireland's — are dictating the agitation to repeal the Test Act: "Whatever Advantage you propose to your selves by repealing the *Sacramental Test,* speak it out plainly, it is the best Argument you can use, for we value your Interest much more than our own. If your little Finger be sore, and you think a Poultice made of our *Vitals* will give it any Ease, speak the Word, and it shall be done; the Interest of our whole Kingdom is, at any Time, ready to strike to that of your poorest *Fishing Town.*"[25]

It is both natural and significant that the author's ironic proposal would sacrifice Ireland's economy as well as her church on the altar of England's expedience. The efforts to abolish the Sacramental Test Act were of a piece with the policy that resulted in the Woolen Act; and such highhanded measures would continue so long as England regarded Ireland as a colony instead of as a sister nation.

Although it could not have improved the church's prospects for gaining the Queen's Bounty, the publication of Swift's *Letter . . . Concerning the Sacramental Test* probably did not harm them; even before its appearance Wharton was determined to do nothing about the First Fruits unless the Irish clergy coöperated with the ministry to remove the Test Act. The *Letter* did, however, have embarrassing consequences for Swift, when, at King's suggestion, he resumed negotiations for the grant, this time with the new lord lieutenant. Despite Swift's efforts to conceal his authorship of the *Letter,* the secret got out and was reported (Swift maintained by Lambert) to Wharton, who heard Swift's representations "with sufficient coldness" and returned him an answer "which amounted to a refusal."[26] At this point Swift realized that he had done all

---

[25] *Ibid.,* II, 113-114. William B. Ewald's interpretation of the role played by the persona is not convincing (see *The Masks of Jonathan Swift* [Cambridge, Mass., 1954], pp. 53-61).

[26] Swift's account of his two interviews with Wharton is in a letter to King (*Corr,* I, 148-149) and in a paper he wrote in 1714, *Memoirs, Relat-*

he could. Three months after the humiliating interview with Wharton, he had embarked for Ireland.

In July, 1709, Swift was back in Dublin, thoroughly dissatisfied with the results of his English sojourn. The affair of the First Fruits was by now regarded as "desperate" (a struggle between the lower house of Convocation and Lambert had deepened the lord lieutenant's hostility toward the Irish clergy),[27] and the Sacramental Test Act was still under fire. In his first speech to the Irish Parliament, Wharton had urged the necessity for unity among the Protestants of Ireland — the necessity, in other words, for the repeal of the Test Act. He reiterated this theme at the end of the session in 1709, a sure indication that the ministry would renew its efforts when Parliament convened the following year. Before the new session of Parliament opened, Swift wrote, but did not publish, another tract intended to strengthen opposition against the repeal. In December, 1709, Alan Brodrick, whose activities to remove the Test Act had so angered Swift two years earlier, had been made chief justice of the Queen's Bench in Ireland. With his removal from the Irish Commons, the House had now to elect a new speaker. The advocates for repeal were supporting John Forster, Recorder of Dublin and Brodrick's protégé,[28] for the office, and Swift was disturbed that the high church party in Commons had not settled on a suitable candidate to oppose Forster. *A Letter to a Member of Parliament in Ireland upon the Chusing a New Speaker There* deplores this indecisiveness and warns of the consequences of electing a speaker who would be hostile to the Test Act.[29] Swift did not publish the tract, either because he realized the futility of his effort or because he did not finish it in time to influence the election. The *Letter* concludes lamely enough to warrant either supposition.

Although Forster was elected speaker of the House of Commons

---

ing to that Change Which Happened in the Queen's Ministry in the Year 1710 (*Prose Works*, VIII, 121).

[27] For an account of the controversy between the lower house of Convocation and Wharton's chaplain, see Landa, pp. 59-60.

[28] F. Elrington Ball, *The Judges in Ireland, 1221-1921* (London, 1926), II, 79.

[29] *Prose Works*, II, 130-131. Swift's claim that he does not know whom the opponents of the Test Act were supporting is disingenuous; such a protest of ignorance was a favorite device of his. The *Letter* was clearly inspired by his fear that Forster would be the new speaker.

when Parliament convened on May 19, 1710, Swift's fears for the Sacramental Test Act proved groundless. The Irish Parliament had remained deaf to all of Wharton's hints, and the ministry was unwilling to take the drastic step of repealing the Test Act through the English Parliament. While the ministry hesitated and Wharton bargained and threatened, a new Tory government, under Robert Harley (later made Earl of Oxford), came into power. Godolphin was dismissed as lord treasurer on August 8, 1710, and the following day Harley was named chancellor of the exchequer (the office of lord treasurer was left vacant until 1711, when it was given to Harley). When the news of these changes reached Ireland in late August, the bishops' hopes for the Queen's Bounty were revived, and once again Swift was chosen to present the church's request to the Crown. He arrived in London on September 7. On October 4, he was granted an interview with Harley, and he was received with "the greatest marks of kindness and esteem." Exactly a month after this first meeting, he wrote to King that Queen Anne had granted the church the First Fruits and Twentieth Parts.[30] This time the report was correct.

Swift's negotiations with Harley affected his fortunes far more profoundly than they did those of the Church of Ireland. The courtesy with which Swift was treated and the ease with which he succeeded in his mission disposed him in favor of the new ministry; and Harley's moderate principles were so in accord with his own that he had no hesitation in accepting Harley's offer "to assert the principles, and justify the proceedings of the new ministers."[31] For the next three years, he was in London as the acknowledged apologist for the Tories.

This new alliance put Swift in the foreground of exciting events, and during the years he edited the Tory paper *The Examiner* and wrote his tract *The Conduct of the Allies,* he had little time to think of Ireland. "If DD were not in Ireland," he wrote to Stella in November, 1711, "I believe seriously I should not think of the place twice a year. Nothing there ever makes the subject of talk in any company where I am." A month earlier he had written to King, "We are so extremely busy here that nothing of Ireland is talked on above a day or two."[32] On one occasion, when the inter-

---

[30] *Corr,* I, 205, 212.   [31] *Prose Works,* VIII, 123.
[32] *Journal to Stella,* II, 405; *Corr,* I, 288. The letters "DD" are Swift's monogram for Stella and her companion, Rebecca Dingley.

ests of the Dublin Corporation clashed with those of the government, Swift adopted almost the tone of the typical English politician. In 1713, a dispute arose between the Tory Lord Chancellor of Ireland, Constantine Phipps, and the Corporation of Dublin over the choice of a mayor. The quarrel grew so noisy that it reached the Irish Parliament, where Phipps was praised in the predominantly Tory upper House and damned as a tyrant and a traitor in Commons, which was in the hands of a Whig majority. Writing to King of the affair, Swift warned, "If your House of Commons should run into any violences disagreeable to us here, it will be of the worst consequences imaginable to that kingdom: for, I know no maxim more strongly maintained at present in our Court, than that her Majesty ought to exert her power to the utmost, upon any uneasinesses given on your side to herself or her servants; neither can I answer, that even the legislative power here may not take cognizance of anything that may pass among you, in opposition to the persons and principles that are now favoured by the Queen."[33]

There are, however, some instances that show Swift's continued interest in Ireland's welfare. In 1712, he reported to Stella that he and the Duke of Ormonde, Wharton's successor as lord lieutenant, had talked "a good deal" about Ireland and that he intended to bring Oxford into the discussion so that the three could come to some conclusions about affairs in that country. The following year he boasted to a friend, "I have done more service to Ireland, and particularly to the Church, than any man of my level."[34] One of the earliest tracts which he wrote in his new role of Tory propagandist is concerned with Ireland's sufferings under Wharton's administration. The former lord lieutenant was regarded by the ministry as a target of prime importance among the displaced Whigs, and he was an especially inviting one to Swift. In the seventeenth number of *The Examiner*, Swift attacked Wharton, portraying him as Verres, the Roman governor of Sicily. The province (which, of course, represents Ireland) "had neither the Benefit of our Laws, nor their own, nor even of Common Right" under Verres' administration, and "in *Sicily*, no Man now possesseth more than what the Governor's Lust and Avarice have overlooked; or what he was forced to neglect out of meer Weariness and Satiety

---

[33] *Ibid.*, II, 79. For a summary of the conflict between Phipps and the corporation, see F. E. Ball, II, 48-50.
[34] *Journal to Stella*, II, 612; *Corr*, II, 76.

of Oppression."[35] Swift continued his attack more openly in *A Short Character of His Excellency Thomas Earl of Wharton* (published shortly after the *Examiner* paper),[36] in which he declared that during Wharton's viceroyalty England had taken a great step "towards finishing the Slavery of that People . . . [who] have for some Time, been distinguished from all her Majesty's Subjects" by arbitrary government and oppression.[37] Although these papers on Wharton's administration were demanded by the exigencies of Tory policy and although the virulence of the *Short Character* was largely owing to Swift's personal animosity, they were written with the conviction and the sense of outrage that characterized the *Letter . . . Concerning the Sacramental Test* and *The Injured Lady*.

On at least one occasion, Swift influenced the ministry in Ireland's behalf. In the first of his tracts published after he returned to Ireland in 1714 as Dean of St. Patrick's, Swift referred to England's tendency to regard Ireland as "one of their *Colonies* of *Out-Casts*" and added, "I observed a little of the same Turn of Spirit in *some great Men,* from whom I expected better; although, to do them Justice, it proved no Point of Difficulty to make them *correct their Idea,* whereof the *whole Nation* quickly found the Benefit."[38] Swift could hardly have meant the First Fruits. The church alone had benefited from Anne's Bounty, and Swift here speaks of "the whole Nation." The reference could be to his conferences with Ormonde and Oxford. More specifically, it could be to an event of 1711 in which he was concerned. The *Journal* of the English Commons records that on February 27 of that year a petition was filed by the woolen manufacturers of several towns in England, asking that a duty be put on Irish yarn; there were subsequent petitions from other manufacturers on March 10 and April 2, and on April 12 a counterpetition was filed by some Irish lords. Swift was active in the affair. "We are now full of the business of the Irish yarn," he wrote to King on April 10, "and I attend among the rest, to engage the members I am acquainted with in our interest."[39] He never reported anything conclusive, the issue being constantly "put off," but apparently the Irish defeated the project.

---

[35] *Prose Works,* III, 28.   [36] *Ibid.,* III, xx.   [37] *Ibid.,* III, 177-178.
[38] *Ibid.,* IX, 21.
[39] *Corr,* I, 248; and cf. *Journal to Stella,* I, 237-238, 239, 241.

There are no more references to it in the Commons' *Journal* after April 12; so it would seem that the lobbying of Swift and his friends had been successful and that at the orders of the Tory leaders, the matter was quietly dropped.

A few statements about Wharton's viceroyalty, "a great deal" of talk, and some lobbying against the proposed duty on Irish yarn — Swift's efforts on behalf of Ireland during his years of power with Oxford seem trivial when compared with those he was to make after 1719. Deeply involved in the vital affairs that led to the end of the war with France and to the Treaty of Utrecht, Swift was, as he told Stella and Archbishop King, too busy to devote much time or thought to Ireland. Ireland was far away; to Swift, as he molded public opinion in favor of the ministry's policies, it must have seemed remote indeed. But time was running out for the ministry, and each new decline in its fortunes brought Swift closer to Ireland. In April, 1713, when the rift between Oxford and his lieutenant, Bolingbroke, had reached serious proportions, Swift was given the deanery of St. Patrick's. He sailed for Dublin in June. In one last effort to mend the irreparable breach between Oxford and Boling-broke, he returned to England in September, but in August, 1714, the death of Queen Anne ended all of the ministry's hopes of remaining in power. Before the end of the month, Swift was back in Ireland, where, except for two short visits to England in the following decade, he would remain for the rest of his life. His services for the Tories from 1710 to 1714 had delayed only temporarily the development of the most articulate champion of the Irish interest since Molyneux.

[II]

Swift went back to Ireland determined to "grow as stupid as . . . affairs will require."[40] Weary of court and party intrigue, bitterly vexed by his own fate and grieved by that of some of his closest friends in the fallen ministry, he had no desire to embroil himself in the affairs of England's poor relation. He had not been in Dublin a month when he wrote to his friend, Charles Ford, "I cannot stop my Ears when People of the wisest sort I see . . . tell me a thousand foolish Things of the Publick: But I hope I shall keep my Resolu-

---

[40] *Corr*, II, 240.

tion of never medling with Irish Politics."[41] He kept this resolution for six years, but in 1720 he meddled so thoroughly that he drew upon himself the hostile notice of the English government. In that year he published his *Proposal for the Universal Use of Irish Manufacture.*

Swift's decision to take up again the cause he had first championed in *The Injured Lady* is not difficult to account for. If anything is surprising, it is that he waited so long to do so. A certain interval, understandably, was necessary in which he could regain his balance after the Tory debacle in 1714; but six years is a long time for a man like Swift to be silent. It is, therefore, important to determine why he remained aloof for so long and what eventually prompted him to take an active — indeed, a dangerous — part in Anglo-Irish affairs.

The overwhelmingly Whig complexion of Dublin politics after 1714 undoubtedly had something to do with Swift's unwillingness to hurry into controversial issues. According to one of his eighteenth-century biographers, at the time of Swift's return to Dublin, party feelings were even more intemperate there than in England.[42] Shortly after the accession of George I, the government made a clean sweep of the Tories in Ireland. The Earl of Sunderland, a Whig of long standing, was made lord lieutenant. Four Whig members of the Irish bar were given the chief judicial posts: Alan Brodrick became chancellor; John Forster, chief justice of the Court of Common Pleas; William Whitshed, chief justice of the King's Bench; and Joseph Deane, chief baron of the exchequer.[43] The majority of the Anglo-Irish approved of these changes. Whig efforts to equate Toryism with Jacobitism had, for the moment at least, succeeded, and most Irish landowners identified the displaced party with the Pretender.

The public scene would have been painful to Swift had he been only a spectator. But he was not allowed to escape the general odium visited upon his former associates in Oxford's ministry — considering his activities as Tory pamphleteer, he could hardly have expected to be. On one occasion his mail was intercepted, and for

---

[41] *Letters to Ford,* p. 60.

[42] Thomas Sheridan, *The Life of the Rev. Dr. Jonathan Swift* (London, 1784), pp. 210-211.

[43] F. E. Ball, II, 77-81.

a time he felt himself in danger of arrest; and although his earliest biographer may have exaggerated the story of Swift's sufferings at the hands of a stone-throwing, taunting mob, Swift has left his own account of how, in 1714, he was threatened by an Irish nobleman.[44]

In addition to these dangers and humiliations, there were the petty annoyances of party hacks. "I am in a hopeful situation," Swift wrote to Bishop Atterbury in 1717, "torn to pieces by pamphleteers and libellers on that side the water, and by the whole body of the ruling party on this; against which all the obscurity I live in will not defend me."[45] The Whig scribes in England had been quick to strike at their once-feared adversary. A passage from one of the earliest of their attacks, *An Hue and Cry After Dean Swift, Occasioned by a True and Exact Copy of His Own Diary* (1714), is indicative of the kind of treatment Grub Street was giving him: "*Mem.* To write a paper when I am in the country to bring with me to town, and to publish at my first appearance, called Dr. Swift's Reasons, viz. for Ingratitude, for Irreligion, for Turning, for Returning, and to serve any turn; to be bound up with the Tale of a Tub."[46] And, if legend is correct, not all of the libels came from England:

> Look down, St. Patrick, look we pray,
> On thine own *Church* and *Steeple;*
> Convert thy *Dean,* on this *Great Day;*
> Or else God help the people!

According to its author, the poem in which this stanza appears was "fixed on the cathedral door, the day of *Dean Gulliver's* installment."[47]

Not all of the antagonism that Swift encountered during his first years at St. Patrick's came from lay sources. He devoted a great deal of time and energy during these years to defending his decanal privileges against encroachments both from within and outside of his chapter. These contentions were particularly disquieting because

---

[44] *Corr,* II, 421-424, 312; John Boyle, Earl of Orrery, *Remarks on the Life and Writings of Dr. Jonathan Swift* (London, 1752), pp. 49-50. For the account of Lord Blayney's attack on Swift, see T. Scott, XI, 388-390.

[45] *Corr,* II, 397.

[46] T. Scott, V, 482. For a list of other pamphlets attacking Swift at this time, see Teerink, pp. 350-352.

[47] The author of this poem was Jonathan Smedley, an Irish clergyman who became Dean of Clogher in 1724. The poem was reprinted in Smedley's *Gulliveriana* (1728), a violent diatribe against Swift and Pope (see p. 78).

of the part Archbishop King played in them.[48] The relationship
between Swift and King had deteriorated sadly since Swift's first
journey to London on behalf of the Irish church. Although the two
had never been close friends, their relations had been amicable.
However, as Swift became more and more deeply involved with the
Tory ministry and as he displayed more and more clearly his formidable powers as a political controversialist, the Whig archbishop
regarded him with increasing uneasiness and disfavor. King was
not happy with Swift's appointment to the deanery of St. Patrick's
(his congratulatory letter is less than cordial),[49] but he was relieved
that Swift had been elevated no higher: "a Dean," he wrote,
"could do less mischief than a Bishop."[50] To inhibit even further
Swift's capacity for mischief, King did all he could to check "that
plenitude of power" which the new dean obviously intended to
assert in his chapter.[51] King probably never seriously believed that
Swift had been engaged in any Jacobite plot. His hint in 1716 that
Swift might have cause to fear if Bolingbroke turned informer was
an ugly weapon, but he used it rather to wound Swift's feelings
than to express a conviction.[52] He was less certain of the loyalty —
or at least the sympathies — of some of his new dean's friends.
When the Customs officials intercepted Swift's mail in 1715, King,
as a member of the Privy Council, examined it. He found that it
was from the household of the Duke of Ormonde, who was under
suspicion of treason, and that it contained several political libels —
all "very bad matter."[53] Such associations as this could hardly have
improved Swift's standing with his archbishop, and there is no
question that the conflicting political allegiances of the two men
made their ecclesiastical disputes more bitter than they would otherwise have been.

Even had Swift had the will to do so, the delicacy of his situation
and the attacks from both ecclesiastical and secular sources left him
little desire to take any prominent part in public affairs at this time.
Furthermore, he felt that his obligations to Oxford had not ended,

[48] For a full discussion of Swift's struggles with his chapter and with King,
see Landa, pp. 68-91.

[49] *Corr*, II, 27-29.

[50] Gilbert Collection, MS 28, King to William Wake, May 8, 1716.

[51] Patrick Delany, *Observations upon Lord Orrery's Remarks on the Life
and Writings of Dr. Jonathan Swift* (London, 1754), p. 88.

[52] *Corr*, II, 343.   [53] *Ibid.*, II, 422.

and for several years after his return to Dublin he was at work on the histories and memoirs which he hoped would someday justify the policies of the Tory ministry. Before the ministry's downfall he had written two of these tracts — *The History of the Four Last Years of the Queen* and *Some Free Thoughts upon the Present State of Affairs.* Shortly after his arrival in Dublin in 1714 he wrote *Memoirs, Relating to that Change Which Happened in the Queen's Ministry in the Year 1710;* and the following year, when he received the news of Oxford's imprisonment in the Tower, he began *An Enquiry into the Behaviour of the Queen's Last Ministry* in defense of Ormonde, Bolingbroke, and Oxford, a work which took up much of his time from 1715 to 1720.[54] These histories of Swift's go far toward accounting for his lack of interest in Irish affairs during his early years as Dean of St. Patrick's. Although they were all too dangerous to be published at this time, he continued to think about them, to revise them, to make plans for their publication. His absorption with them is symptomatic of his unwillingness to accept the fact that the four last years of the Queen had passed and with them the Tories' time of greatness. So long as Swift continued vainly "to assert the principles and justify the proceedings" of Oxford's ministry, he could have few thoughts for Ireland; he was living in the past.

Swift could not, however, remain in the past. At about the time he finished the *Enquiry* there occurred the event that was to compel him to break his six-year silence. In 1720 the Whig government imposed upon Ireland the most inflammatory piece of legislation of the century, the Declaratory Act of 6 George I, the act "for the better securing the Dependency of . . . Ireland."

The act was the outgrowth of a controversy over the appellate jurisdiction of the Irish House of Lords — the old question which had been one of Molyneux's reasons for writing *The Case of Ireland.* Since 1716, the Irish Court of Exchequer and the Irish Lords had been in conflict over the suit of one Maurice Annesley against Hester Sherlock concerning some lands in County Kildare. The Court of Exchequer had found for Annesley, and the Lords had upheld Sherlock's appeal. Annesley then complained to the House of Lords in England that the Irish peers had no appellate

---

[54] Irvin Ehrenpreis, ed., *An Enquiry into the Behavior of the Queen's Last Ministry* (Bloomington, Ind., 1956), pp. xxv-xxvi.

jurisdiction in the case. The English Lords confirmed the decision of the Court of Exchequer and ordered that body to award the disputed estate to Annesley.[55] In July, 1719, the Irish Lords retaliated by ordering the Barons of the Exchequer into the custody of Black Rod, on the charge of interfering with the King's prerogative by "judging in his High Court of Parliament in Ireland." And the following October they made a representation to the King, defending their action; the defense followed much the same lines as Molyneux's argument in *The Case of Ireland.*[56] On his release from confinement, John Pocklington, one of the arrested barons, hastened to London. There he was rewarded by votes of thanks from the English Lords, praising him and his colleagues for their courage in resisting the Irish peers.[57] Shortly after this, on March 26, 1720, the English Parliament passed the Declaratory Act.

This legislation had profound effects on Ireland. Not only did it abolish the appellate jurisdiction of the Irish Lords; it also completed what Poynings' Act had left undone, and it defined unequivocally Ireland's status as a depending kingdom. "I would be glad," Swift wrote in his *Proposal* of 1720, "to learn among the Divines, whether a Law *to bind Men without their own Consent,* be obligatory *in foro Conscientiæ;* because, I find *Scripture, Sanderson* and *Suarez,* are wholly silent in the Matter. The Oracle of *Reason,* the great *Law of Nature,* and general Opinion of *Civilians,* wherever they treat of *limited Governments,* are, indeed, decisive enough."[58]

Those critics who hold that Swift became the defender of Ireland's rights merely in order to discomfort the hated Whig ministry are wrong. To say that he entered the dismal tangle of Irish politics for no more worthy a motive than revenge not only attributes to him a callousness which his character and his later activities in Ireland belie but also oversimplifies the complex motivations that lay behind his decision to write and publish the 1720 *Proposal.*

---

[55] F. E. Ball, II, 88; and J. Roderick O'Flanagan, *The Lives of the Lord Chancellors and Keepers of the Great Seal of Ireland* (London, 1870), II, 15-16. Maurice Annesley was a cousin of King's correspondent, Francis Annesley (see Simms, p. 145).

[56] *Journals of the House of Lords of Ireland* (Dublin, 1783), July 28, 1719. There is a reprint of the Lord's representation to George I in Edmund Curtis and R. B. McDowell, *Irish Historical Documents, 1172-1922* (London, 1943), pp. 214-218.

[57] F. E. Ball, II, 89.

[58] *Prose Works,* IX, 19. Swift is referring to Robert Sanderson (1587-

Assuredly Swift was eager to attack the Whigs, but for deeper reasons than party spite. During his years with Oxford, Swift had been apologist for the principles that he shared with the ministry, political and ethical convictions which he maintained throughout his life. When the Whigs came to power they did more than disgrace and exile Swift's friends; they pursued "a direct contrary system of politics" to that of the Tories.[59] In their treatment of Ireland, Swift saw nothing that caused him to change this opinion. "Your Ministers," he wrote to Oxford's son in 1730, "have ruined this country, which your Lordship's father from principles of justice, prudence and humanity, took care to preserve."[60]

This view of Oxford's Irish policy was both naïve and prejudiced. Archbishop King, as thorough a Whig as Swift was a Tory, was more realistic: "As to Oppressing Ireland," he wrote in 1718, "a Whigge and Tory Parlement and Ministry are much at one."[61] Oxford's administration had, however, been responsible for the remission of the First Fruits, and it had had the negative — but by no means contemptible — virtue of giving Ireland a government free from the odious Wharton, whose failings even King had to admit.[62] On the whole, Ireland, if she did not prosper under Oxford, at least did not suffer unduly; and King's description of the best government that Ireland could hope for is probably not too far short of what the Tories provided from 1710 to 1714: "I do not see how it can be in the power of any chief governor to do us any great good, but any one may do us a great deal of mischief, and if [we] have such a one as will have so much affection for those he governs that he will do us no more hurt than he must . . . we ought and must be thankful to God for him."[63]

Even before the passage of the Declaratory Act the Whig ministry had given sufficient indication that it would use its power to do Ireland mischief. The country's agriculture had long suffered at the expense of grazing interests, through whose influence the Irish Parliament had enacted laws prohibiting tenants from converting

---

1663), Bishop of Lincoln and Regius Professor of Divinity at Oxford, and to Francis Suarez (1548-1617), Jesuit theologian and jurist.

[59] *Ibid.,* VII, xxxiv.   [60] *Corr,* IV, 161.

[61] King Corr, to Francis Annesley, May 6, 1718.

[62] Although King disapproved of Swift's *Short Character* as a libelous "appeal to the mob," he admitted that Wharton "perhaps . . . may deserve this usage" (*Corr,* I, 233-234).

[63] *Ibid.,* I, 321.

pastures into tillable land. In consequence, almost all of Ireland's grain had to be imported from England. By the second decade of the eighteenth century, this practice had proved so injurious to Ireland's economy that in 1716 the Irish Commons unanimously passed heads of a bill invalidating the laws against tillage and providing for the cultivation of five acres out of every hundred. To protect England's grain exports and the monopoly on Irish raw wool — and above all to keep Ireland weak and dependent — the English Privy Council returned the measure in so mutilated a condition that it could not be accepted. In 1719, the Irish Parliament submitted a similar act for the encouragement of tillage; this time the Privy Council did not even bother to return it.[64]

But if the Whigs were indifferent to Ireland's economic needs, they were still the champions of the Ulster Presbyterians. Some two months after the tillage bill had disappeared into oblivion, the Irish Parliament passed an Act of Toleration for Protestant dissenters. The act left the Sacramental Test Act in force, but it relaxed earlier regulations concerning attendance at parish churches and permitted dissenting preachers to administer the Lord's Supper. In the words of Archbishop King, who had led the unsuccessful opposition to the act in the House of Lords, it gave Irish Presbyterians "a full liberty . . . to set up their meetings and propogate what doctrines they please."[65] This measure, of course, had its impetus from England. The lord lieutenant's speech from the throne at the opening of the parliamentary session of 1719 had urged relief for Protestant dissenters, and according to King, the Toleration Act had been passed in Commons because the members had been "so hardly pressed in the lord lieutenant's speech." English influence had made itself felt in the House of Lords as well. The bill would have been

---

[64] J. Middleton Murry is wrong in saying that the Irish Commons rejected the tillage bill at the instigation of the Whig ministry (*Jonathan Swift* [London, 1954], p. 319). The *Journal* of the House of Commons shows that the bill was passed in that house: "Mr. Speaker reported that this House attended his Grace the Lord Lieutenant yesterday at the Castle, with heads of a bill for the encouragement of tillage . . . and desired his Grace to recommend the same in the most effectual manner to his Majesty, as a bill of great benefit . . . to this kingdom" (July 11, 1719). See also James A. Froude, *The English in Ireland in the Eighteenth Century* (London, 1906), I, 446-447.

[65] Beckett, pp. 77-78. King's statement is from a letter to William Wake, quoted in Richard Mant, *History of the Church of Ireland* (London, 1841), II, 357.

defeated there, King wrote to the Archbishop of Canterbury, "if our Brethren that came to us from your side of the water had not deserted us and gone over to the adverse party."[66]

The Toleration Act and the suppression of the tillage bill occurred in the fall of 1719, while Swift was still concerned with vindicating another ministry and "a direct contrary system of politics" and while agitation over the Annesley case was at its height. It is little wonder that in December he wrote to Charles Ford that the public wind was full in his teeth. Five years earlier he had assured Ford that he would never interfere in Irish affairs, but this pledge could be kept no longer: "As the World is now turned, no Cloyster is retired enough to keep Politicks out, and I will own they raise my Passions whenever they come in my way."[67] Within two months after the passage of the Declaratory Act, Swift published *A Proposal for the Universal Use of Irish Manufacture.*

Although the passions which drove Swift to take this step had been raised by political events, the *Proposal* itself was primarily concerned with an economic problem. During the years immediately preceding the appearance of Swift's tract, the condition of the Irish poor had grown intolerable. "I take this kingdom to be more miserable . . . than ever you knew it," King had written to a friend in 1717, and the following year he wrote to the Bishop of Carlisle, "The misery of the people here is very great, the beggars innumerable and encreasing every day. . . . One half of the people in Ireland eat neither bread nor flesh for one half of the year, nor wear Shoes or Stockings; your Hoggs in England and Essex Calves ly and live better than they."[68] The Bishop of Carlisle was William Nicolson, who had just been translated to the see of Derry. He arrived in Ireland later in 1718, and on his journey from Dublin to Londonderry, he was appalled at the "dismal marks of hunger and want" which he met with along the way.[69] The scene was new to Nicolson but not to Swift. Of all the contemporary accounts of the hopeless condition of the Irish peasants at this time, none is filled with the compassion and indignation of a passage in the *Proposal:* "Whoever travels this Country, and observes the *Face* of

---

[66] Beckett, p. 78; *A Great Archbishop,* p. 218.

[67] *Letters to Ford,* pp. 83, 82.

[68] King Corr, to George Tollet, Nov. 7, 1717; to William Nicolson, Feb. 3, 1718.

[69] Quoted by Lecky, I, 184.

Nature, or the *Faces,* and Habits, and Dwellings of the *Natives,* will hardly think himself in a Land where either *Law, Religion,* or *common Humanity* is professed."[70]

Because the economic needs of the country so obviously should take precedence over every other concern, Swift found the recent behavior of the Irish Parliament unaccountable: "I should wish," he wrote in the *Proposal,* "the Parliament had thought fit to have suspended their Regulation of *Church* Matters, and Enlargements of the *Prerogative,* until a more convenient Time, because they did not appear very pressing . . . and, instead of those great Refinements in *Politicks* and *Divinity,* had *amused* Themselves and their Committees, a little, with the *State of the Nation.*"[71] Not only had Parliament passed the despised Act of Toleration, but by defying England over the Annesley case, it had brought about the Declaratory Act. Swift accepted the argument that the Irish Lords had jurisdiction in cases appealed to them from courts in Ireland, but he realized that a tedious lawsuit which had dragged on for over two years was not the issue to inspire any effective widespread popular support; if the blow for Ireland's legislative independence was to be struck, a better weapon would have to be found. Hence, while the protest of the Irish Parliament over the Annesley decision had been a legitimate one, it had done the country no good and a great deal of harm;[72] and while the legislators had amused themselves with this dangerous game, their country's desperate poverty had gone unrelieved. Swift wrote his tract in an effort to recall to the legislators their most pressing duty and to suggest a means by which they could accomplish it.

So long as "the politick Gentlemen of *Ireland*" were determined, in spite of English restraints, to maintain their vast tracts of grazing lands, Ireland's economy would be dependent on wool. But what, the *Proposal* asks, would Ireland do with her chief commodity if English markets should become overstocked or if the haphazard smuggling trade with France should fail? What, for that matter, was she doing even now with the surplus wool that was a drug on

---

[70] *Prose Works,* IX, 21.   [71] *Ibid.,* IX, 16.

[72] Swift's view of the Irish Parliament's reaction to the Annesley case was shared by Alan Brodrick, who feared that the representation would result in even harsher treatment of Ireland (see F. E. Ball, II, 91). For essentially the same reason, Brodrick was one of the signers of the proclamation against the Drapier in 1724.

the market? Swift's answer to these questions is made in the form of a proposal to the Parliament and people of Ireland:

What if the House of Commons . . . thought fit to make a Resolution, *Nemine Contradicente,* against wearing any Cloath or Stuff in their Families, which were not of the Growth and Manufacture of this Kingdom? What if they . . . extended it so far, as utterly to exclude all Silks, Velvets, Calicoes, and the whole *Lexicon* of Female Fopperies; and declared, that whoever acted otherwise, should be deemed and reputed *an Enemy to the Nation?* What if they . . . sent up such a Resolution to be agreed to by the House of Lords; and by their own Practice and Encouragement, spread the Execution of it in their several Countries? What if we should agree to make *burying in Woollen* a *Fashion,* as our Neighbours have made it a *Law?* What if the Ladies would be content with *Irish* Stuffs for the Furniture of their Houses, for Gowns and Petticoats to themselves and their Daughters? Upon the whole, and to crown all the rest, let a firm Resolution be taken, by *Male* and *Female,* never to appear with one single *Shred* that comes from *England; and let all the People say,* AMEN.[73]

In 1721, Swift wrote to Pope that he had written "a discourse to persuade the wretched people to wear their own manufactures instead of those from England."[74] Described in this way, the *Proposal* seems innocent enough, and, in fact, the suggestion that the Irish use their own wool to make clothing and draperies for domestic use was neither fanciful nor original. On November 25, 1719, the *Dublin Courant* had printed "Mr. Parker's Proposals for the Encouragement of Trade in this Kingdom," which recommended that Ireland encourage weaving and discourage the importation of foreign goods, "such as silks, calicoes, printed and striped linens." And in the *Dublin Courant* for March 12, 1720, was the advertisement of one Abraham Bryan, who affirmed that his woolen goods were superior to those imported from England. His pathetic hope that "none will be so *partial,* as to condemn before they try, and after Tryal, for no other Fault, than being the *Manufacture* of this Kingdom" is echoed in Swift's *Proposal:* "It is wonderful to observe the Biass among our People in favour of *Things, Persons,* and *Wares* of all Kinds that come from *England.*"[75] Of more immediate relevance to Swift's scheme, the Irish Parliament had passed resolutions (to no practical effect) in 1703, 1705, and 1707 against importing

[73] *Prose Works,* IX, 16.
[74] *Corr,* III, 115. Swift's letter is reprinted in *Prose Works,* IX, 25-34.
[75] *Ibid.,* IX, 19.

foreign clothing; in fact, the wording of the 1703 resolution may have been used by Swift for his own proposal.[76]

Swift's description of his tract, however, is disingenuous. The *Proposal* was seriously intended as a means for Ireland's self-improvement, but — as its final resolution to abjure every shred of English goods makes abundantly clear — it was also designed to show the Irish that they had within their power a weapon of economic retaliation against the legislative tyranny that had reached its climax with the Declaratory Act. The very title of the pamphlet was calculated to inflame: *A PROPOSAL For the universal Use OF IRISH MANUFACTURE, IN Cloaths and Furniture of Houses, &c. UTTERLY REJECTING AND RENOUNCING Every Thing wearable that comes from ENGLAND.* And it was no accident that it appeared less than two months after the passage of the Declaratory Act, when Irish reaction was violent.

Even while the proposed measure was being debated in the English Parliament, feelings in Ireland had run high. As one of the spiritual peers, William Nicolson was able to send firsthand accounts of the proceedings in the Irish Lords to Archbishop Wake of Canterbury, and his letters reflect the acute discomfort with which he listened to the "Harangues, and Complaints of the daily Increase of our Burthens, and the Oppressions of our English Neighbors." Nicolson, an English-born appointee to the episcopal bench, was an unquestioning supporter of the English interest, and he and the other "forreign bishops" (Evans of Meath, Ellis of Kildare, Goodwin of Kilmore, and Downes of Killala) were regarded with increased hostility during the Lords' debates. Nicolson complained that they were "all treated by Friends & Foes, Whigs & Tories, as Enemies to the publick Interests of this Kingdom." The chief troublemakers, he reported, were "two or three Lords Spiritual" — William King; Edward Synge, Archbishop of Tuam; and John Stearne, Bishop of Clogher.[77] These leaders of the Irish interest were supported by their secular colleague in the Lords, Viscount Molesworth, who in one of his addresses declared, "I do not think myself one jot the more a free man, if an illegal and tyrannical power hangs over me to be exerted at will and pleasure, and my

---

[76] Louis Landa, "Swift's Economic Views and Mercantilism," *Journal of English Literary History*, X (1943), 331.

[77] Gilbert Collection, MS 27, Nicolson to Wake, Jan. 17, 1719/20; Aug. 6, 1719; Feb. 23, 1719/20.

being actually chained like a galley slave to the oar and drubbed at will and pleasure."[78]

Agitation was equally intemperate outside Parliament. Both Synge and King were alarmed at the "universal disaffection of all people thro' the whole Kingdom," and Nicolson wrote to Wake that "a seditious Spirit is arisen (& grown rampant) amongst us; which is dayly animating the Populace to assert their Irish Liberties. . . . Mr. Molineaux's Book . . . is reprinted here and in every bodie's hand."[79] In addition to *The Case of Ireland,* several other tracts appeared in Dublin during 1719-20. The first and second *Letter from a Member of the House of Commons of Ireland* (August 11, 1719, and February 13, 1720) opposed the Declaratory Act with constitutional arguments much in the judicious tone of Molyneux; John Toland's *Reasons . . . Why the Bill Should Not Pass* (1720) accused the English Parliament of encroaching on the royal prerogative; and a pamphlet dated March 5, 1720, shortly before the Declaratory Act had been signed, bitterly announced that "The Peers of Ireland had their Tryal . . . and then they were to be Executed."[80] Edward Waters, who was soon to print Swift's *Proposal,* issued *Hibernia's Passive Obedience,* a half-sheet that may have recommended him to Swift's notice as a printer with courage and the proper sympathies. The piece is substantially a compilation of passages from three of Swift's earlier tracts, *The Sentiments of a Church-of-England Man, The Contests and Dissensions in Athens and Rome,* and the *Letter Concerning the Sacramental Test;* the last of these furnished the angry headnote to Waters' half-sheet: "If Your little Finger be *sore,* and you think a *Poltice* made of my

---

[78] Historical Manuscripts Commission, *Report on Manuscripts in Various Collections,* VIII, 283 (undated notes for Molesworth's speech in the Irish House of Lords).

[79] Gilbert Collection, MS 27, Nicolson to Wake, July 11, 1719; King Corr, to Molesworth, May 10, 1720; Gilbert Collection, MS 27, Nicolson to Wake, Oct. 6, 1719. *The Case of Ireland* seems to have been a valid gauge of Irish opinion during times of national crisis. It had several reprintings in the eighteenth century, one at the time of the halfpence affair.

[80] *Reasons . . . Why the Bill Should Not Pass* was advertised in the *Dublin Courant* for April 27, 1720, as by J——N T——d. Toland's authorship is established in *A Collection of Several Pieces of Mr. John Toland . . . with Some Memoirs of His Life & Writings* (London, 1726), I, lxxvi-lxxvii. The pamphlet of March 5, 1720, is entitled *Several Speeches in the House of Commons in England, For and Against the Bill . . .* (Dublin, 1720). The passage quoted is on p. 3.

Vitals will give you any Ease, speak the Word, and it shall be done."[81]

The *Proposal* appeared during the last week in May,[82] at the height of these "Discontents and Murmurs" (to use Nicolson's phrase), and it was manifestly intended to keep them alive. The indefatigable Nicolson quoted some of the pamphlet's "choicest Beauty-Spots" to Wake: the ironic list of the hardships that the "POOR Kingdom of *England*" suffered on Ireland's account; Swift's application of the fable of Pallas and Arachne to England's treatment of Ireland ("the greatest Part of *our Bowels and Vitals* is extracted, without allowing us the Liberty of *spinning* and *weaving* them"); and his desperate hope that *"Oppression* would, in Time, teach a little *Wisdom* to *Fools."*[83]

The government's response to such sentiments was not long in coming. On May 30, 1720, the Grand Juries of the City and County of Dublin, managed by Lord Chancellor Brodrick (who had been created Viscount Midleton) and Chief Justice Whitshed, presented the tract as "false, scandalous, and seditious," and ordered the printer to be prosecuted.[84] Only technical anonymity saved

---

[81] Aside from the author's introduction, that part of *Hibernia's Passive Obedience* which is not drawn from Swift's tracts is a reprint of selections from Thomas Burnet's *Essays Divine, Moral, and Political* (1714). The anonymous author quotes Burnet's Whig sentiments to show that England's treatment of Ireland is unjust according to the principles of "the most Zealous Patriots." *Hibernia's Passive Obedience* probably appeared before Swift's *Proposal.* For one thing, it makes no reference to the *Proposal,* an odd omission — in view of its excessive use of passages from the other Swift pamphlets — if it was written after the *Proposal.* Furthermore, on the last day of May, Waters was under indictment by the Grand Juries of the City and County of Dublin for printing Swift's pamphlet. It would have been foolhardy for him to publish *Hibernia's Passive Obedience* under these circumstances.

[82] Swift could not have written the *Proposal* later than May 28, for there is a reference in the tract to the King's birthday, "now approaching," which was on that date (*Prose Works,* IX, xv, 16). Swift's reference to *"The Ballad upon* Cotter" (p. 19) indicates that the tract was probably written not much earlier than May 24. Sir James Cotter, a prominent Catholic of County Cork, was executed on May 7, 1720, for rape (see *Mist's Weekly Journal,* May 21, 1720). The trial and execution were of great interest, and on May 24, the mayor of Cork sent a copy of a ballad on Cotter to the officials at Dublin Castle (see Froude, I, 479-481, n. 2).

[83] Gilbert Collection, MS 27, Nicolson to Wake, June 9, 1720. The passages from the *Proposal* to which Nicolson alludes are in *Prose Works,* IX, 18-19.

[84] For a contemporary account of the Grand Juries' proceedings, see the *Dublin Courant* for June 4, 1720.

Swift from being arrested along with Waters. His authorship of the *Proposal* very quickly became an open secret. On June 9, Nicolson had sent Archbishop Wake his account of the tract, which, he said, contained "so much of the Dean of St. Patrick's witty and bantering Strain . . . that the greatest part of its Readers (at the first Blush) give him the Honour of being its author"; and later in the year a newsletter circulating in London reported that "Dean Swift is in tribulation for somewhat writ about the last year's proceedings . . . against the Irish Parliament."[85] Waters was tried at the King's Bench before Chief Justice Whitshed. When the jury returned a verdict in the printer's favor, Whitshed refused to accept it and ordered the jury to deliberate further. Eleven hours later — after nine verdicts of innocent had been rejected — the exhausted jury returned a special verdict, whereby the decision was left to the chief justice. Whitshed, by this time alarmed at the jury's obstinacy, deferred the proceedings to the next term.[86] The case was subsequently dropped, over a year later, by an order of *noli prosequi* from the Duke of Grafton, Ireland's new lord lieutenant, whose intervention Swift had requested in a letter to Grafton's stepfather, Sir Thomas Hanmer. In this letter, Swift made the guarded admission that "the business may be inconvenient, because I am looked on as the author."[87]

Swift could take comfort from the furor the *Proposal* had raised and from the heroic behavior of the jury that refused to indict Waters. However, his suggestion that the Irish use their own manufactures was ignored. He could not have been unduly surprised. After all, three separate Irish parliaments had passed similar reso-

---

[85] Historical Manuscripts Commission, *Report on Portland Manuscripts,* V, 609. More than one of Swift's acquaintances noticed the attack on Ireland as well as England in the *Proposal*. John Evans, Bishop of Meath, said of the tract that "both kingdoms are very ill treated therein" (quoted in *Corr,* III, 65, n. 4). Another contemporary attribution of the *Proposal* to Swift is found in *A Defence of English Commodities,* which appeared in London in the summer of 1720, ostensibly as a reprint from a Dublin edition. It is reprinted in *Prose Works,* IX, 265-277. There is no evidence that Swift's ballad, "An Excellent new SONG on a seditious Pamphlet" (*Poems,* I, 236-238) was printed before Faulkner included it in his 1735 edition of Swift's works. It may, however, have circulated in Dublin in 1720; and it virtually admits Swift's authorship in such lines as "Tho' a Printer and Dean/ Seditiously mean/ Our true *Irish* Hearts from old *England* to wean. . . ."

[86] This account is based on Swift's description of the trial in a letter to Pope (*Corr,* III, 115-116), which is reprinted in *Prose Works,* IX, 26-27.

[87] *Corr,* III, 64-66.

lutions to no purpose. Furthermore Swift must have realized that
there was a serious economic objection to his plan. Irish manufacturers could not possibly compete with their powerful rivals on
anything like an equal footing. Not only could the experienced
and well-established manufacturers in England offer goods of better
quality, but they could also undersell items on the Irish market
because Ireland was prevented from levying adequate protective
duties on English imports.[88] In addition, Irish woolens were in bad
repute because of the unethical business practices of Irish drapers.
In the *Proposal,* Swift called upon the shopkeepers "to improve the
Cloaths and Stuffs of the Nation" and to promise *"not to play the
Knave, according to their Custom, by exacting and imposing upon
the Nobility and Gentry, either as to the Prices or the Goodness."*[89]
He had been anticipated here, too, by the Irish Parliament. In 1703
the House of Commons had noted a number of abuses in the
domestic woolen market, abuses which caused would-be customers
"to wear and consume Manufactures wrought up in other Places."[90]
Obviously the drapers' unsavory reputation had not improved by
1720, and Swift knew that until the merchants acquired a sense of
integrity, any effort to encourage Irish consumption of domestic
goods was all but hopeless.

In his letter to Hanmer, Swift referred to the *Proposal* as a "weak,
hasty scribble," and though this disparagement was no doubt intended to suggest that Whitshed had magnified the importance of a
trivial matter, Swift's estimate of his pamphlet is accurate. Because
the *Proposal* was the result of accumulated causes, it became a ve-
hicle for Swift to express a host of discontents, and consequently it
lacks unity of purpose. Swift touches in rapid succession a number
of topics: the foolish bias the Irish have for all things and opinions
English; England's disposition to treat Ireland like a colony; the
Declaratory Act; absentee landlords and the vicious rack-renters
they relied on for their revenue; the rapidly diminishing supply of
gold and silver; and the current efforts to establish a national bank
in Ireland. There are some passages of effective rhetoric, but for
the most part Swift makes his points mechanically, introducing each
new topic with such phrases as "I would now expostulate" and "I
cannot forbear saying one word." At times, there is no logical

---

[88] O'Brien, pp. 179-180.   [89] *Prose Works,* IX, 17.
[90] *The Journals of the House of Commons of the Kingdom of Ireland*
(Dublin, 1763), March 2, 1703.

transition from one theme to the next. Careful argument, exact marshaling of facts and management of details, logical applications are largely absent; nor is there the brilliant sophistry of the first *Drapier's Letter,* or the terrible and uncompromising logic of a later, more famous proposal.

Judged either artistically or pragmatically, *A Proposal for the Universal Use of Irish Manufacture* is a failure. But even so, it has some significance. It is proof that Swift's interest in Ireland did not cease permanently when he put *The Injured Lady* aside unpublished. Though disorganized and hastily written, it presents an accurate diagnosis of Ireland's economic ills, and it anticipates the themes of many of Swift's later tracts on Irish affairs. Further, it illustrates the ambivalence characteristic of Swift's attitude toward Ireland. His compassion for the wretched victims of England's tyranny was tempered by his condemnation of their own selfish mismanagement and apathy. This moral view was implicit in Swift's allegorical description of Ireland's plight; the Injured Lady was a fallen woman by her own admission. It is more apparent in the *Proposal* and will come to be the dominant theme in Swift's later tracts, reaching a climax in *A Modest Proposal.* Swift's friend and biographer, Patrick Delany, said that although Swift "had . . . abstained from writing, until the year 1720 . . . [he] was very far from having abstained from railing (even in the pulpit) against the wrong politics of Ireland for that time."[91] For Swift, who believed that the chief function of preaching was to persuade people to do their duty,[92] there was nothing incompatible between duty to one's country and duty to one's God. "Is there Vertue enough," he asked in the *Proposal,* "left in this deluded People to save them from the Brink of Ruin?" And the resolution which he urged the Irish Parliament and people to adopt ends with a line from The Book of Common Prayer: "and let all the People say, AMEN."[93]

Nor was the *Proposal* a wholly wasted effort. For one thing, it served to bring Swift into a closer relationship with the leaders of the Irish interest, especially with William King. Even before Swift published his tract, he and King had become more friendly, thanks to their common views on Irish politics. King's opposition to the Toleration Act and his speeches in the House of Lords during the Annesley controversy obviously won Swift's respect; there are approving references to the archbishop in two of his letters to Ford,

---

[91] Delany, p. 105.   [92] *Prose Works,* IX, 70.   [93] *Ibid.,* IX, 16-17.

both written before the appearance of the *Proposal*.[94] After Waters'
trial, Swift wrote to Hanmer that "all the Bishops except the late
ones from England" approved of his "weak, hasty scribble," and
from this time on, Swift and King coöperated closely in their
efforts to help Ireland. Another of the friends that the *Proposal*
won for Swift was Viscount Molesworth. Earlier Swift had disapproved of Molesworth's unsympathetic views toward the Irish
church, and he may have helped deprive the viscount of his seat in
the Irish Privy Council in 1713.[95] But as with Swift and King, the
crisis of the Declaratory Act minimized the differences between
Swift and Molesworth. Molesworth thought so well of the *Proposal*
that for a time he considered having it reprinted in England. On
June 25, he wrote to John Toland, "I will consult friends here
before I determine any thing touching the reprinting the Irish
Pamphlet which I sent you: and if they think it proper I will send
you word." And Molesworth added a remark that confirms Swift's
opinion of the literary merit of his tract: "You may believe it to be
S——'s; for he was here with me to get me to use my interest that
no hardship be put upon the Printer, and did in a manner own it.
I believe it was writ in haste, for persons do not always write
alike."[96]

Swift's tract also afforded him the opportunity to present himself
to the people of Ireland, not as a dangerous Jacobite but as a patriot who had endangered his own safety to defend their rights —
an opportunity worth all the inconvenience caused by the notoriety
of his authorship. From this time on, Swift had the trust and
affection of the common people, and he came to be regarded by
the Dublin weavers as their champion in particular. Despite Swift's

---

[94] *Letters to Ford*, pp. 80, 83-84. At some time between 1719 and 1721,
Swift addressed his highly complimentary *Imitation of Horace* to King
(*Poems*, I, 241-243).

[95] See chapter 1, n. 50.

[96] *A Collection of Several Pieces of Mr. John Toland* . . . , II, 462. The
friendly relations between Swift and Molesworth continued. In December,
1720, Molesworth wrote from London to his wife, "Pray take the first good
opportunity of sending my compliments to Mr. Dean of St. Patrick's. I
have received [a] very kind and civil letter from him to which I design to
return an answer speedily, but I would have some notice taken of his
civility by you, that he may be convinced I am pleased with it" (Historical
Manuscripts Commission, *Report on Manuscripts in Various Collections,*
VIII, 291). Neither Swift's letter nor Molesworth's answer is in *Corr.*
Swift had probably written to Molesworth on Waters' behalf.

approval of the extravagant maxim that the Irish should burn everything English but the people and the coals,[97] the resolution in the *Proposal* has to do only with woolens and cloths. The cathedral and deanery of St. Patrick's were in the heart of the weavers' district in Dublin, and Swift could witness daily the increasing misery of the workers. Had his resolution been adopted, they would have received immediate and particular benefits. They never forgot this effort to serve them. In 1721, one of them, Roger Kendrick, wrote *A Letter to the Reverend Dr. Swift . . . Relating to the Present State of the Manufactures of Ireland,* in which he asked Swift to help correct abuses in the weaving industry and in which he thanked him for his "C[h]aritable Disposition towards me, and the rest of my Fellow-Sufferers in Trade."[98] By that time, Swift had begun the practice of advancing money to tradesmen to set them up in business, and although loans were available for men of all trades, Swift's benevolence was popularly associated with the weaving industry — to the extent, in fact, that Delany felt obliged to deny the charge that Swift provided money exclusively for the weavers in order to maintain his popularity with them.[99] In 1726 the journeymen weavers published an expression of their gratitude, thanking Swift "for the great Favours he had done to the *Corporation* of *Weavers* in Particular, and to the whole Kingdom in general"; and as late as the 1730's Swift was receiving delegations of weavers, who sought his advice "in settling the rates of their stuffs, and the wages of their journeymen" and who looked on him as their "patron and legislator."[100]

No one can be sure, but it is highly probable that when Swift found it necessary in 1724 to speak to the Irish people as one of their fellows, he chose with a special purpose and with a special fondness the alter ego of that respected and patriotic citizen, the woolen draper of St. Francis Street.

---

[97] *Prose Works,* IX, 17. The "late Archbishop of Tuam" to whom Swift attributes this maxim was John Vesey, who died in 1716.

[98] *A Letter to the Reverend Dr. Swift . . . ,* p. 1. Kendrick was made verger of St. Patrick's on May 5, 1732 (see Hugh J. Lawlor, *The Fasti of St. Patrick's* [Dundalk, Ireland, 1930], p. 259; and for further information, *Corr,* Index, s.v. "Kendrick").

[99] *Corr,* III, 99, n. 1, 75; Delany, p. 204.

[100] *An Account of the Journey-Men Weavers Grateful Congratulation of the Rev. Dr. Swift Dean of St. Patrick's Safe Arrival, with His Kind Answer, and Bounty to Their Corporation* (Sept. 5, 1726). See John Hawkesworth's edition of Swift's works (London, 1776-79), I, 42.

CHAPTER III

The Bank Tracts and Other Pieces

[1]

On June 19, 1721, Swift wrote a letter to Bolingbroke. It has not survived, but from Bolingbroke's answer it is obvious that it concerned the condition of Ireland and the uncertain future of Edward Waters, who was still under indictment for printing the *Proposal for the Universal Use of Irish Manufacture.* It is equally obvious that Swift was worried and depressed.[1] He had obtained Sir Thomas Hanmer's promise to use his influence in Waters' behalf, but that had been in October.[2] The case against the printer was still pending, and in January, Sir Constantine Phipps, whom Swift had asked to intervene with the attorney-general, wrote that Waters could expect little help from England.[3] It was not until August, 1721, when Lord Lieutenant Grafton arrived in Dublin, that the government finally dropped its case against Waters. Meanwhile, Swift could only wait, and hope that his printer's fate would not be left in the power of Chief Justice Whitshed.

While he waited, his spirits were in no way relieved by what

---

[1] Bolingbroke's letter is reprinted in *Corr,* III, 88-95. "I mourn over Ireland with all my heart," Bolingbroke wrote, "but I pity you more" (p. 92).

[2] Hanmer's letter is reprinted in *ibid.,* III, 69-70.

[3] *Ibid.,* III, 70.

he saw around him: "Our present calamities are not to be represented. . . . Numbers of miserable objects crowd our doors, begging
us to take their wares at any price, to prevent their families from
immediate starving. . . . [We] have before our eyes the dismal
prospect of universal poverty and desolation." This sounds like a
passage from *A Modest Proposal,* but it comes instead from *The
Present Miserable State of Ireland,* an anonymous tract first published in Dublin in the summer of 1721, when Ireland's economy
had come to a critical pass with the collapse of the South Sea
Bubble.[4]

By June, 1720, the South Sea madness was at its height in
England. At the end of the month, an anxious British Parliament
passed the Bubble Act in an effort to check the growth of new stock
companies being formed to accommodate eager investors, but the
damage had been done. Millions of capital had already been in-
vested in the South Sea Company and its imitators, and speculation
in these companies continued to flourish even after the passage of
the Bubble Act. The inevitable collapse came soon after; in August,
the Bubble burst.[5] Irish speculators had been as greedy as their
counterparts in England, and they reaped the same harvest.

Ireland's economy was far less able to survive the crash than was
that of England. Burdened as it was by English restraints, it was in
so precarious a condition at all times that it could be upset by
very little. Consequently, what in England was a crisis amounted
in Ireland to an almost irreparable catastrophe. "Conversation is
full of nothing but South Sea," Swift wrote Vanessa, "and the ruin
of the kingdom, and scarcity of money."[6] *The London Mercury*
for April 29, 1721, reported that "Letters from Dublin advise that
they feel there more and more the woeful effects of the South Sea
affair. Their gentlemen went late into the stocks, bought dear,
extracted all the foreign gold out of Ireland . . . to make those

---

[4] *The Present Miserable State of Ireland* is reprinted, as Swift's work, in
T. Scott, VII, 151-165. It was not, however, accepted by Herbert Davis
in his edition of the *Prose Works.* For discussions of its provenance and
authorship, see H. R. Wagner, *Irish Economics: 1700-1783* (London, 1907),
pp. 5-6; and Herbert Davis, "The Canon of Swift," *English Institute
Annual, 1942* (New York, 1943), pp. 128-129.

[5] For a recent summary of the South Sea crisis, see J. H. Plumb, *Sir
Robert Walpole* (Cambridge, Mass., 1956), I, 293-301.

[6] *Corr,* III, 68.

purchases, so that money is become extreme scarce."[7] *The Present Miserable State of Ireland,* written in the form of a letter from a Dublin woolen dealer to a friend in London, may well have been one of the "Letters from Dublin" alluded to by the English newspaper. At any rate, it tells the same story: "We went late to the South Sea market, and bore a great share in the losses of it, without having tasted any of its profits." If many English speculators had been ruined, some had realized tremendous profits; and even those who had suffered could expect redress from an "uncorrupted Parliament and ministry, strenuously endeavouring to restore public trade to its former happy state."[8] Not only did Ireland lack this ameliorative influence, but the country was faced with a critical shortage of money, which brought domestic trade to a virtual standstill. The starving tradesmen were unable to sell their goods at any price: "We cannot part with our money to them, both because we know not when we shall have vent for their goods; and, as there are no debts paid, we are afraid of reducing ourselves to their lamentable circumstances."[9]

It is significant that the author of *The Present Miserable State* adopted the character of a draper. For all the restraints under which it operated, the weaving industry was still one of the most vital in Ireland's economy; it provided employment for approximately seventeen hundred families in Dublin alone.[10] It was these weavers, now jobless because of the dearth of trade, who afforded the dramatic illustration of the economic crisis as they crowded the Dublin streets in search of bread. "The poverty of this Kingdom," wrote Archbishop King, "is not to be imagined. The cry of the Weavers of all Sorts, Linnen, Woollen, & Silk was intolerable. They sold and pawned all they had for bread, Houshold Stuff, Cloths, looms and tools and there remained nothing behind but to Starve." According to the archbishop, nearly six thousand persons in Dublin were affected by the collapse of the weaving industry, and "the other Trades have their proportion of poor."[11]

---

[7] Quoted by F. Elrington Ball, *Swift's Verse* (London, 1929), p. 175, n. 43.

[8] T. Scott, VII, 165. This encomium on the English Parliament and ministry makes Swift's authorship extremely unlikely.

[9] *Ibid.,* VII, 164.

[10] King Corr, to Col. Flower, April 8, 1721: "The Number of familyes belonging to the Weaving Trade . . . upon inquiry, are found to be near 1700." This letter is reprinted in *Corr,* III, 75, n. 2.

[11] King Corr, to Col. Flower, April 8, 1721.

This was misery on a scale to which even the most experienced Dubliners were unaccustomed. The Jacobite rebellion of 1715 had seriously injured Irish trade, but, as the author of *The Present Miserable State* noted, that crisis was insignificant in comparison with the one now facing the country.[12] Private citizens and officials alike exerted themselves to aid the weavers. Archbishop King took to Dublin Castle a petition from three hundred distressed families, and he arranged for special collections to be taken in the churches throughout the city.[13] "Everybody bestirred themselves to get them a Supply," he wrote. "The Dissenters, the R[oman] C[atholics], the Deans & Chapters, the Colleges, nay the playhouse gave a play to this purpose which raised £73. . . . The Gent and Ladys did their part by clothing themselves in the Manufactures of the Countrey. . . ."[14] The benefit performance to which King referred was a production of *Hamlet* given at the Theatre-Royal on April 1, 1721, with a prologue written by Swift's friend, Thomas Sheridan. Swift himself wrote the epilogue, a poem of forty-six lines which urged the theme of his 1720 *Proposal:*

> O! Cou'd I see this Audience Clad in *Stuff*,
> Tho' Moneys scarce we shou'd have Trade enough;[15]

The efforts of men like Swift and King, the public and private contributions, even the noteworthy instance of the gentry's condescending to wear Irish goods, were not sufficient to meet the country's need. Thomas Medlycott, Commissioner of Customs at Dublin, described the performance of *Hamlet* to Secretary of State Southwell and added that the weavers were "not in any wise relieved." He included a copy of Swift's epilogue, correctly attributed, and suggested that it would, if it were "advertis'd in London [handsomely?] . . . do good to this poor country."[16] Probably as a consequence of Medlycott's letter, the poem was reprinted in four London newspapers during April and May;[17] but obviously it

---

[12] T. Scott, VII, 164.
[13] See King's letter to Archbishop Wake, March 23, 1721, reprinted in *A Great Archbishop*, p. 226.
[14] King Corr, to Col. Flower, April 8, 1721.
[15] *Poems*, I, 275. Swift had written two other poems, both in 1720, on the South Sea crisis, "The Run upon the Bankers" (*ibid.*, I, 238-241) and "The Bubble," which was revised and printed under the new title "The South Sea" in *Miscellanies, the Last Volume, 1727* (*ibid.*, I, 248-259).
[16] Southwell Papers, B.M. Add. MS 34,778, letter dated April 3, 1721.
[17] For the textual history of the "Epilogue," see *Poems*, I, 273-274.

could do no good for Ireland. "We have got a fund," King wrote to a friend, "which, I hope, will amount to near fifteen hundred, but what will this be amongst so many?"[18]

Swift's letter to Bolingbroke, following these melancholy events, must have been pessimistic in the extreme. Bolingbroke professed concern for his friend and advised him loftily to "leave off instructing the citizens of Dublin,"[19] but Swift did not follow this advice, however much he may have been tempted. By late autumn of 1721, he was again instructing his fellow citizens, this time on a matter more controversial than the advocacy of native manufactures.

At the conclusion of the 1720 *Proposal* Swift had referred briefly and contemptuously to "a *Thing* they call a *Bank*."[20] On May 7, 1720 — around the time that the *Proposal* was published — *Whalley's News-Letter* had reported "a Scheam for errecting a Bank in Ireland to save our Moneys in the Kingdom." The project had first been discussed early in 1719, and on September 8 of that year a group of backers had submitted a petition to the King for a charter. Plans called for a nominal capital of £500,000, of which £100,000 was to be raised by subscription. The bank would issue notes not in excess of its nominal capital, and it would lend money to merchants at a maximum rate of 5 per cent per annum.[21] On July 27, 1721, a charter was granted, subject to the approval of the Irish Parliament and stipulating that the entire capital of £500,000 be subscribed for on or before November 10, 1721.[22] When Parliament convened the following September, both Houses submitted favorable reports on the proposals. There were dissentients, however, and for the next two months the issue was strenuously debated, both in Parliament and in the press. On December 9, Commons voted 150 to 80 against the heads of a bill for establishing a bank. On December 15, the same action was taken by the Lords.[23]

John Hely-Hutchinson, the late–eighteenth-century Irish states-

---

[18] King Corr, to Col. Flower, April 8, 1721.
[19] *Corr,* III, 89.   [20] *Prose Works,* IX, 21-22.
[21] F. G. Hall, *The Bank of Ireland, 1783-1946* (Dublin, 1949), pp. 15-16. Swift was undoubtedly telling the truth when, in the 1720 *Proposal,* he averred that he was a stranger to the details of the bank project, for he said that according to report, "one Half of this Money will be *real,* and the other Half altogether imaginary" (*Prose Works,* IX, 22). This estimate of the bank's operating capital was much more liberal than the actual amount provided by the sponsors of the scheme.
[22] Hall, p. 18.   [23] *Ibid.,* pp. 19-21.

man, has pointed out that the surprising thing about the history of
the bank bill is not that it was defeated but that it was ever seriously
considered by the Irish Parliament.[24] Coming as it did on the heels
of the South Sea disaster, the scheme was pointedly reminiscent of
the Bubble. According to Archbishop King, the initial favorable
report on the bill was made possible only because "the House [of
Lords] was still thin," attended chiefly by members who were subscribers to the bank.[25] King expressed the reaction of a great many
men in Ireland at the time when he said, "France had it's Missis-
sippi & Britain it's South Sea but it is thought this Bubble will be
Sufficient to do our business."[26] As early as 1720, he had warned
that the bank would "only put it in the power of a few to cheat
the whole kingdom, and bring in the villainous trade of Stock
Jobbing and paper credit to the ruin of the nation."[27]

Swift, of course, with his mistrust of projectors — especially those
associated with the monied interests — shared his archbishop's
opinion. However, he was unjustifiably pessimistic in believing that
King was "likely to be the sole opposer of the bank" in the House
of Lords.[28] The final votes in both Houses show that King's was the
majority position. In answer to an anguished letter from King that
"the pernicious Bank is tumbling upon us," John Stearne, Bishop
of Clogher, offered an ingenious plan to defeat "the present pernicious project": He proposed that the directors of the Bank of
England be warned that a national bank in Ireland would cause
them to lose their Irish deposits![29] Another ally among the clergy
was Edward Synge, Archbishop of Tuam. Looking back on the
debate a year later, he wrote, "Last Session of our Parliament we
had a Struggle to get free from the Design of establishing a Bank
here; which if it had taken effect, would have drawn very evil
consequences after it."[30]

Nor was the opposition to the bank confined to representatives of
the Irish interest — men like Swift, King, Stearne, and Synge.

---

[24] John Hely-Hutchinson, *The Commercial Restraints of Ireland* (Dublin,
1779), p. 41.
[25] King Corr, to Molesworth, Nov. 18, 1721.
[26] King Corr, to Stearne, Oct. 5, 1721.
[27] King Corr, to Richard Gorges, Sept. 30, 1720. Gorges was Lieutenant-
General of the Forces of Ireland.
[28] *Corr*, III, 101.
[29] King Corr, to Stearne, Oct. 5, 1721; Stearne to King, Oct. 9, 1721.
[30] Gilbert Collection, MS 28, Synge to Wake, Oct. 21, 1723.

Viscount Midleton, although he was too genuinely concerned for Ireland's welfare to be called a supporter of the English interest, never approved of what he regarded the extreme methods of the Irish interest. When the bank bill was first outlined in Parliament, he was in favor of it, but he soon joined the opposition. During the later agitation over Wood's halfpence, he declared that Wood's patent enabled him to carry off Ireland's gold and silver in exchange for base metal, "as the bank would have done in exchange for the banker's paper."[31] Even Bishop Nicolson, who was not only a sycophantic adherent to the English interest but also a bitter personal enemy of King and Swift, feared the effects of the proposed bank. "Our Law-givers . . . in both Houses of Parliament," he wrote Archbishop Wake in 1722, "have been alarm'd with the noise of approaching Famine; from which it was suppos'd nothing but a National Bank could save us. This Experiment most of us were unwilling to try: And, as yet, we subsist pretty chearfully without it." Nicolson's opposition even led him so far as to praise a tract attributed to Swift, *Subscribers to the Bank,* a copy of which he sent to Wake with the comment, "The inclosed Notes on the men and their circumstances, are generally believ'd to be as true as they are biting."[32]

Had it been established, the bank might have proved beneficial to Ireland. The proposals appear to have offered a sound means of stabilizing interest rates and making currency more available for domestic trade, and the organizers of the project seem to have been disinterested in their efforts to help the country. In fact, the pamphlets of Henry Maxwell, one of the most active of the bank's supporters, present calmly and logically a series of arguments based on fact or sound probability; whereas those of his principal antagonist, Hercules Rowley, often avoid Maxwell's central arguments and appeal, very skillfully, to peripheral issues.[33] For example,

---

[31] Coxe, II, 369-370. Grafton in 1723 charged that Brodrick changed his stand on the bank project only after "he discover'd a flame raised against it . . ." (*ibid.,* II, 355). Apparently, however, Brodrick's change of heart was prompted by the same motives that influenced other members of Parliament who had at first favored the bank. Throughout his long career in Irish politics, Brodrick displayed a heroic and obstinate independence of thought and action.

[32] Gilbert Collection, MS 28, Nicolson to Wake, Jan. 6, 1722, and Nov. 21, 1721.

[33] Rowley, a member of the Irish Commons, played an active part in

Rowley argued that Catholics, who were forbidden to buy land, would invest heavily in the bank and gain control as its principal stockholders. Then, after this appeal to Protestant bias, he exploited the fears of landowners with the prediction that the monied interests would eventually control the bank and enforce a land tax.[34]

To assume too confidently, however, that the bank would have been the blessing its supporters claimed is to ignore the hard facts of life in the Ireland of the 1720's. The attitude of the bank's opponents can be explained not only by their fear of another South Sea but also by events in Ireland's recent past. The Declaratory Act had unequivocally defined Ireland's legislative status, a point which Rowley put to effective use in one of his pamphlets:

> As Ireland is a dependant kingdom . . . we ought . . . to be very cautious how we pin any thing down upon ourselves, the consequences whereof are at least very doubtful; for if in process of time we should find it ever so disadvantageous and ruinous; yet if it either increases the power, or tends to the profit of those who have the negative on us, we must bear the burthen. . . . If the intended bank prove advantageous to us . . . and should in the least interfere with . . . the trade of England, then we may expect they will procure a repeal of the charter.[35]

This was perhaps an emotional appeal, but the events of 1719 made it an understandable one. It was, as a matter of fact, a commonplace objection. Francis Annesley, a regular correspondent of King's, wrote the archbishop from London that the bank would have to depend on England for its subsistence — a dependence which would "make you all more slaves than at present you are"; and he added, "such a bank will do more mischief with your Legislature than any one thing that can be invented."[36] And for a time, it appeared that the promoters of the bank would turn Ireland's dependence to their advantage. Despite the mounting oppo-

---

domestic politics in the 1720's. In 1722, he was appointed Sheriff of Meath by the lords justices (see *Mist's Weekly Journal*, Dec. 1, 1722). Maxwell, also a member of the Commons, was Rowley's nephew (see William Monck Mason, *The History and Antiquities of the Collegiate and Cathedral Church of St. Patrick* [Dublin, 1820], p. 326, n. t). In 1704, he published *An Essay Towards the Union of Great Britain and Ireland*. For a list of pamphlets on the bank controversy — including those by Rowley and Maxwell — see Wagner, pp. 6-14.

[34] Hercules Rowley, *An Answer to a Book, Intitl'd, Reasons Offer'd for Erecting a Bank in Ireland* (Dublin, 1721), pp. 38-40.

[35] *Answer to a Book* . . . , quoted by Mason, p. 326, n. t.

[36] King Corr, Francis Annesley to King, May 30, 1721.

sition in Parliament to the project, the commissioners of the bank
opened their subscription books; determined, King wrote Annesley,
"to cramb it down our throats by their own Strength and Countenance of Court from your side."[37]

Another objection — and it is related to the dependency issue —
echoed Swift's favorite thesis of Ireland's uniqueness. The anonymous author of *A Letter from a Lady in Town to Her Friend in the
Country* asked "how a Country wholly Crampt in every Branch
of its Trade, of Large Extent, ill Peopled, and abounding in Commodities, which they had neither Liberty to Export, nor Encourage-
ments to Manufacture; could be benefitted by a Bank, which [is]
. . . only useful in free Countries where the Territory . . . [is]
small, and the Trade General, and Unlimited."[38] The bank's
opponents may have been misguided, but their motives for attacking the project were by no means "factious" or "purely political,"
as a recent historian has characterized Swift's part in the controversy.[39] The conflict was in part one between the landed and the
monied interests, which accounts to some extent for the position of
the high church party, traditionally allied with the landed group.
But there was something more than this rivalry at stake. There was
also the conviction that the bank would mean disaster for Ireland
— a conviction shared by the government man, Nicolson; the Whig,
William King; and the "disaffected Tory," Swift.

It is easier to establish the fact of Swift's opposition to the bank
than it is to determine his contribution to the mass of pamphlets
occasioned by the controversy. Shortly after the bill was defeated
in Commons, Swift wrote to a friend, "You hear the bank was
kicked out with ignominy last Saturday. This subject filled the
town with pamphlets, and none writ so well as by Mr. Rowley
though he was not thought to have many talents for an author. As
to my own part, I mind little what is doing out of my proper
dominions, the Liberties of the Deanery."[40] This expression of
indifference cannot be reconciled either with Swift's past performance or with his known opinion of the bank. A year and a half

---

[37] King Corr, King to Annesley, Oct. 28, 1721.

[38] *Prose Works*, IX, 302.

[39] Hall, pp. 22, 28. Dr. Hall is at least consistent in his judgment that
Swift's motives for intervening in Irish affairs stemmed from his anger at
the Whig triumph of 1714. He attributes Swift's opposition to Wood's
halfpence to the same cause.

[40] *Corr*, III, 108.

earlier, he had "minded" what occurred outside the liberty of St. Patrick's, and one of the issues that disturbed him then was the report that efforts were afoot to establish the bank. When the report became fact, Swift was certainly involved in the pamphlet war that followed. Indeed, his name seems to have been linked to one of the tracts written by Rowley, whom he had known as early as 1714.[41] Rowley's tract, *An Answer to a Book, Intitl'd, Reasons Offer'd for Erecting a Bank in Ireland,* itself provoked an answer, *A Letter to the Gentlemen of the Landed Interest in Ireland.* This piece hints that Rowley was not the sole author of the *Answer to a Book.* The "Criticks of this Town," it reports, acknowledge Rowley's "known Candour and Probity" in the "Gentlemen-like Strokes" in the *Answer;* "but the bold Accusations of the *English* Parliament, and the dreadful Consequences with which the Mob is frighted, they attribute to some zealous Pen, that is angry and discontented."[42] The one pen in Dublin that best answered this description was the Dean of St. Patrick's. The hint, therefore, while it may be groundless, is clearly in reference to Swift; and it makes one phrase in his letter praising Rowley rather suspicious: "none writ so well as by Mr. Rowley *though he was not thought to have many talents for an author.*"

It is well to remember, however, that while Swift could be disingenuous about his pamphleteering, he could also complain with justice that "all the scurvy things that come out of here" were being fathered on him at this time.[43] The problem of authorship is made even more difficult by the fact that of the bank tracts ascribed to Swift, only two — *The Wonderful Wonder of Wonders* and *The Wonder of All the Wonders* — were later included in the Swift-Pope *Miscellanies, the Third Volume* (1732) or in the authoritative Dublin edition of Swift's works published by George Faulkner in 1735.[44] The absence of the rest of the tracts from either of these editions does not absolutely preclude their having been written by Swift, but it does make them suspect. Certainly, contemporary attribution of a tract is not sufficient warrant for assuming Swift's

---

[41] *Ibid.,* II, 251.

[42] *A Letter to the Gentlemen of the Landed Interest in Ireland, Relating to a Bank* (Dublin, 1721), pp. 16-17.

[43] *Corr,* III, 125.

[44] For a discussion of the authority of Faulkner's edition, see Sir Harold Williams, *The Text of Gulliver's Travels* (Cambridge, 1952), especially chapter III.

authorship. The bank controversy occasioned a good many "scurvy things," and both Dublin and London booksellers had already learned the value of Swift's name on a title page.

Hence, a piece like *The Swearer's Bank,* which appeared in late July or August, 1720, and which was almost immediately ascribed to Swift,[45] is almost certainly not by him. For one thing, the Dublin edition was printed by Thomas Hume, a printer with whom Swift seems never to have had dealings; for another, the style of *The Swearer's Bank* is not characteristic of Swift's work.[46] Another tract, *A Letter from a Lady in Town to Her Friend in the Country, Concerning the Bank,* may have been written by Swift, although it was not attributed to him at the time of its publication and was not included in any edition of his works before Walter Scott's. It was one of several pieces printed by John Harding from November to December, 1721. Harding had printed Swift's "Epilogue" for the weavers' benefit the preceding April, and he was later to be the Drapier's printer. The bank tracts for which there is the strongest evidence of Swift's authorship all came from his press.

A Letter from a Lady was probably published on December 9, the day the bank bill was defeated in Commons.[47] It is a very well-written pamphlet. The Lady has been commissioned by a friend to subscribe to the bank; but, as she explains, she has not done so, because a Dublin acquaintance told her the history of the project and warned her of its dangers. Phrases like "a Jargon which I did not comprehend" and "Masterly Stroaks in Political Calculations" bear a resemblance to Swift's style, and in one passage, the *Letter* touches on the recurrent theme in Swift's Irish tracts: Ireland's uniqueness. The Lady's informant describes Maxwell as "a Gentle-man whose Intentions were better than his Abilities. . . . From

---

[45] It was reprinted in London by James Roberts as "written by Dean Swift." *Boyer's Political State* for August 25, 1720, reprinted it with the statement that it had appeared "About the beginning of this Month" and that it was "said to be written by the facetious Dean Jonathan Swift." Boyer's attribution probably derives from the Roberts reprint, which came out around August 10, the date of the companion piece prefacing Roberts' edition, *An Essay on English Bubbles.*

[46] Herbert Davis notes these objections to Swift's authorship (*Prose Works,* IX, xix). Although the style of *The Swearer's Bank* is dissimilar to Swift's, the tract offers an interesting anticipation of the "statistical" device Swift was later to use in *A Modest Proposal* (see *ibid.,* IX, 295-296).

[47] Although it is dated December 1, 1721, it was advertised in *Harding's Weekly Impartial News Letter* for December 9, as "This Day . . . [to] be Publish'd by the Printer hereof."

poring upon *Dav'enant, Petty, Child,* and other *Reasoners* from *Political Arithmetic* he hath drawn Conclusions by no Means Calculated for the Circumstances and Condition of *Ireland.*"[48]

In her *Letter,* the Lady affirmed the "Notorious Truth" of the allegations of a pamphlet entitled *Subscribers to the Bank.*[49] This tract and its ironic answer, *A Letter to the King at Arms,* were printed by Harding about the middle of November[50] and have traditionally been accepted as Swift's. At least three contemporaries attributed *Subscribers to the Bank* to him.[51] Inaccurately based on the printed roll of subscribers that appeared prior to the election of a governor and a board of directors,[52] it lists the subscribers not by name but "according to Their Order and Quality." The phrase indicates the ironic technique. First listed are the subscribing nobility, who number only seven, including one *"French* Baron." The gentry fare even worse: Only two are subscribers, and the author remarks that while the "Total of Baronets and Knights . . . [is] uncertain . . . [it is] in common Computation supposed to be more than Two." And so the compiler continues, itemizing with studied contempt the handful of subscribers among the ranks of the clergy, the army, and the merchants.[53] Stylistically, *Subscribers to the Bank* resembles Swift's work. It is far more characteristic than is *A Letter to the King at Arms,* an ironic defense by one of the "Reputed Esquires" whose dignity was ruffled by the earlier tract. The transparent *double-entendres* of the *Letter* reveal that "A. B. Esquire" is the son of a postilion and a bankrupt innkeeper and that he himself is a footman.[54] It is a negligible achievement, which, as its close connection with *Subscribers to the Bank* suggests, was written either by Swift or by one of his circle. "Mr. Sheridan's

---

[48] *Prose Works,* IX, 300, 303.   [49] *Ibid.,* IX, 304.

[50] The copy of *A Letter to the King at Arms* at Trinity College, Dublin, is dated November 18, 1721. Herbert Davis accepts this date (see *ibid.,* IX, xx), although it does not appear in his copy text, "the original half-sheet" in the Yale University Library.

[51] The anonymous author of *A Letter to Henry Maxwell* intimated that Swift wrote *Subscribers to the Bank* (Wagner, pp. 8-9; and *Prose Works,* IX, xx), as did the author of *The Bank of Ireland's Answer* (*ibid.,* IX, 317) and a newsletter of December 6, 1721 (*Corr,* III, 108, n. 4).

[52] It fails to list, for example, the Earl of Abercorn, one of the signers of the original petition and the bank's most important supporter (see Hall, p. 16). The official list of subscribers is reprinted in Wagner, pp. 9-11.

[53] *Prose Works,* IX, 288-290.   [54] *Ibid.,* IX, 291-293.

hand," Swift complained a few months after the defeat of the bank, "sometimes entertains the world, and I pay for all."[55]

The two pieces which, of all the bank tracts, can most surely be assigned to Swift, are *The Wonderful Wonder of Wonders* and *The Wonder of All the Wonders that Ever the World Wondered at.* Not only were they reprinted in *Miscellanies, the Third Volume* and in Faulkner's 1735 edition of Swift's works, but in Swift's copy of the *Miscellanies* they are marked, with minor corrections, as by Swift.[56] Despite this strong presumptive evidence of Swift's authorship, some scholars have been reluctant to admit two such "questionable trifles" to the canon, especially when they are of the crude variety of these two items.[57] However, Swift was not above writing trifles, and when these two are read in relation to the subliterary forms which they consciously parody, their crudeness is understandable.

The London reprint of *The Wonderful Wonder of Wonders* carries the subtitle, "Being an Accurate Description of the Birth, Education, Manner of Living, Religion, Politics, Learning, &c. of Mine A —— se."[58] With the thoroughness and obviousness of schoolboy scatology, it describes and personifies a rump as "a Person lately arrived at this City." As it appears in the *Miscellanies,* it has no apparent relevance to the bank controversy, but a sentence in the London reprint shows that it was, in fact, an attack on the bank: "He lives from *Hand* to *Mouth,* but however, the greatest and wisest People will trust him with all their ready Money, which he was never known to *Embezzle,* except, very rarely, when he is sacrificing to his Goddesses below."[59]

The Wonder of All the Wonders advertises the marvels performed by one John Emanuel Schoitz (a name altogether in the style of *The Wonderful Wonder of Wonders*). The wonder-

---

[55] *Corr,* III, 125.

[56] The marked copy of *Miscellanies, the Third Volume* (1732) is in the possession of Lord Rothschild. See *The Rothschild Library* (privately printed at Cambridge University Press, Cambridge, 1954), I, 366-367.

[57] See *Prose Works,* IX, xvii. Professor Davis accepts the pieces tentatively, printing them among the bank papers as "probably written by Swift" (see *ibid.,* IX, 281-287).

[58] There is no known Dublin edition of this tract extant, although it was almost certainly first printed in Dublin. The bank issue was too topical for Swift to have arranged for the tract to appear first in London. It was doubtless reprinted there because by 1721 anything by Swift was marketable. For an account of the London reprints, see Teerink, items 905, 906.

[59] Quoted in *Prose Works,* IX, 378.

worker's feats have in common a single characteristic: Schoitz will do great violence in one form or another to the assembled company — such as running a sword through a gentleman's body, throwing scalding oil on the ladies, drawing the teeth of his audience — and then restore his victims unscathed. Such is the version that appears in the *Miscellanies* and in Faulkner. If the modern reader knows that the piece is related to the antibank pamphlets, he can see its deeply implicit meaning: Schoitz's claims, like the promises of the bank's advocates, will have catastrophic results if they are accepted. The eighteenth-century reader could have read at least one version containing a passage that makes the point explicit: "FINALLY, HE takes from any Gentleman, Ladies, Widows or Orphans, all the Ready Cash they can muster, with Bond and Judgment for all they are or ever will be Worth; which he secures to his own Use, for the Advantage of the said Widows, &c. and the Benefit of the whole Kingdom: And this he as certainly performs to their Satisfaction, as any of his indubitable Operations before-mention'd."[60]

Both *The Wonderful Wonder of Wonders* and *The Wonder of All the Wonders* are parodies of two familiar types of eighteenth-century broadsides. *The Wonder of All the Wonders* is an imitation of the handbills circulated by mountebanks to advertise their feats. The marvels that it promises are scarcely more fantastic than those in the genuine advertisements of the time. One such wonder-worker was invited to appear before the Dublin Philosophical Society in 1685. This artist, who according to the minutes of the society was a German (cf. Schoitz?), "charged a Pistol with a bullet, and discharged it at a Sheet of Paper, The Bullet came out

---

[60] Quoted in *ibid.*, IX, xviii. The tract was reprinted by J. Roberts in London (as was *The Wonderful Wonder of Wonders*) in 1722. A copy of the reprint is in the Yale Library. Roberts claims to print "from the 2d *Edition*" with *Additions* of the *Dublin* copies." The "2d Edition" is presumably the copy in the British Museum, printed by A. Moore "from the Original Copy from Dublin." Besides the unique addition of the paragraph in Roberts' edition, there are slight variations in Moore's and Roberts' versions, but the two have more in common with each other than does either with Faulkner's 1735 printing, which was probably based on Swift's penciled corrections in *Miscellanies, the Third Volume* (1732). There is no known Dublin edition extant, but *Mist's Weekly Journal* for November 6, 1725, reprints the piece with the claim that it is a copy received from "a Gentleman who came from Ireland" some "two or three Years since." This version, which does not contain the deleted paragraph, is at marked variance with both the London and Faulkner reprints; the variations occur exclusively in accidentals.

in shott, making above an hundred Holes in the Paper." Following this, he anointed his hands with urine and onion juice and "suffered melted lead to fall on them."[61] Another entertainer, Cormock McMahon, described his special talents in *A Wonderful Account of the Grand Devourer of Butter-Milk*. McMahon "slits a hot *Potatoe* and puts his Tongue into it, and while his Tongue is a *Parboiling*, sings the *Irish Cry* to Admiration."[62] This broadsheet seems a representative model of the kind imitated by *The Wonder of All the Wonders*. Each begins by announcing the arrival of the celebrity; and after recounting the marvels to be offered, each notes the success of previous performances (Schoitz has won the applause of "most Kings and Princes in *Europe*," whereas McMahon more modestly limits his triumphs to Derry, Cavan, Enniskillen, Kilkenny, and Limerick); finally, each tells where the performance will be given and quotes the prices of tickets.

The Wonderful Wonder of Wonders is patterned after that staple item of eighteenth-century chapbooks, the accounts of freaks and monstrous births. There is a *Wonder of Wonders* in John Ashton's *Chap-Books of the Eighteenth Century*, along with a *Miracle of Miracles* — the "true accounts," respectively, of a mermaid and of an Essex girl "brought to Bed of a Strange Monster."[63] *The Wonderful Wonder of Wonders* is not a faithful copy of its prototype, but its title and the "improbable, and unnatural" character of the "certain Person lately arrived at this City" are sufficient to make the parody clear.

When the deleted paragraphs are restored, Swift's purpose in writing these "questionable trifles" becomes apparent. When they are read as parodies of popular genres, their crudeness and lack of wit and style are vindicated. The reader should no more expect polish and subtlety from them than he should expect true wit from the inanities of *Polite Conversation*. Swift's "bills of wonders" have no literary value (this is the price of verisimilitude to their models), but they express perfectly Swift's contempt for the charla-

---

[61] Minutes of the Dublin Philosophical Society for March 23, 1684/85 (B.M. Add. MS 4811, fol. 169). I am indebted to Professor Irvin Ehrenpreis for calling my attention to this information.

[62] This broadsheet, which is undated, is in Marsh's Library, Dublin.

[63] John Ashton, *Chap-Books of the Eighteenth Century* (London, 1882), pp. 74-77, 60.

tans who were urging the citizens of Dublin to give their money to that unnatural monster, the bank.[64]

[II]

About the time the author of *The Present Miserable State of Ireland* was writing moving accounts of the crowds of beggars that swarmed the streets of Dublin, the city was faced with an even more serious problem. An inevitable result of the widespread unemployment was an increase in the crime rate. In 1721, *The London Mercury* reported that street robberies in Dublin had grown so common that it was dangerous to be abroad after ten at night.[65] The robbers, working in gangs, "would seize on Gentlemen, and take them into remote Corners, and after they had robbed them, would leave them bound and gagged."[66] Because of these conditions, an item in *Whalley's News-Letter* for Monday, April 30, 1722, may have held more than usual interest for Dublin readers:

> On Wednesday [April 25], were Tryed at the King's-Bench, for Stealing a Mare from Councillor Sweeny, Rich. Otway a Boy, and Ebenezer Alison who about two Years since was Pardon'd upon becoming an Evidence against Macmanaus and his own Apprentice, who thereupon were Executed at Stephens green, for several Robberies committed by Alison, and them in company; in about this City; and also Stephen Mauley and

---

[64] Of the remaining pieces on the bank controversy that have at one time or another been attributed to Swift, "The Bank Thrown Down," a poem celebrating the project's defeat, may have been written by him; Sir Harold Williams accepts it "with some hesitation" (*Poems*, I, 286). There is nothing in three prose papers of December, 1721, to suggest Swift's authorship: *The Last Speech and Dying Words of the Bank of Ireland,* although printed by Harding, was obviously written by a proponent of the bank. Because it attacked the House of Commons for defeating the bank bill (for example, "I believe we have Less Sense, and more evil Nature in this Kingdom, than in any Part of Europe" [*Prose Works*, IX, 307]), the broadside was on December 9 condemned by the House as "a false, scandalous and malicious Libel" (quoted in *ibid.*, IX, xxi). The two remaining papers are *An Account of the Short Life, Sudden Death, and Pompous Funeral of Michy Windybank, &c.* (see *ibid.*, IX, 308-310) and *The Bank's Ghost.* The latter, published after the bank had "lain ten Days in the Dust," was an answer to *The Last Speech and Dying Words of the Bank of Ireland,* which had been condemned in Commons on December 9. It therefore probably appeared on December 19. There is a copy of the broadsheet in the National Library of Ireland.

[65] Quoted by F. E. Ball, *Swift's Verse*, pp. 175-176.

[66] Faulkner's note to *The Last Speech and Dying Words of Ebenezor Elliston,* reprinted in *Prose Works*, IX, 37.

Patrick Mauley, for Stealing 2 Silver-Tankards from *John Capine,* and Cormick Roch for Robbing his Master, a Gardiner in Ballybough Lane. The first viz. the Boy, was acquitted, but the other 4 found Guilty and Sentenc'd to be Hang'd on Wednesday next.

Of the four condemned malefactors, "Ebenezer Alison," a member of a Dublin street gang since 1719, was the most notorious. His real name seems to have been Ebenezor Elliston. When he was caught with Counselor Sweeny's mare, he denied any criminal intent. He had borrowed the mare, he said, to avoid a Dublin thieftaker who sought him for an earlier robbery. Arrested in Clonmel, where he had fled with his young accomplice, Otway, he was brought to Dublin for trial. These details are found in *The Last Farewell of Ebenezor Elliston to This Transitory World,* an apparently authentic account which Elliston gave of his criminal career shortly before his execution on May 2.[67] It was printed by John Harding for another bookseller, Elizabeth Sadlier.

Swift was not in Dublin on May 2, the day Elliston was hanged. He had left the city a day or two previously for a journey to the north of Ireland that was to keep him away until October. While he was still in Dublin, however, he saw a copy of *The Last Farewell* before it was issued by Elizabeth Sadlier. The last speech of a condemned felon was usually printed prior to the day of his execution so that it could be hawked among the crowd at the gallows, and Mrs. Sadlier had probably given Harding the text of *The Last Farewell* soon after Elliston's conviction on April 25. Harding, who had been Swift's printer since the spring of the preceding year, may have sent Swift a copy of the broadsheet as a matter of course; or Swift may have seen it on a visit to Harding's shop. When Swift read the broadsheet that Harding was printing, he saw a means of putting Elliston's forthcoming execution to even better use than the authorities intended. Accordingly, he wrote his own account of the criminal's valediction and gave it to Harding.[68] On April 28,

---

[67] This account (reprinted in *ibid.,* IX, 365-367) was "Delivered in the Presence of *George Derry,* Clerk." The name "Otway," as it appears in *Whalley's News-Letter,* is here spelled "Oroway."

[68] This is admittedly an hypothesis. Swift may in some other way have seen the broadsheet that Harding was printing for Elizabeth Sadlier. He had, however, to have seen it before he wrote his own version, as will subsequently be demonstrated. He probably composed this version between April 26 (Elliston was convicted on April 25) and April 28; he must have left Dublin for his northern journey no later than April 29 (see *Corr,* III, 131).

Harding's *Impartial News-Letter* advised its readers that "The last and true Speech of Ebenezor Ellison will be Printed by the Printer hereof (containing several Things for the Common Good) and by no other in this City. N.B. This Publick Notice is given that the Town may not be impos'd on by any sham one Printed by one Fitzgerald in Montrath-Street, who makes it his constant Practice to Impose on the Publick."

On May 2, Elliston was hanged, and Dublin readers could choose between two versions of his dying words: Sadlier's *Last Farewell* and the broadsheet Harding had advertised four days earlier, *The Last Speech and Dying Words of Ebenezor Ellison,* "Publish'd at his Desire for the Common Good."[69] (If "one Fitzgerald" issued yet another account of Elliston's last words, it has not survived.)[70] *The Last Speech* was different from *The Last Farewell*

It does not seem likely to suppose that Swift wrote both versions, using the "authentic" one as a foil for the other. This would have involved unnecessary trouble, especially since Swift had so short a time in which to work.

[69] There can be no doubt that the advertisement referred to Swift's broadsheet and not the one Harding printed for Elizabeth Sadlier. Not only do the title and the phrase "for the Common Good" echo the opening sentence of the advertisement, but also both the advertisement and *The Last Speech* spell "Elliston" as "Ellison."

Until recently, it was not known that Harding printed Swift's broadsheet, the earliest known source for *The Last Speech* being Faulkner's 1735 edition of Swift's works. However, Daniel L. McCue, Jr., has discovered the broadsheet that came from Harding's press in 1722. He reports this discovery and provides a photostat of Harding's edition of *The Last Speech* in the *Harvard Library Bulletin,* XIII (1959), 362-368. Aside from minor differences in punctuation, the important variants between Harding's and Faulkner's printings are as follows: Harding spells the criminal's name "Ellison," whereas Faulkner — agreeing with the spelling in *The Last Farewell* — spells it "Elliston"; Harding's title contains the phrase "Who is to be Executed this Second Day of May, 1722," whereas Faulkner's title is emended to *"who was Executed the Second Day of* May, 1722"; Harding's broadsheet contains a paragraph at the end — omitted by Faulkner — which lists the names of two other criminals sentenced to die: they are Patrick Mc. Clanen and Stephen Mc. Clanen, obviously the "Patrick and Stephen Mauley" of *Whalley's News-Letter* (they were not members of the gang, as McCue suggests [p. 366], but were convicted of separate offenses, as Whalley's news item makes clear); finally, the statement in Harding's broadsheet which reads, "I hope you shall see me Die like a *Man* tho' a Death *contrary,"* is revised in Faulkner's edition to read, "I hope you shall see me die like a Man, the Death of a Dog."

[70] I have been unable to find not only any reference to an Elliston broadsheet printed by Fitzgerald but also any reference, aside from Harding's, to a Dublin printer of that name. No Fitzgerald is listed in Plomer's *Dictionary of Booksellers and Printers, 1668-1725,* or in Dix's *Dictionary of Booksellers and Printers, 1726-1775.*

in a number of ways, but what most distinguished it was the remarkable threat that it contained for Elliston's confederates who
were still at large — "Elliston's" solemn declaration that he has
left a list of their names and offenses with "an honest Man," who
has promised, on hearing of the arrest of any on his list, to turn
the entire paper over to the authorities.[71] The threat must have
carried added weight with Elliston's associates in crime who recalled that two years earlier he had not only informed against
"Macmanaus" but had at the same time threatened to discover
four other gangs.[72]

When the two broadsheets are compared, it is clear that *The Last
Farewell* not only suggested the idea but also provided the specific
model for Swift's grim parody. *The Last Farewell* is the usual
kind of gallows oratory. It contains a brief summary of Elliston's
early life, an account of his crimes, and the reiterated protestation
of his sincere repentance; and its grammar and orthography are
atrocious. Swift's Elliston, on the other hand, begins his con-
fession with a denunciation of the stereotyped speeches attributed
to condemned criminals, which, he says, invariably contain "a pretended Account of our Birth and Family; of the Fact for which
we are to die; of our sincere Repentance; and a Declaration of
our Religion" — and which are so badly written that even an
"illiterate and ignorant" criminal would be "ashamed to have such
Nonsense and false *English* charged upon him." The Elliston of *The
Last Farewell* avers that he was brought to his present condition not
by "the Delusions of Women," but by the wiles of Satan; whereas
the Elliston of *The Last Speech* warns his readers that "Nothing
is more dangerous to idle young Fellows than the Company of those
odious common Whores we frequent." *The Last Farewell* presents
a thoroughly chastened and penitent sinner, whereas *The Last
Speech* reveals a hardened criminal who regrets not his misdeeds but
the ill luck that has brought him to the gallows. As for the threat of
Swift's Elliston to turn informer, the Elliston of *The Last Farewell*

---

[71] *Prose Works,* IX, 39. All references are to this edition, which is based
on Faulkner's 1735 printing of *The Last Speech.* Aside from those discussed in n. 69, the variations between Faulkner and Harding are minor.

[72] See *Whalley's News-Letter,* March 5, 1719/20: "[He] says he was in
above 24 Robberies, in which he will discover 4 Gangs and some of 'em
Sons of Men of Note in this City, but The Particulars keepes Secret as
yet." I am indebted to Professor George Mayhew for calling my attention
to this item.

makes a specific point of refusing to publish the names of his former accomplices.[73]

The antithetical points in *The Last Speech* and *The Last Farewell* are too exactly matched to be merely coincidental. Swift had recently parodied "bills of wonders" in his attack on the bank. Now he was parodying an equally popular subliterary species in an effort to combat Dublin's crime wave.

The Last Speech is a serious variation of the kind of hoax Swift had played so well in the Bickerstaff pamphlets. Unlike the patently pseudonymous Bickerstaff, Elliston is altogether credible; the success of the hoax depended on his being so. Swift achieved this credibility not through biographical details but through psychological realism, portraying with remarkable verisimilitude a man incurably addicted to crime. Although he is incapable of repentance, Elliston fully recognizes the wickedness and sterility of his way of life. At one point, his *Last Speech* reads like a scene from a tragic *Beggar's Opera:*

> If any Thing in this World be like Hell, as I have heard it described by our Clergy; the truest Picture of it must be in the Back-Room of one of our Ale-houses at Midnight; where a Crew of Robbers and their Whores are met together after a Booty, and are beginning to grow drunk; from which Time, until they are past their Senses, is such a continued horrible Noise of Cursing, Blasphemy, Lewdness, Scurrility, and brutish Behaviour; such Roaring and Confusion, such a Clatter of Mugs and Pots at each other's Heads; that *Bedlam,* in Comparison, is a sober and orderly Place: At last they all tumble from their Stools and Benches, and sleep away the rest of the Night; and generally the Landlord or his Wife, or some other Whore who has a stronger Head than the rest, picks their Pockets before they wake. The Misfortune is, that we can never be easy till we are drunk; and our Drunkenness constantly exposes us to be more easily betrayed and taken.[74]

Even with this terrible awareness of the wages of sin, however, Elliston admits that if he could secure a pardon "at the Foot of the Gallows," he would resume his old habits by nightfall — although he tells his former comrades (in one of the cleverest touches in the *Speech*) that he will behave at his execution "after the usual Manner, Kneeling, with a Book in my Hand, and my Eyes lift up."[75] One feels that his desire to expose his friends "for the Common Good" is compulsive rather than altruistic, so bitter is his detesta-

[73] *Prose Works,* IX, 37-38, 366, 39, 365-367 *passim,* 38, 365-366.
[74] *Ibid.,* IX, 41.   [75] *Ibid.,* IX, 41, 38.

tion of the vice which has ensnared him: "upon the whole, we ought to be looked upon as the common Enemies of Mankind; whose Interest it is to root us out like Wolves, and other mischievous Vermin, against which no fair Play is required."[76]

According to Faulkner's note to his reprint of *The Last Speech,* Swift's deception was so successful that "very few Robberies of that kind" had been committed since.[77] This claim must be exaggerated, but Swift's broadsheet might have been a temporary deterrent. It is easy to imagine its sobering effect on Elliston's acquaintances.

[III]

The tracts that Swift wrote between the publication of the *Proposal for the Universal Use of Irish Manufacture* and *The Drapier's Letters* show an interest in Ireland's welfare quite independent of his hatred of the Whigs in England. The bank tracts, the weavers' "Epilogue," and Elliston's *Last Speech* all dealt exclusively with Irish affairs. When he published the *Proposal* of 1720, Swift committed himself to Ireland's cause, and he remained firm to the commitment throughout the rest of his active life. Another lifelong concern was the Church of Ireland, and although Swift's higher loyalty was always to his church, he did not regard the interests of church and state as necessarily incompatible; indeed, he felt that the economic well-being of both was closely related.[78] He had already labored in behalf of the established church before he came to Ireland as Dean of St. Patrick's, to gain the remission of the First Fruits and — with less Christian charity, perhaps — to oppose the removal of the Sacramental Test. In 1723, he became involved in another ecclesiastical issue, when he published *Some Arguments Against Enlarging the Power of Bishops in Letting of Leases.* The tract was written in opposition not to the Irish bishops (as its misleading title would suggest) but to the lay landlords who sought the repeal of an act passed during the reign of Charles I to prevent the alienation of church lands.[79]

Swift found occasion in his tract to disagree respectfully with his

---

[76] *Ibid.,* IX, 41.   [77] *Ibid.,* IX, 37.

[78] Landa, *Swift and the Church of Ireland,* p. 97.

[79] The tract is reprinted in *Prose Works,* IX, 45-60. For a discussion of the act against alienation of church lands (10 and 11 Charles I, *Statutes at Large,* c. 3) and the landlords' attempt to repeal it in 1723, see Landa, pp. 97-110.

ally during the dependency crisis of 1719, Viscount Molesworth. *Some Arguments Against Enlarging the Power of Bishops* was published in October, probably October 26.[80] About a week before it appeared, Molesworth had published *Some Considerations for the Promotion of Agriculture.*[81] Although Swift praised it as "an excellent Discourse . . . full of most useful *Hints,*" he took exception to the viscount's charge that tithes were an unwarranted burden on Irish tenants. Swift was unwilling to abandon the principle that tithes were the church's divine right, a position that was becoming increasingly difficult to maintain in eighteenth-century Ireland.[82] However, the disagreement between Swift and Molesworth was not to alienate them, nor, indeed, even to become a matter for moderate debate. A much more serious issue had already engaged Molesworth's attention, as it was later to engage Swift's. Molesworth had dedicated his tract on agriculture to the Irish Commons, in approval of a stand they had taken a few weeks prior to its publication: "The Writer of the following Sheets, cannot more properly Dedicate them than to You, who have lately given an eminent Instance of Your Wisdom and Love to Your Country, in Your just Censure and vigorous Resolutions against a Patent calculated to destroy Your Trade, rob You of Your Money; and which calls You Slaves and Fools to Your Faces. I know not what good Thing may not be expected further from an Assembly which dares do it's Duty."

A great deal in addition to this was soon to be expected from the

---

[80] William Nicolson wrote to Archbishop Wake on October 26, 1723, "My Brother of Elphin [Henry Downes] sends your Grace a smart Pamphlet of Remarks, this day publish'd; which is supposed to be the Dean of St. Patricks" (Gilbert Collection, MS 27). *Some Arguments* was probably composed on October 21, the date printed at its conclusion. Like virtually all of the Irish bishops, Nicolson was opposed to the lay landlords' bill. In one of his rare moments of agreement with Swift, he wrote Wake that the pamphlet was "allow'd to atone for a Multitude of By-past Transgressions" (*ibid.*).

[81] Nicolson wrote to Archbishop Wake on October 19, 1723. In his letter he reported that Molesworth's tract was "this Day publish'd" (Gilbert Collection, MS 27). In Historical Manuscripts Commission, *Rpt. on Mss. in Various Collections,* VIII, 362, a draft of *Some Considerations* is described. It is a manuscript, with corrections, on the back of a letter dated August 15, 1723.

[82] *Prose Works,* IX, 58-60. Landa gives a detailed account of this controversy between the clergy and laity of Ireland (pp. 123-135).

entire nation — from the Parliament, the gentry, the shopkeepers, the tradesmen, "the whole People of Ireland." The action for which Molesworth praised the Commons had occurred on September 23, 1723, when that body sent a "humble Address to the King," objecting to a patent that had been granted to William Wood to issue copper farthings and halfpence in Ireland.

CHAPTER IV

The Drapier

After the passing of the Declaratory Act, Anglo-Irish relations became abnormally strained. Ireland's reaction to the Annesley case and the Declaratory Act predisposed the ministry to assign any new Irish protests to "disaffection," and after 1720 the leaders of the Irish interest became acutely sensitive to any new threats to Ireland's legislative status. This uneasy relationship between the two countries is reflected in a letter of 1721 from Francis Annesley to Archbishop King:

> Your Ld. Lieut. will now soon be with you. I believe he goes over with very good dispositions to do every thing he can to make your Kingdom happy, but some people fear he will meet with difficulties from your Jurisdiction being damn'd, how farr that should be made easy to him deserves consideration. I assure your Grace Ireland has few friends here and restiveness on your part may endanger the loss of your legislature and subject your Kingdom to be taxed here, which will be a fatall blow.[1]

Lord Lieutenant Grafton met with no important difficulties during the parliamentary session of 1721, for the legislators were then taken up with the purely domestic controversy of the proposed national bank. Annesley's anxiety, however, proved to have been

---

[1] King Corr, Annesley to King, May 30, 1721.

well founded, if premature. When Grafton arrived in Dublin in 1723 to open Parliament, he encountered a "restiveness" that made him frantic with alarm; and he was recalled from office a year later at the end of one of the stormiest sessions accorded any lord lieutenant during the Protestant Ascendancy.

If Walpole's biographer William Coxe can be believed, at the time Grafton was appointed lord lieutenant in 1720 he became involved in the issue responsible for his year of troubles. According to Coxe, during the viceroyalty of the Duke of Bolton (1717-19), the disposal of a patent to issue copper coins in Ireland had been given to the Duchess of Kendal, the influential mistress of George I. This favor had been bestowed on the duchess by the Earl of Sunderland, first lord of the Treasury, who urged Bolton to support the project in Ireland. Bolton, however, realizing that the scheme "would greatly embarrass his administration," refused to countenance it, but when Grafton succeeded him in 1720, "he consented to bring it forward, and was promised the support of the king's friends in Ireland."[2]

Whether or not Coxe's account of Grafton's early part in the affair is accurate, there is no doubt that Robert Walpole inherited the thorny problem of Ireland's proposed copper coinage. In 1721 he succeeded Sunderland, and although he had no personal enthusiasm for the project, he did not oppose it, "being unwilling," Coxe said, "to offend the duchess of Kendal."[3] On July 12, 1722, William Wood, an English iron dealer, was granted a patent to coin 360 tons of copper for Ireland to the value of £100,800. This action proved to be, after the Declaratory Act, the most disruptive event in Anglo-Irish relations since the Revolution of 1689.

[1]

Since the history of the halfpence crisis is so complicated, since (as one historian has said) "Passion and argument were very strangely mixed throughout the course of the whole affair,"[4] and since Swift himself wilfully manipulated "passion and argument" to serve his ends, it is important to understand that Ireland's objections to Wood's patent were both political and economic. For

---

[2] Coxe, I, 218.

[3] *Ibid.,* I, 218; and A. Goodwin, "Wood's Halfpence," *The English Historical Review,* LI (1936), 655.

[4] Archibald Ballantyne, *Lord Carteret* (London, 1887), p. 104.

various reasons and in varying degrees, almost everyone — private citizens, members of the Privy Council, and representatives in both Houses of Parliament — was opposed to the patent. The case against Wood's coin rested on a foundation sufficiently broad to accommodate "the whole People of Ireland."

The underlying cause for Ireland's dissatisfaction with the patent was the absence of a national mint. For gold and silver the Irish had to depend on the fortuitous and fluctuating circulation of coins from almost every country in Europe. To provide smaller currency, it was customary for the Crown to grant patents to private citizens to mint farthings, halfpence, and pence for the exclusive use of Ireland. When, therefore, George I awarded Wood his patent, no one in Ireland questioned his right to do so; he had precedents in similar grants as recently as the reigns of Charles II and James II. But, as the Drapier wrote in his third *Letter*, "*St. Paul* says, *All things are* Lawful, *but all things are not* Expedient. We are Answered that this Patent is *Lawful*, but is it *Expedient?*"[5] Precedent and prerogative notwithstanding, Wood's patent was highly inexpedient. It underscored the insulting fact that Ireland was denied the privilege, "possessed by every *petty* Prince abroad," of coining her own money, a privilege for which the country had petitioned since the early part of the seventeenth century.[6] Even had there been no objections to the terms of Wood's patent, the very fact that he had been given one was a humiliating reminder of Ireland's dependent status. Moreover, the secrecy with which the affair had been negotiated and the reception given their subsequent official protests seemed to the Irish a deliberate affront to national dignity. This is a recurring theme in their complaints. "We shal speak our minds freely," Midleton threatened, "in what maner the nation hath been treated in the matter of Mr. Wood from the beginning to the end."[7] King, more outspoken, declared that the Irish had been treated "with the utmost contempt; endeavoured to be imposed on as fools and children, as if we had not common understandings, or knew when we were abused."[8]

It is doubtful, however, that the issue of national dignity could have had a very widespread popular appeal in the Ireland of the

---

[5] *Drapier's Letters*, p. 54.   [6] *Ibid.*, p. 155; and O'Brien, p. 345.
[7] Coxe, II, 425.
[8] King to Gorges, Jan. 28, 1724. Quoted by Mason, p. 331, n. w.

1720's; certainly it alone could not have served as an effective rallying point for concerted action. The virtual unanimity of Irish resistance to the patent did not spring from so abstract a cause but from concrete objections to the patent itself. These objections were not political but economic. *"Money,"* the Drapier wrote in the fourth *Letter,* "the great *Divider* of the World, hath by a strange Revolution, been the great *Uniter* of a most *Divided* People."[9]

One of the most persistent objections to Wood's patent was that it allowed an excessive issue. The first official protest — that of the Commissioners of Revenue in 1722 — maintained that there was "not the least want of such small species of Coin for Change"; and Archbishop King seconded this assertion, saying that Ireland needed silver currency, not copper halfpence and farthings.[10] These claims were not true; one of the greatest hindrances to Ireland's domestic trade throughout the eighteenth century was a scarcity of small change of all denominations.[11] But even so, there was no justification for the amount of money that Wood intended to issue. Ireland's total currency was approximately £400,000; the £100,800 authorized by Wood's grant thus amounted to one-fourth of all the money in the kingdom.[12] Even when Wood later agreed to limit the amount of his coinage to £40,000, the Irish were justified in rejecting the compromise. According to Swift, £40,000 was almost twice as much copper money as Ireland needed; and Hugh Boulter, who had been appointed Primate of All Ireland in 1724 because of his unswerving devotion to the English interest, estimated that £10,000 or £20,000 in copper money was sufficient for the country's needs.[13]

Another fault of the patent was that it set at too low a rate the intrinsic value of the coins. At the mint in England twenty-three pence per pound of copper was the authorized yield; Wood's patent permitted him to coin thirty pence from each pound.[14] Not only did this increased yield allow Wood what seemed to the Irish an

---

[9] *Drapier's Letters,* p. 77.

[10] *Ibid.,* p. xiii; Goodwin, p. 654.

[11] O'Brien, p. 351. O'Brien suggests that Wood's patent may have been granted partly to replace the debased coinage issued under previous grants (p. 350). Even the Drapier admitted that Ireland needed small change (see, for example, *Drapier's Letters,* pp. 4, 20, 152).

[12] O'Brien, p. 351. O'Brien notes that in England the copper coinage amounted to one hundredth part of the total currency.

[13] *Drapier's Letters,* pp. 20-22; Boulter, I, 9.   [14] O'Brien, p. 351.

unreasonably large profit, but the low intrinsic value of his half-pence posed a threat to Ireland's supply of gold and silver. The nation's specie was already being depleted at an alarming rate even without the threat of Wood's halfpence. When the English Parliament forbade the exporting of English coin, the East India Company turned to Ireland for its supply and paid a premium for the foreign gold and silver in circulation there. Furthermore, the rate of exchange between gold and silver was different in England and Ireland, so that an Irishman could save threepence in the guinea by paying his English debts in silver instead of gold; although the gain was a small one, the practice was sufficiently widespread to cause a heavy drain on Ireland's silver.[15] Wood intended to flood Ireland with copper coins amounting to one-fourth (by his revised plans, one-eighth) of the nation's currency. It did not require any knowledge of Gresham's Law for the informed Irishman to predict the effect of this on the country's diminishing stock of gold and silver money.

The low intrinsic value of Wood's halfpence was a potential threat to Ireland's economy in still another way. In a letter to Grafton's secretary the Irish Commissioners of Revenue recalled Ireland's sufferings because of the "small base Coin" issued by earlier private grants; and *Ireland's Consternation,* a pamphlet by James Maculla, warned that Wood's halfpence and farthings — "part . . . lighter than the rest, stampt with the Harp forward on one side, and backward on the other, Edges snagled, and bulg'd" — would offer an irresistible temptation to counterfeiters, who, according to Maculla, "are or will be at Work making that Money."[16]

Wood's patent seemed particularly liable to such abuse. Not only were the coins to be manufactured in England, where any Irish complaints would be difficult to redress; Wood was further authorized to manufacture the coins at Bristol instead of at the Tower under government supervision, and the comptroller who was to assay them was one of his own employees.[17] This almost complete absence of safeguards virtually insured a currency even more

[15] Goodwin, p. 651.

[16] *Drapier's Letters,* p. xii; James Maculla, *Ireland's Consternation* (Dublin, 1723), p. 4.

[17] See *A Defense of the Conduct of the People of Ireland* (Dublin, 1724) by an anonymous author. Quoted by Mason, p. 331, n. w. See also Goodwin, p. 653.

debased than the patent allowed.[18] In addition to these opportunities for fraud, Wood was not required to redeem his coins with
legal tender on demand, a safeguard "worth a Hundred Times all
other Limitations whatsoever";[19] nor was there any practicable way
to insure that Wood not exceed the terms of the patent. He was
authorized to coin 360 tons of copper over a fourteen-year period,
but this stipulation was obviously no stronger than the patentee's
integrity, since once his coins got into circulation, there was nothing
to prevent him from surreptitiously introducing more of his money
into Ireland. The Drapier expressed a general conviction when he
predicted that Wood "will never be at rest but coin on . . . and
while there is a *Silver* Sixpence left these BLOOD-SUCKERS will
never be quiet."[20]

This, then, was Ireland's case against the halfpence. The objections had become commonplace long before Swift entered the
controversy; in fact, they were being urged even before Ireland was
officially notified of the patent. Although Walpole was so indifferent to protocol (or so circumspect) that some of Wood's coins were
actually in circulation before a copy of the grant was sent to
Dublin,[21] reports of the intended project reached Ireland as early as
the summer of 1722; and rumors quickly spread that the coinage
was to be an inferior job and that Wood expected to realize tremendous profits — large enough to enable him to pay £10,000 to
the Duchess of Kendal for having secured him the patent.[22] On
July 10, two days before the patent was granted, Archbishop King
wrote to Grafton, "I hear there is a design to coin brass money for
Ireland . . . if it be not managed with the utmost caution, it will
drain the Kingdom of the little gold and silver that is left in it."[23]
A month later, the Commissioners of Revenue in Dublin sent their
letter of protest to Grafton's secretary. In September the com-

---

[18] The Irish were confirmed in their suspicions when an assay ordered by
the Commons in 1723 disclosed that Wood had in fact issued coins of four
different kinds, varying in size, weight, and quality of workmanship (see
Goodwin, p. 653; *Drapier's Letters*, p. 41).

[19] *Ibid.*, p. 39. For an abstract of Wood's patent, see pp. 190-191.

[20] *Ibid.*, p. 9.

[21] *Ibid.*, p. xii. The Commissioners of Revenue were so ill informed that
in their letter of August, 1722, they referred to the patent as "about to be
passed," when it had already been passed the preceding month.

[22] Coxe seems to be the earliest source for the now generally accepted
account of this bribe (Coxe, I, 222).

[23] Quoted by Goodwin, p. 667.

missioners sent a second letter, this time to the Treasury in London, warning that "this matter has already made a great noise here."[24]

The English government ignored both these letters, and Wood began quietly making arrangements for the manufacture and shipment of his coins on a large scale. He and the government were so quiet that it was rumored that the design had been dropped. At the beginning of 1723, Edward Southwell, Chief Secretary for Ireland, wrote to Archbishop King, "For the New Copper Coyn intended, it is some time ago, that I was not displeas'd to hear that the patentee, having employ'd his Current Cash in procuring, was hawking about his patent at a Mortgage to raise supplys to go on, but could not find any who had a superfluity of Cash to venture on so precarious a thing."[25] By the following summer, however, there was no longer any doubt that Wood was proceeding with his plans. In August, James Maculla published *Ireland's Consternation,* which warned that some of the coins were already in circulation. Arriving in Dublin to find the subject of the halfpence "in every bodys mouth," Grafton predicted unhappily to Walpole that the business would cause "some disagreeable proceeding" in the impending session of Parliament.[26]

Grafton was an inept statesman, but on this occasion he was no bad prophet. When Parliament convened in September, the House of Commons ordered an investigation of Wood's patent, submitted some of the halfpence to a Dublin chemist for analysis, and sent an address to the King, accusing Wood of fraud and asking that his patent be revoked. The Lords sent a similar address, to which two of the members, Archbishop King and the Earl of Abercorn, almost succeeded in adding an amendment censuring all who had been responsible for the patent. In October Grafton wrote to Walpole, "All that I would presume to advise is that such an answer [to the addresses] might be obtained as will not irritate a country where there is such a visible coolness of affections, nay so much ill blood stirring, as may sometime prove very hurtful to His M's service and interest here."[27] His Majesty's answer arrived on November 16, while Parliament was in recess. On reconvening December 12, both Houses were assured that the King would do "every thing

---

[24] *Drapier's Letters,* pp. xii, xiv.
[25] King Corr, Southwell to King, Jan. 1, 1722/23.
[26] *Drapier's Letters,* pp. xvii-xviii.   [27] Quoted by Goodwin, p. 657, n. 5.

. . . in his power for the satisfaction of his people." A week later, Parliament returned votes of thanks, but the temper in Commons found expression in an amendment which requested the King "to give Directions to the several Officers concerned in the Receipt of His Majesty's Revenue, that they do not, on any Pretence whatsoever, receive or utter any of the said Copper Halfpence or Farthings, in any Payments to be made to, or by them."[28]

Walpole allowed six months to pass before acting on these addresses. Archbishop King thought the "affair was dead,"[29] but in March, 1724, Walpole ordered the English Privy Council to conduct an inquiry into the protests from the Irish Parliament. At this point, the Irish leaders moved deliberately to obstruct Walpole's intentions. The request for all "Papers and witnesses as shall be thought proper to support the objections made against the Patent" was refused, and Grafton confessed his inability to persuade the Irish to produce them.[30] To Walpole and the Privy Council, such noncoöperation seemed not only defiant but also incomprehensible. The subsequent report of the inquiry termed it "extraordinary . . . that in a matter which had raised so great and universal a clamour in Ireland, no one person could be prevailed upon to come over from Ireland in support of the united sense of both houses of parliament of Ireland."[31]

There were very sound reasons for this seemingly odd behavior, however. As Archbishop King explained, the Irish Parliament was in adjournment at the time of the inquiry and thus could not officially appoint witnesses and deliver papers to the Privy Council. No individual was willing to assume the responsibility of appearing at the inquiry as an official witness without the authorization of the Irish Parliament.[32] A further explanation — and one that more clearly reveals the Irish leaders' strategy — was given by St. John Brodrick, Midleton's son and a member of Commons: "If any body *on behalf of Ireland,* had appear'd at a certain place [i.e., the Cockpit, where the Privy Council held the inquiry], which I know was both expected and desir'd by Wood and his accomplices, it would only have furnisht some people with a plausible excuse for doing what they were in all events determin'd to do; whereas now all the world thinks and says the hearing was only ex parte."[33]

---

[28] *Drapier's Letters,* pp. xxii-xxiii.   [29] *Ibid.,* p. 230.
[30] Goodwin, pp. 658-659.   [31] Mason, p. lxxxvii.
[32] Quoted by Goodwin, p. 660.   [33] Coxe, II, 392.

This open defiance marked the end of the preliminary maneuvers in the struggle between England and her dependent kingdom. With their refusal to send witnesses to the inquiry, the Irish leaders had begun a policy of noncoöperation that was soon to be adopted by the Irish people.

[II]

Considering the difficulties they were faced with, the behavior of those forwarding Wood's patent was curiously inept. At the height of the agitation, Midleton remarked in wonder and contempt, "No project was ever carryed on so sillily as this hath been."[34] He appears to have been thinking primarily of Wood and possibly Grafton, but he could just as well have included Walpole himself, who, even his apologist Coxe admits, did not act "with his usual caution."[35]

At the outset, Walpole underestimated the seriousness of Irish objections to the patent. He assured Grafton in 1723 that the agitation was merely "a popular run without consideration," and a year later, when the stubborn resistance of the Irish Privy Council forced him to recognize the gravity of the state of affairs, he attributed the opposition to political rather than economic motives: "It is not new to see small matters aggravated and carried to a very great height, but these things seldom happen by chance, and when there is in reality little or no reason to complain, nothing but secret management and industry can kindle a general flame in a kingdom."[36] At this time, Walpole's most formidable rival in English politics was John, Lord Carteret. Carteret was a friend of Midleton, one of the leaders of the opposition to Wood's patent. Walpole thought that Carteret, seeking to supplant him in his position of chief adviser to George I, was conniving with Midleton and other antiministerial Whigs in Dublin to embarrass his administration by exploiting the unpopularity of the halfpence; and he apparently believed that to accomplish this, his rivals had seized on the dangerous weapon of Irish "independency." Alert to any recurrence of the agitation of 1720, Walpole and his advisers were as quick to see the political motives behind Ireland's resistance to Wood's coin as they were slow to see the economic ones. The Duke of Newcastle, Secretary of State for the Southern Department, spoke for the entire ministry when he said that Wood's patent "can

---

[34] *Ibid.*, II, 370.   [35] *Ibid.*, I, 223.   [36] *Ibid.*, II, 348, 363.

have no real objections to it, even to the Irish, but what are the natural consequences of the dependency of that kingdom."[37]

The Irish themselves were in some measure to blame for the fact that their economic objections to the halfpence were not taken seriously. In their first anger and fear, they made some hasty and foolish arguments. Maculla, for example, computed in *Ireland's Consternation* that the country would lose £200,000 by the project, whereas the total amount authorized by the patent was only £100,800.[38] The ministry remained unpersuaded by such hysterical arithmetic — and later the Drapier's Brobdingnagian calculations that twelve hundred horses would be required to transport £40,000 of Wood's copper probably confirmed English opinion that the economic arguments against the halfpence were frivolous. The opinion was dangerously fallacious, for it at once oversimplified the motives and underestimated the strength of Irish resistance. Boulter, a shrewd observer, gave a more informed account of the nature of the opposition and made it clear that while "those of the best sense and estates" abhorred the notion of "independency" which "some foolish and other ill-meaning people" advanced, they nevertheless genuinely feared the economic consequences of the patent.[39] This report — and the unlikely alliance between men like King and Midleton — should have told Walpole that Ireland had a just grievance, but his morbid sensitivity to English intrigue and Irish rebellion caused him to miss the obvious: political differences notwithstanding, all Ireland was united in opposing Wood's halfpence. In the face of such unity, Walpole's miscalculations caused irreparable damage to the success of his plans. The damage was aggravated by the blunders of Grafton and Wood, which, if less crucial than Walpole's, were more public.

If ever the wrong man was in the wrong job at the wrong time, it was the Duke of Grafton in 1723-24. To have threaded successfully through the maze of hidden motives, misunderstandings, and conflicting allegiances in the halfpence crisis would have taxed the abilities of the most accomplished diplomatist, and the lord lieutenant was decidedly no such diplomatist. Swift later described him as "almost a slobberer."[40]

Grafton's initial misstep was in aligning with the wrong political group in Dublin. The struggle for power between Walpole and

---

[37] *Ibid.*, II, 350.   [38] Goodwin, p. 649.   [39] Boulter, I, 8-11.
[40] T. Scott, X, 275.

Carteret in England was paralleled in Ireland by the rivalry between Midleton and William Conolly, Speaker of the House of Commons and one of the lords justices. Midleton, a determined anti-Walpole Whig, did not approve of the Irish interest; but he was not indifferent to Ireland's welfare, and he opposed the halfpence. In addition to commanding considerable power in Parliament (he had a brother and a son in the Commons, and he himself was, of course, a member of the Lords), he was lord chancellor, and of the three lords justices, the man largely responsible for their inflexible stand against Wood's patent. Conolly, on the other hand, was loyal both to the English interest and to Walpole. It was natural that the lord lieutenant should rely on him in forwarding the patent, but Grafton seems to have gone out of his way to antagonize Midleton. While he was still in England in 1722, he took offense at a real or imagined slight by Midleton and foolishly wrote a letter of complaint to Archbishop King. King, thoroughly aware of the Walpole-Carteret, Midleton-Conolly imbroglio, was quick to see that the quarrel between Grafton and Midleton could be used to Ireland's advantage. There is only Coxe's authority for the story that King "exaggerated the disaffection of the lord lieutenant," but he certainly made no attempt to conceal Grafton's enmity from Midleton. The hostility between the two finally became so violent that it led Grafton to make an unsuccessful attempt to have Midleton censured by the Irish Parliament.[41] Coxe himself probably exaggerates when he says that "these jealousies . . . laid the foundation of a successful opposition to the introduction of Wood's coinage";[42] Midleton had opposed the patent from the beginning, and he would have done so regardless of Grafton's behavior. But the lord lieutenant's open attack on Midleton is typical of the maladroitness with which he conducted the business of the halfpence. He had begun negotiating his delicate commission by alienating one of the most powerful men in the Irish government.[43]

Grafton's ineptness is further illustrated by the way he handled

---

[41] Coxe, II, 346-347, and I, 222.

[42] *Ibid.*, I, 222.

[43] As events turned out, Grafton could not keep even Conolly's support. The speaker, whose self-interest proved stronger than his loyalty to Walpole, was so fearful of going against the unanimous sentiment in Commons that he allowed himself to be dragged along with the opponents of the patent. Walpole said that his defection "almost excuses what the Brodericks have done" (*ibid.*, II, 286).

the question of the patent before the Irish Parliament. The legislature convened in September, 1723, determined to bring up the matter of the halfpence. When the Commons unanimously resolved itself into a committee of the whole House to investigate the patent and demanded a copy of Wood's grant, Grafton insisted that he had no copy, only (after repeated pressure from the Commons) to produce one a few days later with the clumsy story that it had been mistakenly sent from England to his secretary's servant.[44] It was not long after this display of his diplomacy that Grafton began to admit his inability to cope with the crisis. "I think myself most unfortunate," he lamented to Townshend, "that such an affaire happen'd in my time"; and he confessed to Walpole, "It is above my reach."[45] By this time, his procrastination and his blunders were so obvious that Walpole actually suspected him of having betrayed the ministry.[46] When the lord lieutenant was finally relieved of office in 1724, Midleton's son, St. John Brodrick, gave the fitting valediction: "I doubt we shall never have his fellow."[47]

In his unofficial capacity, William Wood damaged his cause almost as severely as did Grafton. The patentee wrote several letters in 1723 to his brother-in-law, John Molyneux, a Dublin tradesman (and no relation to the author of *The Case of Ireland*). In these letters he boasted of strong government support, going so far as to assure Molyneux that he could secure a royal proclamation if that were necessary to force his coins on Ireland. Not only was Molyneux, presumably with Wood's approval, imprudent enough to make these letters public; he did so before Ireland had received official notification of the patent. One of the letters, dated August 10, implicated Grafton in Wood's scheme, an error in tactics that was to prove doubly embarrassing when the lord lieutenant denied any knowledge of the patent at the opening of Parliament the following month.[48] Wood's behavior was even less intelligent after the patent had become public knowledge. In October, 1723, he made a reply in an English newspaper (*The Flying-Post*) to the addresses of the Irish Parliament. Feeling that his "Credit and Reputation" had been injured, he arrogantly accused Parliament of misrepresenting the terms of his patent. The Irish, he charged,

---

[44] *Ibid.*, I, 223.   [45] *Ibid.*, II, 349; Ballantyne, p. 107.
[46] Goodwin, pp. 656-657.   [47] Coxe, II, 380.
[48] *Drapier's Letters*, pp. xv-xvi; Coxe, II, 370-371.

opposed his coinage only because the grant had been given to an Englishman.[49]

Wood's insolence shows how very certain he was of his strength. He could not believe that the Irish would be able to withstand the power of the English government. Their dependent status, their traditionally and notoriously subservient Parliament, their ancient and bitter divisions seemed guarantees that the agitation was indeed only "a popular run without consideration." But the impossible was to come to pass. An incredulous Boulter was later to marvel "that the people of every religion, country, and party here, are alike set against *Wood's* halfpence, and that their agreement in this has had a very unhappy influence on the state of this nation, by bringing on intimacies, between Papists and Jacobites, and the Whigs, who before had no correspondence with them."[50]

The groups responsible for the most effective opposition to the patent were the lords justices and the Privy Council. With their support, Walpole might have forced Wood's brass down Ireland's throat (as he once threatened to do), despite parliamentary remonstrances, popular agitation, and even the Drapier himself. Certainly, successful opposition from any quarter would have been impossible without the stubborn resistance of the Irish executive.[51]

The leaders of the resistance, however, realized that to be most effective the struggle against the patent should also be waged at the popular level. Several pamphlets attacking the halfpence had already appeared in 1723. James Maculla later declared, quite accurately, that he was "the earliest Person that Discovered [i.e., disclosed] the ill Consequences" Wood's patent held for Ireland; and in addition to *Ireland's Consternation,* at least two — probably four — anti-Wood tracts were published in 1723 or early in 1724.[52]

---

[49] *The Flying-Post,* Oct. 5-8, 1723. Wood's letter was reprinted in Abel Boyer's *Political State* (London, 1723), XXVI, 341-352. It occasioned a reply in *Mist's Weekly Journal* on October 26. The reply, signed "J. G.," noted the "extraordinary Manner" in which Wood, a private citizen, argued with the Parliament of Ireland. "J. G." 's reply was also reprinted by Boyer (XXVI, 435-443).

[50] Boulter, I, 7.

[51] For example, in August, 1724, the Privy Council refused to respond to a directive from England ordering the Commissioners of Revenue to receive Wood's coin. Had this command been obeyed, the commissioners would have had to pay the army with the halfpence, thus insuring its ultimate circulation throughout Ireland (see Goodwin, pp. 662-663).

[52] James Maculla, *A Coinage or Mint, Proposed* (Dublin, 1728), p. 4. Fol-

But to arouse and organize the people of Ireland into effective resistance required something more than scattered pamphlets, most of them calmly persuasive. To find someone who could make the people aware of their common danger and their common duty, the leaders of the official opposition to Wood's patent had to look no further than Dublin, where, in the southeastern part of the city, in the heart of the weavers' district, lived the most expert — and notorious — propagandist of the day.

Less than six months after the appearance of Wood's arrogant letter to *The Flying-Post* — and while Walpole was making arrangements for his inquiry — the citizens of Dublin were reading another letter, addressed to "The Shop-Keepers, Tradesmen, Farmers, and Common-People of Ireland," by M. B., Drapier.

[III]

There can be no doubt that Swift was asked by King and Midleton to intervene in the controversy. In a letter written to Charles Ford shortly after the appearance of the *Letter to the Shopkeepers, etc.*, he revealed that he had been in consultation with the archbishop and the lord chancellor "about the Farthings."[53] Indeed, King may have suggested the strategy that Swift used in *The Drapier's Letters.* The possibility of boycotting Wood's coin had occurred to King a year and a half before the publication of the Drapier's first *Letter,* and while there is nothing particularly original in the idea itself (Swift had recommended a boycott in the *Proposal for the Universal Use of Irish Manufacture*), it is significant that as early as 1722, King defined the legal grounds on which a boycott could be founded — the people's *right* to refuse the halfpence: "We have only one remedy, and that is not to receive these [coins] in payments; the Patent oblidges none but such as are willing of themselves, if therefore landlords . . . refuse to take their rents in brass . . . it will break the neck of the Project."[54]

lowing *Ireland's Consternation,* two tracts appeared in Dublin in 1723: *Ireland's Case Humbly Presented to . . . Parliament* (Sept., 1723), also by Maculla; and *The Patentee's Computation of Ireland* (Dec./Jan., 1723/ 24). *A Creed for an Irish Commoner* and *The True State of the Case Between the Kingdom of Ireland of the One Part, and Mr. William Wood of the Other Part* both appeared early in 1724, probably before the first *Drapier's Letter.* For a list of tracts against Wood's patent, see *Drapier's Letters,* pp. 352-373; and Wagner, pp. 15-26.

[53] *Letters to Ford,* p. 106.

[54] King to Annesley, Sept. 3, 1722. Quoted by Goodwin, p. 668, n. 1.

But if Swift's advisers supplied him with the strategy, Swift himself chose the tactics for his attack: the persona of M. B., Drapier.

The simplest kind of characterization for his alter ego was sufficient. Swift provided the Drapier with the sparsest of biographical data, and he was not particularly concerned with consistency of detail, so long as the Drapier maintained a consistency of tone reasonably appropriate to his station in life.[55] Of more relevance than a character analysis of the Drapier is the question of why Swift chose any persona at all. Simple anonymity would have afforded him the protection he needed, and, as a matter of fact, the safety provided by the Drapier's mask was only a technical one. Everyone knew the Drapier's identity, but without legal proof even an Irish court could not prosecute Swift as the author of the *Letters*.

Swift chose a pseudonym partly because he always preferred the pseudonymous to the anonymous as a more effective rhetorical device for his own peculiar brand of irony — the brand which, as the author of *A Tale of a Tub*, the apologist for nominal Christianity, the Drapier, Gulliver, and the Modest Proposer all attest, he was born to introduce. More specifically, in the campaign against Wood, the persona of the Drapier offered particular advantages. The absolute union of everyone from the lords justices to the Dublin beggars was essential to the success of the boycott against the halfpence. Resistance at the legislative and executive levels was well organized; effective persuasion was crucially needed among the middle and lower classes, where Wood's rumors and Walpole's threats could do most harm and where morale was already seriously impaired by the failure of the Irish Parliament to get reassurances from England that the patent would not be forced on the people.[56] Swift provided the average Irishman with a spokesman of his own kind. Not, of course, with the intention of deceiving him. Some readers of the first *Letter* may have thought they were reading the work of an actual "M. B.," who resided at St. Francis Street; but even the most naïve cannot have been fooled long. By using as his mouthpiece a decent, hard-working, moderately prosperous shopkeeper, Swift could accomplish two aims that were essential to the

---

[55] In the first *Letter*, for example, the Drapier knows no Latin (*Drapier's Letters*, p. 11), but in the fifth, he states that he had "acquired some little Knowledge in the *Latin Tongue*" in school (*ibid.*, p. 102).

[56] See the Drapier's explanation of why he entered the controversy (*ibid.*, p. 137).

success of his appeal: he could achieve a tone familiar to his audience, and he could dramatize for the ordinary middle-class Dublin citizen the economic catastrophe that the halfpence threatened:

> For my own Part, I am already resolved what to do; I have a pretty good Shop of *Irish Stuffs* and *Silks,* and instead of taking Mr. WOODS's bad Copper, I intend to Truck with my Neighbours the BUTCHERS, and *Bakers,* and *Brewers,* and the rest, *Goods for Goods,* and the little *Gold* and *Silver* I have, I will keep by me like my *Heart's Blood* till better Times, or till I am just ready to starve, and then I will buy Mr. WOODS's Money as my Father did the Brass Money in K. JAMES's Time, who could buy *Ten Pound* of it with a *Guinea,* and I hope to get as much for a *Pistole,* and so purchase *Bread* from those who will be such Fools as to sell it me.[57]

One passage like this carried more weight with the Dublin citizenry than a dozen parliamentary addresses.

Finally, the Drapier was the perfect antagonist for William Wood. Throughout the *Letters,* Swift emphasized Wood's mean origin and social status. This strategy was designed at once to reassure the Irish that their opponent could easily be defeated and to show the indignity of England's putting the claims of one "insignificant hardware man" above those of an entire nation. The Drapier was for Swift a defiant gesture: an obscure Dublin tradesman fittingly matched against an obscure English rogue. In a sense, Swift's persona was no more a fiction to the Irish people than was Wood. If anything, the Drapier was more credible than the patentee, whose natural obscurity and cultivated secrecy endowed him with the terror but also the insubstantiality of a nightmare. The Drapier was only a shadow, but he was a shadow cast by the familiar and reassuringly concrete figure of the Dean of St. Patrick's.

There is a further appropriateness in Swift's decision to fight Wood with an imaginary antagonist: in the contest between England and Ireland, Wood was no more England's real champion than was the Drapier Ireland's. The actual combatants were Walpole and Swift.

[IV]

The English ministry must have been particularly vexed at the realization that Wood's patent itself afforded the Irish the means to defeat it. By English statute, the King's subjects were required to accept as legal tender only coins made of gold or silver. Coins of

---

[57] *Ibid.,* p. 8.

base metal were issued merely as a convenience for trade; no one was compelled to receive them in payments. Wood's patent contained the proviso, customary with all such grants, that his coins should "pass and be received as current money, by such as shall be Willing to Receive the same."[58] When the Irish refused to accept the halfpence, their position was legally unassailable, as England's tactics throughout the controversy prove. In his efforts to force the halfpence on Ireland, Walpole never attacked directly the principle on which the Drapier based his arguments. Instead, he attempted by rumors and threats to weaken Irish resistance. The closest he came to an open abrogation of this constitutionally guaranteed right was when, in August, 1724, he tried to unload Wood's brass on the Commissioners of Revenue, who would in turn have had to use it to pay the army quartered in Ireland. This scheme, however, was blocked by the same constitutional guarantee that protected the private citizen: the Commissioners of Revenue were obliged to accept only coin of gold or silver.[59] So long as the commissioners refused to coöperate with the ministry, Walpole had to resort to indirect methods.

To inform the people of their constitutional safeguard was one of the two main objects in the Drapier's first *Letter*. The other was to persuade them to use it. The *Letter* opens in a homiletic vein. It is the people's duty "as *Men,* as *Christians,* as *Parents,*" and as patriots to follow the Drapier's counsel.[60] The tone is reminiscent of the *Proposal for the Universal Use of Irish Manufacture.* In that pamphlet Swift had also urged boycott as an almost sacred duty, ending his proposed resolution with the phrase, "and let all the People say AMEN." The Drapier takes occasion in the *Letter to the Shopkeepers, etc.* to reprove the people for their indifference to the 1720 *Proposal,* and he emphasizes the ruin facing them if they fail to respond to the present call. His appeal combines the motifs of Christian duty and survival: The halfpence *"are like the* accursed Thing, *which as the* Scripture *tells us, the* Children of Israel *were forbidden to touch, they will run about like the* Plague *and destroy every one who lays his Hands upon them."* The people must not "be so *Foolish* and *Wicked"* as to accept Wood's coin.[61]

In discussing Wood's patent in this *Letter,* the Drapier touches

---

[58] *Ibid.,* p. 191.   [59] Goodwin, p. 663, also n. 4.
[60] *Drapier's Letters,* p. 3.   [61] *Ibid.,* pp. 15, 10.

only lightly on the political issue of a national mint. His argument
is based almost exclusively on the familiar economic objections to
the halfpence. He notes the ease with which Wood can exceed the
terms of his patent, warns of the dangers of counterfeiting, and
dwells at length on the low intrinsic value of the coins. It is in
developing this last point that Swift achieved some of the most
brilliant strokes in the *Letter*. The Drapier tells his readers that
twelve pence of Wood's coin have the intrinsic value of a penny
"of good Money"! With this ratio of one pence to one shilling,
he estimates that Wood's total authorized coinage will cost Ireland
approximately £81,000.[62] So vast a sum as this was beyond the
comprehension of an audience of shopkeepers and farmers. Hence,
the Drapier scales down his figures to their intellectual and economic level, and to make his points easier to grasp, he gives concrete and appropriate illustrations: a hatter sells a dozen hats at
five shillings apiece; if he is paid with the halfpence, he receives
the value of only five shillings. If the halfpence is issued to the
army and a blustering soldier offers it for a twopenny quart of ale,
the alewife must charge twenty pence in Wood's coin to get her
full value.[63]

The next examples from the Drapier's primer are "logical" results in terms of his distorted ratio. Having diminished the value
of Wood's coins, the Drapier now magnifies their bulk: the halfpence weigh five to the ounce (another wilful distortion); thus
three shillings and four pence weigh a pound, and twenty shillings
weigh six pounds "Butter Weight." The arithmetic soars to dizzy-
ing heights, and the slow-witted farmer who a moment before was
wondering over the anomaly of twopenny ale for twenty pence now
finds himself grappling with six hundred pounds of adulterated
copper, his half-year's rent in the coin; and while he is still trying
to comprehend this phenomenon, the Drapier heaps more tons on
the scales: "Squire C[onolly]" will require two hundred and forty
horses to transport his half-year's rent to Dublin, not to mention
"Two or Three great *Cellars* in his House for Stowage." The cal-

---

[62] "This Sum of *Fourscore* and *Ten Thousand Pounds* in good Gold and
Silver, must be given for TRASH that will not be worth above *Eight* or
Nine Thousand Pounds real Value" (*ibid.*, p. 5). Swift's error as to the
amount Wood was authorized to issue was fairly widespread in 1724 (*ibid.*,
p. 191). Actually, the grant authorized the issue of £100,800.

[63] *Ibid.*, pp. 5, 7.

culations take one more spiral upward as the Drapier shows twelve hundred horses toiling to cart £40,000 of Wood's brass to the Dublin bankers.[64]

These examples are like elongated shadows, which are distortions but are nevertheless produced by a tangible substance. Wood's halfpence threatened the common man's meat and drink. No amount of exaggeration could falsify this plain fact; and no amount of comedy could obscure the deadly seriousness of the issue. The *Letter* was written not to amuse but to alarm. If Swift's more sophisticated readers enjoyed the Drapier's fantastic calculations, his simpler audience assuredly did not. The threat of the copper money touched them too directly. There is in this letter to the common people a hint of class appeal. Swift does not emphasize it; his purpose is to unite, not divide, the classes. But in depicting the dark future facing Ireland, he reminds the common reader that "it is the *Landed-man* that maintains the *Merchant,* and *Shop-keeper,* and *Handycrafts Man.*" If Wood's coins obtain currency, everyone will suffer, but it is the lower classes who will be most severely hit. Once Wood drains the country of all its gold, silver, and goods, the landed gentry will dismiss their tenants, convert their farms into pasture, and ship their wool and dairy produce directly to England, keeping only a few ill-paid hands to oversee their flocks. "The *Farmers* must *Rob* or *Beg,* or leave their *Country.* The *Shop-keepers* . . . must *Break* and *Starve.*"[65] The humblest station, the most complete obscurity, will afford no protection. Even if some tradesmen are foolish enough to accept Wood's copper in payments, they will have to inflate their prices beyond the common man's ability to pay; and the landlords will not accept it for their rents, "so that it must certainly stop some where or other, and wherever it stops it is the same thing, and we are all undone."[66]

Having set forth in the starkest terms the economic disaster that threatens them, the Drapier next explains to the people the constitutional guarantee by which they can avert it: "But your *great Comfort is,* that as his MAJESTIES *Patent* does not oblige you to take this *Money,* so the *Laws* have not given the *Crown* a Power of forcing the *Subjects* to take what *Money* the KING pleases." The succeeding eleven paragraphs supply the proof for this central point. The references to precedents and the excerpts from English

<hr>

[64] *Ibid.,* pp. 7, 8. [65] *Ibid.,* p. 9. [66] *Ibid.,* pp. 14, 7.

statutes were doubtless too technical for the Drapier's unlearned readers, but even though it was beyond them, the Drapier's impressive display of his learning must have convinced the shopkeepers and farmers of the soundness of his position. And to make certain that these readers are clear as to their course of action, the Drapier summarizes his argument in three simple steps which lead directly to the flat imperative, "One and All, refuse this *Filthy Trash.*"[67]

The first *Letter* was published early in March. On April 2, Swift wrote to Charles Ford that two thousand copies had already been sold; but he was not sanguine over the prospects of victory, because "People are more in fear than ever" and "one can promise nothing from such Wretches as the Irish People."[68] It is not certain whether at this stage he intended writing any more letters under the Drapier's name, but that he was still active in opposing Wood's patent is shown by a letter he wrote on April 28 to Lord Carteret, Grafton's successor as lord lieutenant.[69] During his years with Oxford's ministry Swift had become friendly with Carteret,[70] and he now presumed on this friendship to write to the new lord lieutenant about the halfpence, emphasizing that he was doing so at the request of "many of the principal persons" in Ireland. In his letter he enclosed two pamphlets. One was by the Earl of Abercorn; the other was the first *Letter,* "entitled to a weaver . . . but thought to be the work of a better hand."[71]

Whatever Swift's plans for his persona after the publication of the first *Letter,* events were soon to compel the Drapier's reappearance. While the *Letter to the Shopkeepers, etc.* was being read throughout Ireland,[72] the Privy Council in England was holding the inquiry ordered by Walpole. Unable to secure any witnesses from Ireland, the Privy Council found four in London, three of them Irishmen, the fourth a London merchant who admitted that he was speculating in Wood's coin. As for the three Irishmen, one was Wood's Dublin agent, another had formerly been tried for em-

---

[67] *Ibid.,* pp. 10, 13, 14.
[68] *Ibid.,* pp. lxix-lxx; *Letters to Ford,* p. 106.
[69] Grafton had received official notification of his dismissal on April 9 (see *Drapier's Letters,* p. xxiv).
[70] *Journal to Stella,* I, 153, n. 42.
[71] *Corr,* III, 191-193.
[72] Swift wrote to Ford that copies of the first *Letter* had been "dispersd by Gentlemen in severall Parts of the Country" (*Letters to Ford,* p. 106).

bezzlement, and the third later declared that he had been forced to appear.[73] The witnesses all testified that there was a shortage of copper money in Ireland. On April 21, the *Dublin Journal* reprinted from a London newspaper an account of the proceedings of the inquiry, and it added an angry gloss which was probably written by Swift.[74] The London account had also noted that Walpole had ordered an assay of Wood's coins. The assay was conducted on April 27 under the direction of Sir Isaac Newton, Master of the Mint. His findings were not officially released until August, when they were incorporated into the report of the Privy Council's inquiry. However, they were made known to Archbishop King — and by him, presumably, to Swift — in a letter written on April 30 by Edward Southwell, who was present at the assay;[75] and on July 25 several London newspapers carried an account of the meeting of the Privy Council the preceding day, at which Newton's report had been presented. No one in Ireland was surprised to learn that the assay had found Wood's coins to be of good quality, for the patentee had chosen the samples that Newton analyzed.

At the meeting of the Privy Council on July 24, Wood had made four proposals in order to mollify the Irish. He now offered to limit his coinage to £40,000, unless "the Exigencies of Trade" required a further issue; or to sell his coins at Bristol for two shillings and one pence a pound; or to sell his bulk copper for one shilling and eight pence a pound; or, out of regard for Ireland's "Apprehensions," to take Irish goods in exchange for his coin and to require no one to accept more than fivepence halfpenny in any one payment.[76] In his *Dublin Impartial News Letter* for August 1, John Harding reprinted this account from London. Harding was the Drapier's printer. On August 4, the *News Letter* advised its readers that another letter from M. B. would appear "on Thursday next."[77]

A Letter to Mr. Harding the Printer, upon Occasion of a Paragraph in His News-Paper of Aug. 1st., though addressed to Harding, is really, like the first *Letter,* to the people of Ireland. The testimony of the witnesses at the inquiry, Newton's assay of the coin, and Wood's proposed concessions all made England's position ap-

---

[73] *Drapier's Letters,* pp. 226-229; *Corr,* IV, 25-26.
[74] *Drapier's Letters,* pp. xxv-xxvii.
[75] King Corr, Southwell to King, April 30, 1724.
[76] *Drapier's Letters,* p. 203.   [77] *Ibid.,* p. xxxiii.

pear unshakable; and to add to Ireland's fears, there was a current rumor that the King intended to force the halfpence on the country by a proclamation. The Irish executive and legislature were standing firm, but the bulk of the people were in danger of wavering. The second *Letter* was written to reassure them and to urge a specific plan of resistance. In the first *Letter,* the Drapier had explained Ireland's rights and called upon the people individually to refuse the halfpence. In the *Letter to Harding* he proposes a collective boycott.

First, however, he must meet the new threats posed by the results of the inquiry and Wood's recent proposals. He has a relatively easy task in disposing of Newton's assay and the Privy Council's witnesses. These last are "only a few Betrayers of their Country, Confederates with *Woods*",[78] and even if the Irish do need copper money, as the witnesses testified, they do not need that issued by Wood. Newton's assay had found that the patentee *"had in all Respects performed his Contract."* The Drapier retorts that Wood has no contract with the Parliament or people of Ireland. The assay itself is equally "impudent and insupportable." The coins tested by Newton were specially minted by Wood for the occasion, "and these must answer all that he hath already Coyned or shall Coyn for the Future."[79]

Wood thought that Newton's report had vindicated his honesty; he hoped that his proposed concessions would prove his reasonableness. But in offering his compromise to the Irish, he played directly into Swift's hands. After volunteering to limit his issue to £40,000

---

[78] *Ibid.,* pp. 19-20. Wood's name is spelled thus throughout the first two *Letters.*

[79] *Ibid.,* pp. 21-22. Swift is here simplifying Ireland's objections to Newton's assay: Wood had minted four varieties of coins in 1722 and 1723, but the ones he submitted for the assay had been minted after March 25, 1723; further, in testifying as to the amount of copper he had already coined, Wood did not include that coined in 1722 (*ibid.,* pp. 207-209).

Swift did not attack Newton in this or subsequent *Drapier's Letters;* but in part III of *Gulliver's Travels,* which contains a transparent allegory of the halfpence crisis, the account of the astronomical tailor's error in calculating the sizes of Gulliver's clothes is probably a veiled attack on Newton (see A. E. Case's edition of *Gulliver's Travels* [New York, 1938], p. 168, n. 7). There is also an ironical reference to Newton in a late parody of Swift's, *A Discourse to Prove the Antiquity of the English Tongue;* and in the introduction to *A Complete Collection of Genteel and Ingenious Conversation* (1738), Swift calls Newton "an obscure Mechanick," a phrase he had applied to Wood in 1724 (*Prose Works,* IV, 231, 122-123).

(unless "the Exigencies of Trade" required more), Wood had imprudently noted that his patent empowered him to issue a much larger quantity. To this, the Drapier responds contemptuously that Wood may issue any quantity he pleases; the Irish people will not receive his copper. As for Wood's revised total, £40,000 is nearly twice what Ireland requires in small change, and "the Exigencies of Trade" is a dangerous proviso, for Wood "will judge of our Exigencies by his own." The Drapier barely acknowledges Wood's second and third alternatives — to sell his copper, minted or rolled, by the pound — because the first *Letter* had already made abundantly clear that Wood's halfpence was adulterated.[80] He is more concerned with examining Wood's final proposal — to *oblige* no one to receive more than fivepence halfpenny of his coin in any one payment. This proposal convicted Wood of "perfect *High Treason*," for he claimed for himself a power outside even the royal prerogative.[81]

In the first *Letter,* Swift had not concerned himself overly with attacking Wood. The *Letter to the Shopkeepers, etc.* leaves no doubt that the patentee is a common swindler of undistinguished origin: He is *"a mean ordinary Man, a Hard-Ware Dealer";* he and his accomplices are "BLOOD-SUCKERS," and their project is "abominable."[82] But these epithets are scattered and undeveloped; the Drapier is aloof in his contempt for Wood. The need to warn and advise the people is too urgent to permit much attention to this "ordinary fellow." Fear is the primary emotive force that propels the arguments in the first *Letter.* But in the second, inspired by Wood's outrageous concessions, it is anger. The Drapier is now writing, he tells the people, to keep up their "Spirits and Resentments,"[83] and in consequence, the attack on Wood reaches an intensity that is not found in the *Letter to the Shopkeepers, etc.*

Wood is almost as convenient a device for Swift as is the persona of the Drapier. In the first *Letter,* Swift used him as a figurehead on whom the Drapier could place the responsibility for the patent. Now that the Drapier can add to his former charges of insolence, avarice, and fraud the "treason" of meddling with the prerogative, he can also implicate Walpole and George I, the powers behind Wood. He achieves this by the simple, brilliant, and comparatively safe means of emphasizing both Wood's insignificance and the

---

[80] *Drapier's Letters,* pp. 22-23.   [81] *Ibid.,* p. 24.
[82] *Ibid.,* pp. 4, 9, 10, *et passim.*   [83] *Ibid.,* p. 28.

enormity of his threat to the nation. Wood has reason to be arrogant in his treatment of Ireland, "for sure there was never an Example in History, of a great Kingdom kept in Awe for above a Year in daily Dread of utter Destruction, not by a powerful Invader at the Head of Twenty thousand Men, not by a Plague or a Famine, not by a Tyrannical Prince (for we never had one more Gracious) or a corrupt Administration, but by one single, diminutive, insignificant Mechanick."[84] In the first *Letter* the Drapier had gravely told his countrymen that Wood had gained the patent through his "GREAT FRIENDS" and that the King had been imposed upon in granting it.[85] In the *Letter to Harding*, however, he does not attempt to explain the paradox of an obscure swindler terrorizing a nation under the protection of a gracious prince and an uncorruptible administration. He does still keep Wood apart from Walpole and the King, but the distinction is one of name only. The patentee is endowed with some suggestive attributes and titles: he dares "prescribe what no King of *England* ever attempted"; he is a "little Arbitrary *Mock-Monarch*"; he "takes upon him the *Entire Legislature,* and an absolute Dominion over the Properties of the whole Nation." Then the Drapier asks, "Good God! Who are this Wretch's Advisers?"[86] Only someone naïve enough not to have known the answer to this wholly rhetorical question would have failed to see its audacity.

And the Drapier is not through. His threat to "Shoot Mr. *Woods* and his Deputies through the Head, like *High-way Men* or *Housebreakers*" is incautious, but it is a sentence later in the same paragraph that climaxes the dangerous game of identifying Wood with the King: "If the Famous Mr. *Hambden* rather chose to go to Prison, than pay a few Shillings to King *Charles* Ist. without Authority of Parliament, I will rather chuse to be *Hanged* than have all my Substance Taxed at Seventeen Shillings in the Pound, at the Arbitrary Will and Pleasure of the Venerable Mr. *Woods.*"[87] Had Wood been his real target here, Swift could hardly have chosen a more inappropriate allusion. There is no place for the insignificant patentee in this exalted context. As Hampden opposed Charles I, so the Drapier will suffer the fate of political martyrs rather than submit to the *arbitrary will and pleasure of* — the explosive analogy

---

[84] *Ibid.,* p. 24.   [85] *Ibid.,* pp. 5-6.   [86] *Ibid.,* pp. 23-25.
[87] *Ibid.,* pp. 25-26.

stops one word short of treason, and the name of Wood fills the blank, much as Dryden, in *The Battle of the Books,* wore Virgil's helmet "like a Mouse under a Canopy of State."[88]

The Drapier is calmer but scarcely more respectful when he deals openly with George I. He assures his countrymen that there is no truth in the rumor that the King will force the halfpence on them, because "the King never Issues out a *Proclamation* but to enjoyn what the *Law* permits him."[89] In other words, he *cannot* issue such a proclamation. If one "should happen by a Mistake," the Irish are not obliged to obey it, for it will have no more validity than Wood's proposal to oblige them to accept his coin. So long as the people remain firm, they are safe. If, the Drapier adds realistically, the halfpence are accepted, the names of those who received and passed them should be made public as "Betrayers of their Country," but to prevent that evil day, the people should organize a general boycott. With characteristic diffidence the Drapier asks that "some Skilful Judicious Pen" frame a resolution to be circulated against the coins — a resolution much like the one he then judiciously provides.

One of the first responses to the Drapier's call came not from the shopkeepers and farmers but from a group of Dublin bankers who on August 15 signed a resolution not to accept the halfpence. The newspapers in which this resolution was printed added that "The Merchants and all considerable Traders in this City . . . are now signing a Declaration to the same Effect against Importing or Passing the said Bad Money," and they predicted that this example would be followed in cities and towns throughout Ireland.[90] Meanwhile, there had been a significant development at a meeting of the lords justices. On August 14 they had received the order from the English Privy Council directing the Commissioners of Revenue to accept and issue Wood's coin without hindrance. The decision of the Irish executive to ignore this command brought the controversy to an impasse.

At this juncture, the findings of Walpole's inquiry were being circulated in Dublin. On August 19, lengthy excerpts from the report of the Privy Council were printed in the *Dublin Intelligence.*

---

[88] *A Tale of a Tub,* eds. A. C. Guthkelch and D. Nichol Smith. Second ed. (Oxford, 1958), p. 247.

[89] *Drapier's Letters,* p. 27.

[90] See the *Dublin Intelligence* and the *Dublin Gazette* for August 15, 1724.

Ten days later Harding's *News Letter* announced that a third letter from the Drapier was soon to be published. *Some Observations upon a Paper, Call'd the Report of the Committee of the Most Honourable the Privy-Council in England* appeared at the end of August or early September. On September 7, Marmaduke Coghill, Judge of the Prerogative Court in Ireland, sent a copy of the *Letter* to Southwell. He attributed it to Swift and said that although it contained "many observations that are very proper, yet . . . it may give offence & do us hurt."[91]

This new *Letter* is directed to "the Nobility and Gentry" of Ireland, a more responsible audience than the Drapier had hitherto addressed, and a more appropriate one on the "very pressing Occasion" of the English government's open support of the patent.[92] For this more knowledgeable audience, the Drapier is himself more learned, and while the *Letter* is by no means altogether dispassionate, it is generally more restrained in tone than either of the first two. Since the Privy Council had incorporated the results of the inquiry and Newton's assay into its report, the Drapier refurbishes some of the arguments he had made in the second *Letter*. He now identifies three of the witnesses by name and gives a brief account of their unsavory pasts; he greatly expands his earlier treatment of the assay; and he makes a detailed comparison of Wood's patent with former grants.

In the opening paragraphs of the *Letter*, it appears that Wood is still the Drapier's primary antagonist. The Drapier repeats a rumor that six years earlier Wood had competed with three other applicants for a patent to coin halfpence for Ireland and that his terms were the worst of any submitted; and he recalls (or invents) a highly discreditable story that Wood was once dismissed from his office of collector in Shropshire for bringing a fraudulent suit against the county.[93] But Wood is not central to the Drapier's pur-

---

[91] *Drapier's Letters*, pp. xxxiii-xxxv, lxxxv; Southwell Papers, B.M., Add. MSS 21,122.

[92] *Drapier's Letters*, p. 35.

[93] *Ibid.*, p. 37. Herbert Davis cites letters from Newton in 1717-18 concerning an application by Wood to coin halfpence for England, but he has found no records of an application for an Irish grant (*ibid.*, p. 229). The Drapier's story about Wood's activities in Shropshire seems a pure fabrication. The libel was elaborated in Harding's *Dublin Impartial News Letter* of September 12, 1724, the issue that announced the publication of the Drapier's third *Letter:* "We hear that there is just now Publish'd in the

pose in this *Letter*. The publication of the Privy Council's report has forced the patentee into the background, for now the English government is officially and overtly committed to imposing the half-pence on Ireland. The struggle is no longer between an obscure mechanic and the Irish people; it is now between England and the kingdom of Ireland. For this reason the Drapier plays only briefly with the suspicion that the report is another of Wood's under-handed maneuvers (it is written "with the Turn and Air of a Pamphlet").[94] Actually, he is quite willing to grant its authenticity; now he can discuss freely the delicate issue of Ireland's constitu-tional status.

Up to this time, the Drapier's grand theme has been the liberty of the subject. In answer to the Privy Council's implicit distinction, throughout its report, between the rights of Englishmen and the rights of Irishmen, the theme of the third *Letter* is the liberty of *Irish* subjects. The report referred to the protests of the Irish Parlia-ment and Privy Council as a "Clamour." If this term were applied to the actions of the English Parliament, the Drapier asks, "How many *Impeachments* would follow?" What if the legislators of England petitioned the King to remove a patent which the whole nation feared? Would the King hesitate, or would any minister advise him to ignore such a request? "And is there even the small-est Difference between the two Cases?" The Drapier's comparison of the two cases ultimately takes him far beyond the question of the halfpence:

> Were not the People of *Ireland* born as *Free* as those of *England?* How have they forfeited their Freedom? Is not their *Parliament* as fair a *Representative* of the *People* as that of *England?* And hath not their Privy Council as great or a greater Share in the Administration of Publick Affairs? Are they not Subjects of the same King? Does not the same *Sun* shine on them? And have they not the same *God* for their Protector? Am I a *Free-Man* in *England,* and do I become a *Slave* in six Hours by crossing the Channel?[95]

The Drapier has spoken in such a tone before, but only against

---

Good Town of *Shrewsbury, A Hue* and *Cry* after 'Squire *Wood* the *Coiner,* who attempted to Cheat the County by a pretended Robbery. In which a full Account is given of his whole Tryal, Conviction and Rogueries, in FOLIO. N.B. This shall be publish'd here as soon [as] the Copy comes over, with a large De-[dica]tion to his Friend in Meath-Street." John and Daniel Molyneux lived in Meath Street (*ibid.*, p. xxxvii).

[94] *Ibid.*, p. 35.   [95] *Ibid.*, pp. 39-40.

Wood. Now that the Privy Council has voluntarily emerged as Ireland's real adversary, he too becomes more explicit in his condemnation of the power that made Wood's grant possible. Swift allows his persona to retain some of the characteristics he displayed in the first two *Letters*. He can still be humble (when he remembers to be), but even his apology for undertaking a task that he might have left to his betters has a dignity that belies his professed humility: "I was in the Case of *David* who *could not move in the Armour of* Saul, and therefore I rather chose to attack this *Uncircumcised Philistine (Wood* I mean) *with a Sling and a Stone.*"[96] In answering the Privy Council's report, the Drapier has gained in stature, and he has also at last verified Walpole's worst suspicions: he has raised the theme of "independency," and he has given it its most forthright expression since Molyneux's *Case of Ireland.* Coghill was not being overly apprehensive in fearing that the third *Letter* might give offense. It was intended to do so.

The third *Letter,* like the second, had concluded with a plea for declarations against the halfpence. Throughout August and September there was a spectacular response to this plea, accelerated partly, no doubt, by the influential example of the Dublin bankers and even more by growing rumors that the Commissioners of Revenue would be forced to receive Wood's coin. The Grand Jury and other inhabitants of the liberty of St. Patrick's (the area including and adjacent to the cathedral) presented Swift with a declaration on August 20. Two days later the powerful Holy Trinity Guild of Merchants filled half the *Dublin Gazette* with their resolution and signatures. Men of all trades and classes — coopers and brewers, bricklayers and smiths, brazers and pin makers, grand juries and corporations from a host of towns and counties — were equally zealous to make public their determination not to accept the halfpence.[97]

---

[96] *Ibid.,* p. 63. Swift continues this brilliant analogy of David and Goliath by showing how Goliath, like Wood, was clad in brass and *"defied the Armies of the Living God."* The metaphor was anticipated in a tract published on August 19 (see Harding's *Dublin Impartial News Letter,* Aug. 18, 1724), *A Word or Two to the People of Ireland.* It refers to the Drapier's first two *Letters* and adds, "He [Wood] only thinks fit to tread the Stage as . . . [his confederates'] great *Goliath,* but who knows but he may meet a *David* among us, who thus defies all our *Hosts"* (*A Word or Two* . . ., p. 13).
[97] *Ibid.,* pp. xxxiii-xl; and see the *Dublin Intelligence* and the *Dublin*

Among the myriad serious declarations, three facetious ones are worth noting, for they were a clever and doubtless effective part of the campaign against the halfpence. The traditional enmity between the weavers and butchers of Dublin was notorious and violent.[98] Faced, however, with the common danger of the halfpence, the "weavers" sent a magnanimous offering of amnesty to their old enemies:

Gentlemen,
Altho we have been at Difference this some Time past, yet we can't in our Honour or Consciences stand by and see you oppress'd, as you must certainly be, if this Damn'd Scheme of Wood's having the Army paid with his Coin comes to perfection. We all know they must live, but why should you or any one be made Sacrifices to the Ambition of that *pitiful Hardware Man.* Therefore, if you have any Intimation of having your Meat forcibly taken away, and Dross, Dirt, or Nothing left in exchange, send for US, and to the risque of our Lives &c we will help and assist you to defend your selves.[99]

Whoever wrote this had read enough of the Drapier's first two *Letters* to borrow some of his familiar epithets for Wood and his copper. Someone also took a hint from the warning in the *Letter to the Shopkeepers, etc.* that even the beggars must suffer if Wood's coin were circulated. Harding's *Dublin Impartial News Letter* for September 12 printed a "Declaration of the Beggars, Lame and Blind, Halt and Maimed, both Male and Female, in and about the City of Dublin, with all their Children Legitamate and Merrybegotten," expressing their concern over the "Mischievous Consequences" of the halfpence on their "Antient Fraternity" and begging all "well disposed Charitable Christians" not to give them alms in Wood's coin. This declaration could well have been written by Swift or one of his friends. It is signed by *Tho. Ticklepitcher, Roger Humpshoulder, Timothy Blinker,* and *Jerimia Hopp* — names very like the *Cancerina, Stumpa-Nympha,* and *Pullagowna* of Swift's "Seraglio" of Dublin beggars.[100] And the same hand may have been responsible for the "Advertisement from the *Church-Wardens* of the City," which appeared in Harding's *News Letter* on

---

Gazette, Aug.–Sept., 1724, *passim.* Swift himself was one of the signers of the resolution passed on September 3 by the "High-Sherriff, Justices of Peace, Grand Jury, Nobility, Clergy, Gentlemen and Freeholders of the County of Dublin" (*Dublin Gazette,* Oct. 14, 1724).
[98] Lecky, I, 322.   [99] *Needham's Post-Man,* Sept. 2, 1724.
[100] Swift's "Seraglio" is described by Delany, p. 133.

September 5: "Whereas some Persons indiscreetly put some of *Wood's Counters* into the Poor-Boxes last *Sunday,* This is to Caution those who made this Mistake, not to do it again, The POOR of every Parish refusing to except [*sic*] of any of them."

Among all these declarations, serious and facetious, none could have pleased Swift more than two advertisements which appeared in late August. One was a self-righteous statement from Wood's brothers-in-law, John and Daniel Molyneux, disavowing any connection with Wood and his patent and declaring that they never possessed any of his coins, "except one Halfpenny and one Farthing . . . receiv'd in a Post-Letter," which they dutifully turned over to the lords justices. The other was from one Thomas Handy, who indignantly reported that he had recently received from "an Entire Stranger" a bill of lading for eleven casks of Wood's halfpence, which he returned to the sender immediately on receipt.[101] If, as he protested, Handy was innocent, he was the victim of assuredly the cruelest practical joke possible in Dublin at that time.

Wood was being attacked by resolutions, poems, and pamphlets;[102] and the opposition occasionally took a more violent form. In Cork a mob prevented a shipment of halfpence from being unloaded, and threatened to burn the ship; and in Dublin Wood was hanged in effigy — an event which Swift celebrated with *A Full and True Account of . . . the Execution of William Wood.*[103] But despite their unanimity and determination, the Irish were in desperate circumstances in the fall of 1724. Marmaduke Coghill wrote to Secretary Southwell in September, "We are still under great confusion, & an entire stop is putt to trade here. You know we all deal upon Credditt, & people are unwilling to trust for their goods, least the Brass Money shou'd become current, & they be forced to take them for payment, besides the bankers who generally negotiate bills, dare not do it now, nor advance any money on them, fearing every body that has money in their banks may draw it from them."[104] Not long after this, a report reached Ireland that neither clarified the chaotic economic situation nor allayed Irish fears that England would compel acceptance of the halfpence. Not daring to

---

[101] *Drapier's Letters,* p. xxxvii.

[102] A list of verse and prose attacks on Wood is given in *Drapier's Letters,* pp. 352-381.

[103] Goodwin, p. 665; *Drapier's Letters,* p. xxxvi, 173-180.

[104] Southwell Papers, Coghill to Southwell, Sept. 17, 1724, B.M. Add. MSS 21,122.

leave the administration in the hands of the lords justices any longer, Walpole determined to send Carteret to Dublin fully a year earlier than the new lord lieutenant would normally have assumed his duties.[105]

[v]

Since Swift had reopened their correspondence the preceding April, he and Carteret had exchanged several letters, reassuring each other of their friendship and anticipating the pleasure of resuming their association in Dublin. Whenever Swift referred to Wood's patent, Carteret made pleasant, evasive answers.[106] Both men were aware of the quiet comedy which circumstances had forced them to enact. Even had the lord lieutenant not already known of the Drapier-Dean when Swift sent him the *Letter to the Shopkeepers, etc.,* he could not have missed the significance of his friend's hint that the tract was "thought to be the work of a better hand." Carteret certainly recognized the challenge — and the sober warning — in a letter written before Swift knew how imminent his arrival was: "My Lord, we are here preparing for your reception [i.e., a year hence, when Carteret was scheduled to come to Ireland], and for a quiet session under your government; but whether you approve the manner I can only guess. It is by universal declarations against Wood's coin."[107] Probably not even Swift guessed at this time how dramatic their encounter would be; there is no doubt that Carteret was not prepared for the boldness of the Drapier's next move.

If he can be believed, the Drapier had expected the *Letter to the Nobility and Gentry* to be his last. In his three letters he had shown the people their duty, he had answered the new arguments of Wood, and he had refuted the Privy Council's report paragraph by paragraph. As he said in the third *Letter,* "It is needless to argue any longer. The Matter is come to an Issue."[108] The resolutions and declarations of support that followed the second and third *Letters* gave every promise that the country was determined and united in its resistance; and Wood's compromises seemed an indication of weakness. There were grounds, if not for optimism, at

---

[105] Goodwin, pp. 663-664.   [106] *Corr,* III, 191-214, *passim.*
[107] *Ibid.,* III, 214.
[108] *Drapier's Letters,* pp. 62, 59; and see the opening of the fourth *Letter* (p. 67).

least for cautious hope; so it could be that Swift did think, in the fall of 1724, that the Drapier had made his final appearance. All this was changed in late September, when Swift learned, apparently from private sources,[109] that Carteret was bound for Dublin a year before he was expected.

Swift knew that the new viceroy would be a more dangerous adversary than Grafton had been. Further, he realized that any lord lieutenant in Dublin at this time would put the Irish at a serious psychological disadvantage. The very rumor of Carteret's imminent arrival had already caused "some weak People" to lose heart; everyone believed that his "coming at an *Unusual* Time must portend some *Unusual* Business to be done." Clearly, something was needed to counteract the effect of Walpole's latest maneuver. As the Drapier explained his fourth appearance before his fellow citizens, "Cordials must be frequently apply'd to weak Constitutions."[110] Swift, however, intended the fourth *Letter* to do more than strengthen the fiber of Irish resistance. Carteret's precipitate departure for Dublin was an indication of the extraordinary lengths to which Walpole was prepared to go to force the halfpence on Ireland. The *Letter to the Whole People of Ireland* was designed to shock the chief minister into recognizing the probable consequence of his actions. To do this, Swift deliberately crossed the narrow line that distinguished opposition from sedition: he made the central theme of the fourth *Letter* Ireland's legislative independence.

Swift finished writing *A Letter to the Whole People of Ireland* on October 13 (at least, it is so dated). Then he waited for Carteret. It is generally held that the *Letter* was published on October 22, the day the lord lieutenant arrived in Dublin; this is what Carteret himself reported to the ministry. He may, however, have been misinformed, for Archbishop King, Marmaduke Coghill, and William Nicolson all made the positive statement that the *Letter* appeared the day before Carteret landed — actually a more strategic time for it to come out, since it would have been in circulation

---

[109] In a letter to his friend, Knightley Chetwode (undated but endorsed by Chetwode on September 22), Swift wrote that Carteret was "coming suddenly over" (*Corr*, III, 216). This was more than a week before Dublin newspapers carried the information that the lord lieutenant's arrival was imminent.

[110] *Drapier's Letters*, pp. 67, 71-72.

for some twenty-four hours before Carteret's arrival and would thus have gained a full day of publicity.[111] Whenever it first appeared, the fourth *Letter* was being read by the citizens of Dublin as Carteret proceeded to Dublin Castle for his installation ceremonies; and it was being sold even within the castle walls. According to Midleton, Carteret was first shown a copy on October 23. Four days later, the lord lieutenant called the Privy Council in a special meeting, read "some few of the many exceptionable passages" in the *Letter,* and made it clear that he regarded it as treasonable.[112] After much discussion, a majority of the Council voted to have Harding arrested for printing the *Letter* and to issue a proclamation offering a reward of £300 to anyone who should discover the Drapier's identity.[113]

Had Swift confined himself in the fourth *Letter* to reassuring the people that they had nothing to fear from Carteret, he almost certainly would not have found himself with a price on his head. His treatment of the lord lieutenant was impudent but not treasonable. With characteristic ingenuousness, the Drapier refuses to believe that Carteret is actually coming to Dublin; the report that he is doing so must be yet another of Wood's rumors, for who could suppose "that a Lord Lieutenant is to be dispatched over in great

[111] On October 28, 1724, Carteret wrote to Newcastle that the *Letter* was published "the very day" of his arrival (*S.P.D.*[P.R.O.] 63/384). Coghill's conflicting account is in a letter to Southwell, dated October 31 (Southwell Papers, B.M. Add. MSS 21,122). On November 24, King referred to the various pamphlets that had been published: "Two have come out since my lord lieutenant came here. . . . Four were printed before, by somebody that calleth himself a Drapier" (quoted by Mason, p. 344, n. n). Nicolson's statement occurs in a letter to Archbishop Wake, written October 30, 1724: "Care was taken to publish [the fourth *Letter*] the very day before the Lord Lieutenant landed" (Gilbert Collection, MS 27). Midleton wrote on October 31 that the *Letter* came out the day of Carteret's arrival, though he admitted that he himself did not see a copy until October 24; his authority is somewhat shaken, however, by his writing a month later that the *Letter* was published the day of Carteret's arrival, "or very soon after" (Coxe, II, 396, 408). Although Nicolson's authority might be questioned because he was in Londonderry at the time, both King and Coghill were in Dublin on October 21; and King's statement carries special authority because of the close coöperation between Swift and King throughout the struggle against the patent.

[112] Coxe, II, 396-397.

[113] *Drapier's Letters,* p. xlii. The passages in the fourth *Letter* which Carteret marked as "exceptionable" are indicated in Davis' notes to his edition of *The Drapier's Letters.* The proclamation is reprinted on pp. 265-266.

Haste before the Ordinary Time . . . meerly to put an Hundred thousand Pounds into the Pocket of a *Sharper?*"[114] Swift was not trying, of course, to deny the truth of the report; he knew that Carteret was en route to Dublin at the very moment he was writing. Rather, he was setting an embarrassing trap for his friend. Carteret's appearance would reveal the limits of the Drapier's experience with *Realpolitik,* but it would also put the lord lieutenant in the unenviable role of a sharper's lackey. And if he is naïve, the Drapier does have the foresight to plan for the unlikely eventuality of the rumor's being fact. If Carteret were really coming to Ireland, he says, the people would have nothing to fear, for if the King cannot compel his subjects to receive base money, much less can his viceregent. Nor would Carteret be able to use his persuasive talents to good effect, because most of the lucrative sinecures in Ireland (the usual bait for bribery) were already in English hands, and even if new "Employments" were specially created for him to bargain with, they would be no inducement, since the salaries they yielded would be paid in *"Wood's* Brass, at above Eighty per Cent. Discount."[115]

This reference to English place holders in Ireland was among the "exceptionable" passages noted by Carteret, but he probably would not have issued his proclamation had Swift stopped here. His preference was always for tact, not force, and he had come to Ireland with the intention of settling the halfpence crisis as quietly as possible.[116] But the Drapier's headlong recklessness compelled Carteret to issue the proclamation against the author of the fourth *Letter.* He did not require Archbishop King's warning that the action was impolitic. In a letter to Newcastle on October 28, he regretted "the unfortunate accident" that had forced him to take this public measure against the most popular figure in Ireland.[117]

Although Swift had maneuvered Carteret into this awkward position, he himself had to some degree been forced by circumstances to go as dangerously far as he did in the fourth *Letter.* Two issues were basic to his attack on the patent: his conception of Ireland's legislative status and his condemnation of Walpole and George I for their cynical negotiations with Wood. As long as possible, Swift stayed on the near side of sedition — if at times only barely — in

---

[114] *Ibid.,* p. 72.　[115] *Ibid.,* pp. 73-75.　[116] Ballantyne, p. 117.
[117] *Drapier's Letters,* p. xliii; *S.P.D.*(P.R.O.) 63/384.

handling these issues, limiting the question of Ireland's constitutional status to a strict and, for the most part, unexceptionable discussion of the prerogative, and attacking the corruption of the throne and ministry through Wood. But as Ireland's official protests had, one after the other, been ignored, Swift developed these issues more openly. In *A Letter to the Whole People of Ireland,* they are as explicit as Swift's irony will allow. Midleton did not distort the *Letter* when he said that it "seem'd to treat the king in an undutiful and dishonourable manner . . . [and] asserted an independencye of this kingdome."[118]

The Drapier still has some barbs for Wood, whom he accuses of circulating, among other false reports, the threat that Walpole will force the halfpence on Ireland. But such familiar epithets as "obscure *Iron-Monger*" are mild in comparison with the stinging irony of his defense of Walpole: "as his *Integrity* is above all *Corruption,* so is his *Fortune* above all *Temptation.*" He reiterates his definition of the prerogative, but now adds the significant remark that "the Wisest and the Best" monarchs use it as infrequently as possible. He can still entertain his sophisticated readers with the kind of fanciful mathematics he used in the first *Letter,* but now the sum of his ciphers is a warning — almost a challenge — to England: Walpole, the Drapier estimates, will require fifty thousand "Operators" to make good his threat to force Wood's brass down Ireland's throat.[119]

This new outspokenness is most strikingly illustrated by the comparison of a passage from the fourth *Letter* with one from the second. In the *Letter to Mr. Harding,* the Drapier contemptuously defied Wood in these words: "Let Mr. *Woods* and his Crew . . . Coyn old Leather, Tobacco-pipe Clay or the Dirt in the Streets, and call their Trumpery by what Name they please from a Guinea to a Farthing, we are not under any Concern to know how he and his Tribe or Accomplices think fit to employ themselves." In the fourth *Letter,* there is a passage similar in substance and identical in tone. The important difference is that Swift is now treating not Wood but George I in "an undutiful and dishonourable manner": "We are so far from disputing the King's *Prerogative* in Coyning,

---

[118] Coxe, II, 397.

[119] *Drapier's Letters,* pp. 87, 69, 86. Midleton commented on the Drapier's "insinuation" that Ireland was "to be born down with main force" (Coxe, II, 397).

that we own he has Power to give a Patent to any Man for setting his Royal Image and Superscription upon whatever Materials he pleases, and Liberty to the Patentee to offer them in any Country from *England* to *Japan,* only attended with one small Limitation, That *no body alive is obliged to take them.*"[120]

Like the attack on Walpole and the King, the theme of "independencye" had become increasingly explicit in the earlier *Letters.* The *Letter to the Nobility and Gentry* had come close to sedition, with its invidious comparison of the rights of English and Irish subjects; and the series of rhetorical questions beginning "Were not the People of *Ireland* born as Free as those of *England?*" might well have brought on government prosecution had a lord lieutenant been in Dublin at the time. Here Swift took the theme as far as the context of his argument warranted. In the *Letter to the Whole People of Ireland* he takes it even further because the context is broader, thanks to the charges from England (the Drapier attributes them to Wood) that in refusing to accept the halfpence the Irish were *"Ripe for Rebellion"* and preparing "to *shake off their Dependance upon the Crown of* England." This made an answer necessary — or, perhaps more accurately, possible — for Swift was obviously eager to discuss the dangerous topic that his adversary had introduced. The point toward which he has been moving since the *Letter to the Shopkeepers, etc.* has finally been reached. The constitutional principle on which the Irish interest based Ireland's case against the halfpence has now been brought into the open. "And this gives me an Opportunity," the Drapier exclaims, "of Explaining . . . [a] Point, which hath often *Swelled in my Breast.*"[121]

The "Point" that cries out for explanation is England's claim that Ireland is a "Depending Kingdom." The Drapier confesses his inability to comprehend the phrase. It must be "a *Modern Term of Art,*" for the Drapier has found no law in English or Irish statutes "that makes *Ireland depend* upon *England* any more than *England* does upon *Ireland.*" The two countries depend equally — and only — upon the King; neither Parliament is subservient to the other. "Dependency," whatever meaning it may have for some people, means for the Drapier allegiance only to the throne:

Let whoever think otherwise, I *M. B. Drapier,* desire to be excepted,

---

[120] *Drapier's Letters,* pp. 22, 70.   [121] *Ibid.,* p. 78.

for I declare, next under God, I *depend* only on the King my Sovereign, and on the Laws of my own Country; and I am so far from *depending* upon the People of *England,* that if they should ever *Rebel* against my Sovereign (which God forbid) I would be ready at the first Command from his Majesty to take Arms against them. . . . And if such a Rebellion should prove so successful as to fix the *Pretender* on the Throne of *England,* I would venture to transgress that *Statute* so far as to lose every Drop of my Blood to hinder him from being *King* of *Ireland.*[122]

Of all the "exceptionable" passages in the fourth *Letter* none was more provocative; it, more than any other, put a price on the Drapier's head and sent John Harding to prison.[123] It is not difficult to see why, for here is Molyneux's thesis of legislative independence expressed with an insolence that Molyneux would not have dared. *The Case of Ireland* had been dedicated to William III with sincere assurances of the author's allegiance to the sovereign and his respect for the English Parliament. The Drapier wears his loyalty with a difference. He is signally lacking in the proper deference to Parliament, but in his zeal for the King he outstrips Molyneux. Ireland can serve but one master, George I, whom the Drapier unites in common cause with Ireland against the rebellious Parliament of his hypothesis. Swift was following *The Case of Ireland* very closely at this point. In the paragraph following his hypothesis, the Drapier refers to the power which England has assumed, "within the Memory of Man," to legislate for Ireland and which was first opposed by "the Famous Mr. *Molineaux.*" The conclusion of the paragraph suggests that Swift was writing with *The Case of Ireland* open before him. Molyneux had hopefully reasoned that his book could not be taken amiss by the English, for *"We are in a Miserable Condition indeed, if we may not be Allow'd to* Complain, *when we think we are Hurt."* The Drapier is more pessimistic, "For those who have used *Power* to cramp *Liberty* have gone so far as to Resent even the *Liberty* of *Complaining,* altho' a Man upon the Rack was never known to be refused the Liberty of *Roaring* as loud as he thought fit."[124]

Swift's indebtedness to Molyneux is important in helping determine the nature of his "treason." Swift never advocated an Irish rebellion, in 1724 or at any other time. He never questioned the legality of the Hanoverian succession, and, like all the Anglo-Irish,

---

[122] *Ibid.,* pp. 78-79.   [123] *Ibid.,* pp. 90, 107.

[124] Molyneux, p. [xi]; *Drapier's Letters,* p. 79.

he knew that his security in Ireland depended on the Protestant Ascendancy. He did question, however, England's disposition to deny the Anglo-Irish their rights as English subjects. In thus challenging the constitutionality of the Declaratory Act, he was guilty of the same kind of "treason" that Molyneux had been in challenging the constitutionality of the Woolen Act of 1699.

It has been argued that Swift's position was extreme and that Midleton's and King's reaction to the fourth *Letter* shows that Swift did not represent Irish feeling at the time of the halfpence controversy.[125] Swift's arguments, however, were neither advanced nor unrepresentative. They were first set forth by Molyneux in 1698, since which time they had been identified with the Irish interest. Midleton's disapproval of the Drapier's fourth *Letter* was predictable. In 1719 he had refused to join with the Irish Lords in protesting England's interference in the Annesley case; in 1720 he had favored the prosecution of Edward Waters for printing Swift's *Proposal for the Universal Use of Irish Manufacture;* and in 1724 he voted to prosecute Harding, and he signed the proclamation against the Drapier. He was as determined an opponent of the halfpence as was Swift, but he shared Carteret's opinion that "to provoke England to that degree as some have endeavoured to do, is not the true way to keep them out."[126]

King did not go so far as Midleton in disapproving of the *Letter to the Whole People of Ireland,* but in letters written in November and December, 1724, he did declare that he disapproved of "several things" in it and he described it as "ludicrous and satyrically writ."[127] It is difficult to imagine what these "several things"

---

[125] Goodwin, p. 670. Goodwin further argues that the ministry granted the patent for economic reasons, and only later, in the face of Irish resistance, defended it on political grounds; and that the Irish, conversely, at first objected to the patent for political reasons, but as the economic dangers grew more apparent, shifted their attack to emphasize this threat (*ibid.*, pp. 666-667). It would be difficult, however, to establish the priority for either the political or the economic objections to the patent. As early as 1722, King advanced both in a letter to Grafton. Goodwin quotes this letter (*ibid.*, p. 667), but he is unwarranted in saying that King urges the constitutional objection at the expense of the economic one. Also in 1722, the Commissioners of Revenue pointed out the economic dangers of the halfpence, as did both Houses of Parliament in their addresses in 1723.

[126] Henry Downes, Bishop of Meath, to William Nicolson, Oct. 25, 1724 (see *Letters on Various Subjects, Literary, Political, and Ecclesiastical, to and from William Nicolson,* ed. John Nichols [London, 1809], II, 588).

[127] Goodwin, p. 671, ns. 1, 2.

were (one may have been the Drapier's slighting reference to Edward Southwell, King's friend and the recipient of the November letter),[128] for King's actions before and during the halfpence crisis prove beyond question that he accepted the principles expressed in the fourth *Letter*. He had argued these same principles in 1719, during the Lords' debates on the Annesley case. In at least one speech (reported by Nicolson) he made a statement more overtly "treasonable" than anything the Drapier was later to write: "He stood to his old Doctrine of Independency and strenuously avow'd that no Acts made by a Parliament of Gr. Britain signify'd more than By-Laws of a Court of Py-Powder, unless confirm'd by our own two Houses."[129] Such sentiments — and his opposition to the Toleration Act of 1719 — had cost King his place as one of the lords justices in 1720, and they marked him in government eyes as a "disaffected person" for the remainder of his life. The Duke of Grafton described him in 1723 as "to a ridiculous extravagance, national. Upon some points (of which the jurisdiction of the house of lords is a principal one) he looses both his temper and his reason."[130] So well known were his sympathies that Midleton held him equally responsible with Swift for *A Letter to the Whole People of Ireland*. Its "great position," he wrote, was "Mr. Molineaux's notion, that they in England could not bind Ireland by any act made there; which is . . . a darling point of his grace; and from that quarter, I take it, the arrow originally comes."[131]

King, then, was in general agreement with the Drapier's "treason." The "exceptionable passages" may have seemed to him a little too daring; there was a difference between publishing such arguments and making them under the protection of parliamentary privilege. King may, therefore, have questioned the wisdom of Swift's tactics, but he assuredly did not disown his sentiments. His uncomplimentary remarks about the fourth *Letter* are an indication not of the political but the personal relationship between the archbishop and his dean — a relationship which, one scholar has said, "endured, in spite of many strains and much irritation on both sides."[132] Although the two men had become

---

[128] *Drapier's Letters*, p. 73.
[129] Gilbert Collection, MS 27, Nicolson to Wake, Oct. 6, 1719.
[130] Coxe, II, 357.
[131] *Ibid.*, II, 398.
[132] Henry Craik, *The Life of Jonathan Swift* (London and New York,

reconciled after 1719, they remained temperamentally incompatible. Each respected the other's abilities, but their strongest bond was an impersonal one, concern for the Irish church and nation. It is this almost instinctive antipathy that caused King in a letter of 1726 to write, "As to our Irish copper-farthen Dean, he has behaved himself very well in his station, very agreeable to me, and been useful to the public, both by his charity and labours."[133] The mixture of condescension and appreciation here is characteristic of King's attitude toward Swift. In the same letter in which he expressed his disapproval of "several things" in the Drapier's fourth *Letter,* he also credited the tract with raising "the Spirit that this poor Kingdom has shewed . . . on this occasion."[134]

When the Privy Council met on October 27 at Carteret's request, all the members of the Council "owned their abhorrence of the pamphlet, as seditious and of dangerous consequences" — no one, in the presence of the lord lieutenant, could avoid this concession, no matter what his private opinion. But when Midleton made his motion to order a prosecution of Harding, King refused to sign it; and when Carteret asked the Council to issue the proclamation offering a reward for the discovery of the Drapier's identity, King and three others dissented. King's allies were Theophilous Bolton, Bishop of Elphin; Marmaduke Coghill; and John, Viscount Allen. Midleton later described them all as "creatures" of the archbishop; and Boulter called Coghill a "determined supporter of the *Irish* against the *English* interest" and Bolton "as dangerous an *Irishman* as any on the Bench."[135] Their refusal to sign the proclamation was a gesture, as was King's remark to Carteret that he would sign it if the lord lieutenant would guarantee them that Wood's patent

---

1894), I, 158-159. Craik quotes Swift's remark about King, "I hate him as I hate garlick" (*ibid.,* p. 160). Mason also commented on "the symptoms of that jealousy towards Swift" that King was not always able to conceal (Mason, p. 344, n. n).

[133] *Corr,* III, 391, n. 3.

[134] Goodwin quotes this excerpt (Goodwin, p. 652, n. 3) but does not indicate that it is from the same letter that contains King's derogatory remark about the fourth *Letter.* He cites the adverse comment on p. 671.

[135] Coxe, II, 397, 399; *Drapier's Letters,* pp. xliv-xlv; Boulter, I, 227, 134. Lord Allen, incidentally, did not transmit his political virtues to his son, Joshua, who succeeded to the title in 1726. It was he who objected to Swift's being made a freeman of the Dublin Corporation in 1730. Swift retaliated with attacks on Allen in prose and verse (see *Prose Works,* XII, 141, 145, 153; and *Poems,* III, 794-801).

would be revoked.[136]   But it was a gesture that clearly separated the adherents of the Irish and the English interests.

Even those members of the Council who did sign the proclamation revised it so that it was directed not against Swift's tract as a whole but against "several seditious and scandalous paragraphs in it."[137]   The distinction was a nice one, but it was important. No matter how much the fourth *Letter* outraged the loyalties of men like Midleton, the fight against the halfpence was not to be abandoned; and the Privy Council was careful to keep its condemnation of Wood's patent distinct from its disapproval of the Drapier's politics.

This careful distinction, however, had been invalidated long before the proclamation was issued. Swift had so firmly established the Drapier as a symbol of resistance against Wood's coin that in the popular mind betrayal of the Drapier was betrayal of Ireland. As Boulter admitted to Newcastle, "The uneasiness against the halfpence is a protection for any sedition . . . that has any thing against the halfpence intermixed with it."[138]   While Carteret and the Privy Council waited for an informer to claim the £300, the citizens of Dublin were memorizing and quoting to one another a verse of Scripture that had appeared, "fix'd up in publick Places about the City": "And the people said unto Saul, Shall Jonathan die, who hath wrought this great salvation in Israel? God forbid: as the Lord liveth, there shall not one hair of his head fall to the ground, for he hath wrought with God this day. So the people rescued Jonathan, and he died not."[139]   Swift had cause for deep satisfaction as the pledge of allegiance to the latter-day Jonathan circulated throughout the city. He had forced the government into a position that was awkward, if not impossible, to maintain and from which it could retreat only with considerable loss of dignity. And Wood's chances for success were growing more remote daily.

---

[136] King to Samuel Molyneux, Nov. 24, 1724. Quoted by Mason, p. 344, n. n.

[137] *Drapier's Letters*, pp. xlii-xliii.   [138] Boulter, I, 7.

[139] *Mist's Weekly Journal*, Dec. 5, 1724. The account in Mist ponderously explains the passage from I Sam. xiv. 45: "The Conceit lies in this, that the suspected Author of the said Pamphlet is called *Jonathan;* we are told also, that his Sir-Name begins with an *S.*" Reference to the biblical quotation was also made in a letter written on November 1, 1724, by Thomas Tickell, Carteret's secretary (see *Drapier's Letters*, pp. xliv-xlv).

So sure was Swift of the strength of his own position that he now contemplated an extraordinary move. On October 30, Archbishop King called on Lord Carteret and, after some general discussion of the state of affairs, informed him that the Drapier was thinking of laying aside his mask and putting himself "upon his country." It was fortunate that King paid this visit and that the lord lieutenant was Swift's friend, for Carteret made it clear that "no man in the Kingdom how great and considerable soever he might think himself was of weight enough to stand a matter of this nature."[140] The warning came just in time, for Swift had already begun his fifth tract, *A Letter to the Lord Chancellor Middleton*, which was signed, not "M. B., Drapier," but "J. S., Deanry House."[141] As a result of Carteret's warning, Swift withheld the *Letter* (it first appeared in 1735, as the sixth of *The Drapier's Letters*). Had he published it in 1724, he almost certainly would have been arrested. As a vindication of the fourth *Letter*, the *Letter to Middleton* made Swift liable to the same charges that the government had brought against the Drapier. Not only did Swift call the Drapier, himself, and other anti-Wood writers "all true Patriots in our several Degrees," but he also professed his inability to find anything treasonable in the fourth *Letter*, or to comprehend the phrase, "a depending Kingdom."[142] Most significantly, he paraphrased the passage in the *Letter to the Whole People of Ireland* "which . . . gives greatest Offense" and declared that, like the Drapier's, his loyalty would be to the King and not the Parliament, should the Drapier's hypothetical rebellion ever become a reality.[143]

Nowhere in the *Letter to Middleton* did Swift reveal himself as the Drapier. This discrepancy with King's statement that the Drapier was on the point of disclosing his identity may, however, be only apparent. The *Letter to Middleton* was clearly intended not to placate but to provoke. It may be that Swift originally planned to publish the *Letter*, submit to the almost certain arrest, and at his trial dramatically claim the authorship of all the *Letters* and "put himself upon his country." A passage in the *Letter to Middleton* suggests that Swift was eager to force a test case on the

---

[140] *Ibid.*, p. xlvi.

[141] The *Letter* is signed October 26, but this date cannot be accurate, because in the *Letter* Swift quotes from the proclamation, which was drawn up on October 27 (*ibid.*, p. 307).

[142] *Ibid.*, pp. 141, 132, 134.   [143] *Ibid.*, pp. 132-133.

government: "I own, it would be a great Satisfaction to me, to hear the Arguments not only of Judges, but of Lawyers upon [the Drapier's] Case."[144] If this was Swift's original design, Dublin was deprived of a spectacular drama when he abandoned it. However, the government's action early in November started a course of events that was to provide drama enough. On November 7, John Harding, along with his wife, was arrested for printing *A Letter to the Whole People of Ireland.*

Swift had made a wise choice in his printer, who, before issuing *The Drapier's Letters,* had printed Swift's "Epilogue" for the weavers' benefit, at least one of his tracts against the bank, and *The Last Speech and Dying Words of Ebenezor Ellison.* He may first have been brought to Swift's attention in 1719, when it was reported that he was in hiding to avoid arrest for issuing a proclamation by the King of Spain which recognized the Pretender's claim to the English throne.[145] He had been in trouble with the authorities on at least one other occasion: he was imprisoned in 1721 for printing the lord lieutenant's speech without authorization.[146] Obviously, Harding was experienced enough in the dangers of political journalism to recognize an "exceptionable" passage when he saw one; and he was courageous enough to print it. He demonstrated the extent of this courage by his behavior as he lay in prison awaiting the action of the grand jury. He swore that he did not know the Drapier's identity, that all the *Letters* had been sent to him by an unknown hand, and that he had seen nothing objectionable in them. Carteret was convinced that he had been "spirited up to stand the prosecution and persist in concealing the Author."[147]

A few days after Harding's arrest, Swift circulated throughout Dublin an anonymous paper entitled *Seasonable Advice.* It was addressed to the members of the grand jury who were to examine Harding, and it noted "several things maturely to be considered by those Gentlemen." Among the several things it urged were forbearance for the Drapier and compassion for his printer. Harding was "a poor Man *perfectly Innocent"* who had never dreamed that the lawyers could *"pick* out Expressions" from the fourth *Letter* "and make them Liable to Exception." As for the Drapier, the

---

[144] *Ibid.,* p. 133.   [145] *Whalley's News-Letter,* April 4, 1719.
[146] *Drapier's Letters,* p. 201.   [147] *Ibid.,* pp. 92, xlviii.

jurors were reminded that he was guilty of nothing more serious than "an *Inadvertent* Expression" if, indeed, he was guilty at all, for "it ought to be well considered, whether any one Expression in the said Pamphlet, be *really* liable to *just* Exception." His first three tracts had been unexceptionable, and the *Letter to the Whole People of Ireland,* like them, was written solely for the good of the country.[148] The paper's most telling point, however, was more practical. The proclamation against the Drapier had been worded to avoid any reference to Wood's patent, for only by separating the issues of the halfpence and the fourth *Letter's* sedition could Carteret get a majority of the Privy Council to sign the proclamation. What the lord lieutenant and his advisers had been so careful to put asunder, Swift now united in *Seasonable Advice* by cautioning the jurors that if they brought in a true bill against Harding, their decision would be universally interpreted as an indictment of the opposition to the halfpence.[149]

On November 14, Carteret was shown a copy of *Seasonable Advice,* which he thought "of so scandalous and seditious a nature" that at his orders the paper was given precedence over Harding's case and was presented to the grand jury on November 21.[150] The lord lieutenant's move puzzled some of the ministry's friends, who thought that the government's first efforts should have been to seek an indictment of Harding.[151] Carteret may have deliberately postponed Harding's case in order to shield Swift as long as possible. He was personally indifferent to the question of Wood's patent, and he knew that one of Walpole's motives in sending him to Ireland had been to confront him with a situation that was almost impossible to solve to the satisfaction of both England and Ireland.[152] His chief concern, therefore, was to follow the letter of his commission but to pay little heed to the spirit of it. He knew that the *Letter to the Whole People of Ireland* was so clearly seditious that he could not avoid issuing the proclamation. If, however, he had been really determined to arrest Swift, he would not have advised him through Archbishop King not to reveal his identity as the Drapier. But whatever Carteret's reasons for deferring Harding's case — whether he did so by design, or whether he honestly felt that the grand jury should first consider presenting *Seasonable Ad-*

---

[148] *Seasonable Advice* is reprinted in *Drapier's Letters,* pp. 89-92.
[149] *Ibid.,* p. 91.   [150] *Ibid.,* p. 1.   [151] Coxe, II, 405-406.
[152] Ballantyne, pp. 123, 111-115.

vice — the decision provided Swift with a test case that involved the least possible danger both to himself and to Harding, for *Seasonable Advice* had appeared without either author's or printer's name. A presentment of the paper would endanger no one; and if the jury refused to bring in a true bill, the government would suffer a serious loss of prestige which in itself would improve Harding's position.

The grand jury met on November 21. Despite "the concurrent and zealous Exhortation" of Chief Justice Whitshed and his two colleagues on the King's Bench, the jury refused to make a presentment. The chief justice then urged the jurors to reconsider their decision; but, finding them determined against his wishes, he discharged them and ordered a new jury to be impaneled. He would have been wiser to leave bad enough alone. The legality of his action in dismissing the jurors was highly questionable, and, as Carteret gently put it, Whitshed was "censured by some for having exerted himself, as they pretended to think, more than was necessary upon this occasion." Swift responded almost immediately by issuing an extract of resolutions passed by the English Commons in 1680 condemning the dismissal of a grand jury before the end of term as "Arbitrary, Illegal, [and] destructive to public Justice." The parallel between the cases of 1680 and 1724 was obvious, as were the implications of Swift's *Extract:* Whitshed's action was, like that of George I in granting Wood his patent, "a means to Subvert the Fundamental Laws" of Ireland. The *Extract* appeared on November 23, the day the new grand jury met. The jurors were unmoved by Whitshed's eloquence against *Seasonable Advice;* and the chief justice, afraid to risk a rebuff from his second jury, decided to wait until November 28, the last day of Michaelmas term, to submit the paper for their verdict. When the jurors received their instructions from Whitshed on November 28, they returned a presentment, not of *Seasonable Advice,* but of "all such Persons as have attempted, or shall endeavour by fraud or otherwise, to Impose the . . . Half-pence upon US." Any persons who did so would be deemed "Enemies to his Majesty's Government, and to the Safety, Peace, and Welfare of all his Majesty's Subjects of this Kingdom." The jurors concluded with effusive assurances of Ireland's loyalty to his most sacred Majesty, but the warmth of this sentiment was made slightly suspect by their expression of gratitude for the efforts of "all such PATRIOTS, as have been eminently ZEALOUS . . . in detecting the Fraudulent Impositions of . . . Wood." The presentment had been written by Swift and given to the grand jury just before he left Dublin to visit friends in the country.[153]

The Michaelmas term had now ended, and Harding was released without ever having been brought before the grand jury. It had been an altogether disastrous session for the government.[154]

[VI]

The unexpected boldness of the grand jury brought to a standstill the government's efforts to implement Wood's patent. On December 19, Swift returned from his visit to the country, and in a letter of that date he reported to a friend that there was "now a sort of calm" in Dublin.[155] He did not intend, however, to retire the Drapier just yet. When he arrived in Dublin, he had with him the fifth *Letter,* addressed to Viscount Molesworth; it was published — by Harding — on December 31.[156]

The *Letter to Molesworth* is Swift's celebration of his triumph at the King's Bench. Not that the tone of the *Letter* is one of gaiety. On the contrary, the Drapier seems abashed, weary, and ready to quit the struggle. The sense of failure, however, is his, not Swift's. The grand jury's proceedings had delighted Swift, and the impudent virtuosity of this new *Letter* is evidence of his delight. For example, it is in the *Letter to Molesworth* that there occurs the fullest biography of the Drapier, included not so much to enhance the persona's reality as to afford Swift the pleasure of indulging in a thinly veiled account of his own career: "I was bred at a Free-School where I acquired some little Knowledge in the *Latin Tongue,* I served my Apprenticeship in *London,* and there set up for my self with good Success, 'till by the *Death of some Friends,*

---

[153] The account of Whitshed and the grand juries is based on letters from Carteret and Coghill; they are quoted in *Drapier's Letters,* pp. l-lv, *passim.* An *Extract Out of a Book, Entituled, an Exact Collection of the Debates of the House of Commons Held at* Westminster, October *21, 1680. Pag. 150.* is reprinted in *Drapier's Letters,* p. 93. The grand jury's presentment is reprinted on pp. 95-96.

[154] For a discussion of Swift's attacks on Whitshed, see appendix D.

[155] *Corr,* III, 226.

[156] The *Letter* is dated December 14; Swift wrote to Ford that it appeared on December 31 (*Letters to Ford,* p. 116).

and the Misfortunes of Others, I returned into this Kingdom, and began to employ my Thoughts in cultivating the *Woollen Manufacture* through all it's Branches." The account continues, describing the Drapier's activities in terms which all but the dullest of readers would have recognized as equally applicable to Swift's public career. The 1720 *Proposal* becomes, in the Drapier's jargon, "a Piece of *Black and White Stuff,*" and the first four *Drapier's Letters* are similarly described. More knowledgeable readers would have recognized other resemblances between the careers of Swift and his persona: Swift had acquired *his* Latin at Kilkenny School, which would have been beyond the limited means and station of the Drapier; but both men had begun their apprenticeships in London, and after Swift had served his literary apprenticeship, he had "set up for himself with good Success," until the death of Anne and the misfortunes of Oxford's ministry had forced his return to Ireland.[157]

The *"Piece of Stuff"* in hand, the Drapier apologizes to Molesworth, is "made only from the *Shreds and Remnants of the Wooll employed in the Former.*"[158] This is true. The fifth *Letter* contains no new arguments — or epithets — against Wood or his patent. It is instead the Drapier's apologia for the cloth that made up the *Letter to the Whole People of Ireland.* The Drapier portrays himself as an obscure private citizen who offered his small contribution for his country's welfare (he does not make the observation, but he might have noted that he has behaved exactly as the Dean of St. Patrick's had recommended in a sermon recently preached at the cathedral).[159] As a result of his public spiritedness, he now finds himself with a price on his head, and his grief and vexation are aggravated by the knowledge that he lacks the wit to clear himself of the charge of sedition. He admits his despair of explaining to everyone's satisfaction the passage in the fourth *Letter* which gives most offense:

It is said I WENT TOO FAR, when I declared that *if ever the* Pretender *should come to be fixed upon the Throne* of England . . . *I would . . . lose the last Drop of my Blood before I would submit to him as King of* Ireland. . . . Now if in defending my self from this Accusation I should freely confess, that I WENT TOO FAR, that the Expression

---

[157] *Drapier's Letters,* pp. 102-103.
[158] *Ibid.,* p. 104.
[159] For Swift's sermon, *Doing Good,* see *Prose Works,* IX, 127, 232-240.

was very indiscreet . . . and That I shall be careful never to offend again in the like Kind. . . . I say if I should offer such a Defence as this, I do not doubt but some People would wrest it to an ill Meaning by some spiteful Interpretation, and therefore since I cannot think of any other Answer, which that Paragraph can admit, I will leave it to the Mercy of every Candid Reader.[160]

Swift had not derived such comedy from his persona since the *Letter to the Shopkeepers.*

The Drapier is the more discouraged because in none of his *Letters* is there a sentiment so dangerous as those he has read in the works of Locke, Molyneux, and Molesworth himself. Because he got his political education from these liberal Whig philosophers, he based his attack upon the halfpence on the wrong foundation: "I foolishly *disdained* to have Recourse to *Whining, Lamenting,* and *Crying for Mercy,* but rather chose to *appeal* to *Law* and *Liberty* and *the common Rights of Mankind,* without considering the *Climate* I was in." He has since remembered where he is, however, and he is determined henceforth to stay quietly in his shop and to avoid the dangerous influence of Molesworth's ideas — unless the viscount will rent him a small part of his estate in Yorkshire, where he will "feed on plain homely Fare, and Live and Dye a FREE Honest *English* Farmer."[161]

Swift had made his defense of *A Letter to the Whole People of Ireland* in the *Letter to Middleton,* which he had been dissuaded from publishing and which the subsequent action of the grand jury had made superfluous: the Drapier could get no more practical and decisive a vindication than the grand jury's presentment. In the *Letter to Molesworth,* Swift was not seriously concerned with defending the fourth *Letter;* rather, he was gloating over his enemies' discomfort. Those readers who had thought that the fourth *Letter* "went too far" found the same extreme sentiments repeated in the Drapier's hapless apologia; and the ministerial Whigs and their supporters in Dublin were bludgeoned by their own political philosophy when the Drapier attributed his convictions to Molesworth, who was as well known for his "old Whig" principles as he was for his steady opposition to the ministry's Irish policy.[162]

---

[160] *Drapier's Letters,* p. 107.

[161] *Ibid.,* pp. 108, 116-117.

[162] Swift had a few years earlier played with the device of turning accepted Whig principles against the ministry. In 1721, he had written to Pope,

Shortly after Whitshed dismissed the first grand jury, Swift wrote to Ford, "The Government and Judges are all at their Witts end."[163] This sense of satisfaction is apparent throughout the *Letter to Molesworth*. Indeed, of all the *Letters,* none shows more clearly Swift's confidence than this one in which the humble Drapier admits his defeat.

Swift may have intended the fifth *Letter* to be the last; the Drapier's farewell sounds genuine. There was nothing now for the Irish to do except wait for England's next move; and the only possible move that made sense was a revocation of the patent. Carteret had advised this in December, and the next month Boulter — whose counsel would be better attended by Walpole than Carteret's — also recommended that the ministry determine "what compromise can be offered to have *Wood's* patent sunk."[164] Aside from rejecting this advice, the government did nothing, and as the months dragged on and Ireland was still not free from the danger that had threatened since 1722, Swift's confidence waned. In April, 1725, he visited his friend Sheridan at Quilca, in County Cavan, where he remained throughout the summer. Shortly before Parliament was scheduled to meet in August, he wrote to a friend in Dublin that he expected the members to "be slaves as usual, and led where the government pleases." Despite — or because of — this gloomy prediction, he had already written a new *Drapier's Letter*.[165] This one (numbered the seventh) was addressed to the Irish Parliament.

In the earlier *Letters,* the Drapier had appealed to "the whole People of Ireland" — tradesmen, gentry, nobility — in their various capacities as private citizens. He now turned to their official representatives, whose firm union against the halfpence might in some degree make up for their lack of real power. Swift had no illusions about the Irish Parliament, a body he did not much admire even when he thought it "tolerably good,"[166] but if he was really convinced that the legislators would "be slaves as usual," he was careful not to infect the Drapier with his pessimism in the seventh

---

"Intending to make my court to some people on the prevailing side, by advancing certain old whiggish principles, which it seems had been exploded about a month before, I have passed for a disaffected person" (*Prose Works,* IX, 33).

[163] *Letters to Ford,* p. 114.   [164] *Drapier's Letters,* p. lvi; Boulter, I, 10.
[165] *Corr,* III, 264.   [166] *Ibid.,* II, 288.

Letter. The Drapier believes that even if the members of Parliament are only "in some Manner, the *Voice* of *God*," they are still "the *Voice* of the Nation,"[167] and it is as a subject of Ireland that he now addresses to them the nation's wishes. These wishes relate to two issues: the present crisis and the broader question of the condition of Ireland.

Addressing himself first to the compelling question of the halfpence, the Drapier asks Parliament to conduct an inquiry into the circumstances surrounding Wood's patent, to request the establishment of a mint in Ireland, and to censure Whitshed for his unconstitutional proceedings with the late grand juries.[168] These requests are made in good earnest by the Drapier, but for Swift their function is purely rhetorical. Swift knew that the Irish Parliament could not uncover the secret history of Wood's grant and that it would not dare censure Whitshed; and an official plea for a local mint would have even less effect, if less were possible, than the official addresses which both Houses of Parliament had sent to England two years earlier requesting the revocation of Wood's patent. When in the fourth *Letter* he exploited the theme of Ireland's legislative independence, Swift had made the last possible argument against the halfpence. There was nothing left to say, as he admitted when he apologized for the "Shreds and Remnants" in the *Letter to Molesworth.* In that *Letter,* he had said that it only remained for the Irish to keep up the spirit of resistance to Wood's coin "by frequent Remembrances,"[169] and it is for this purpose that the Drapier now makes these first suggestions to Parliament. They breathe the spirit of resistance and anger, as do the superfluous recapitulation of the history of the controversy and the equally unnecessary reminder to the legislators that they can strengthen the boycott against the halfpence by refusing to vote funds for the civil and military establishment. The tone of this part of the seventh *Letter* recalls the sense of outrage expressed in the second, third, and fourth; and once again the Drapier focuses his anger on Wood, using him, as he had done in the second *Letter,* to symbolize the extent of the indignity done Ireland: "The great Ignominy of a whole Kingdom, lying so long at *Mercy,* under so *vile* an Adversary, is such a deplorable Aggravation, that the utmost Expressions of Shame and Rage, are too low to set it forth; and

---

[167] *Drapier's Letters*, p. 154.   [168] *Ibid.*, pp. 145, 149, 155.
[169] *Ibid.*, p. 116.

therefore, I shall leave it to receive such a Resentment, as is worthy of a *Parliament.*"[170]

In the third *Letter* the Drapier had remarked, in answer to the English Privy Council's report that Ireland stood in great want of copper money, "We know our own *Wants* but too well; They are *Many* and *Grievous* to be born, but quite of another Kind." He makes this same point, in the same context and in much the same words, in the seventh *Letter*,[171] as he turns his attention to some problems that had plagued Ireland long before the country was threatened with Wood's halfpence: the declining state of agriculture and domestic industry, and the barbarous condition of the native Irish. Before offering Parliament his suggestions on how to cope with these problems, the Drapier introduces another grievance, the remedy for which is quite out of Ireland's power: the various means by which the Irish "are altogether Losers, and *England* a Gainer" in the two countrys' relations. The expenditures of absentee landlords account for some of the £700,000 which England gains annually from Ireland, but the bulk of the sum derives from England's restrictions on Ireland's trade and from her oppressive interference in Ireland's domestic economy. This account of England's economic policy toward Ireland serves much the same rhetorical purpose as does the Drapier's summary of the struggle over the halfpence: to support the spirit of resistance by reminding the Irish of their wrongs. The tone here is slightly more restrained than in that part of the *Letter* devoted to Wood, but the anger is not far beneath the surface; and the Drapier relates the issue of Wood's patent to the nation's other grievances when he observes that England's economic exploitation of Ireland "bears a Kind of *Analogy* to *William Wood.*"[172]

Although they are developed similarly and exercise a common function, there is an important difference between these two parts of the seventh *Letter*. The general discourse on Ireland's economic ills is intended not only to keep up the spirit of resistance but also to put the legislature and the people in a frame of mind to adopt the program for partial recovery which the Drapier offers: to support domestic industry; to encourage agriculture; to conserve and restore lands and forests; and to educate ("civilize," as the Drapier terms it) the Irish peasantry.[173] The *Letter* calls on Parlia-

---

[170] *Ibid.*, p. 155.   [171] *Ibid.*, pp. 57, 152.   [172] *Ibid.*, pp. 156-158.
[173] *Ibid.*, pp. 169-170.

ment to pass resolutions to these purposes, and it calls on the people to coöperate in effecting them. The 1720 *Proposal* had not accomplished its purpose, but now that the Irish people had demonstrated that they could unite effectively, Swift hoped to create something of real benefit out of their unity, something more productive than a boycott. Such was his hope. And even if it was undoubtedly more of a hope than a belief, it was strong enough to be one of the two themes of the seventh *Drapier's Letter* and to become the central theme of all of the tracts — except the last — that Swift was subsequently to address to the Irish people.

Swift finished writing the *Letter to Both Houses of Parliament* in June and, because he intended to remain at Quilca for the rest of the summer, he entrusted its publication to friends in Dublin, with instructions that it appear "just when the Parliament meets."[174] Parliament was scheduled to convene on August 6, and as the date drew near, Carteret waited anxiously for the ministry to tell him what his next move should be. He had no desire to give the legislators the occasion to cause further trouble, either by passing new resolutions against the halfpence or by refusing to vote supplies for the establishment. He had already prorogued Parliament from March 24 to August 6, and to gain additional time, he extended the prorogation until September 7. When Swift, still at Quilca, learned of this new postponement, he repeated his instructions that the seventh *Letter* not be published until "the first day the Parliament meets."[175] This was on August 27. He did not yet know that two days earlier Carteret had received his long-awaited orders from England. On August 26, 1725, the Irish Privy Council made the official announcement that Wood had surrendered his patent.[176] The news reached Swift a few days later, and he immediately canceled the plans to publish the *Letter to Both Houses of Parliament*.

Swift's decision not to publish the seventh *Letter* (it was first printed in Faulkner's 1735 edition of his works) is not difficult to account for. From the beginning of his short career, the Drapier had been identified in the popular mind as the antagonist of William Wood, and though the seventh *Letter* included issues unrelated to the halfpence, it, like the Drapier, had its origin in the controversy with Wood. With Wood's defeat, the Drapier retired from

[174] *Corr*, III, 247.   [175] *Ibid.*, III, 264.   [176] *Drapier's Letters*, pp. lx-lxi.

the public scene as abruptly as he had entered it. "The work is done," Swift wrote to a friend on August 31, "and there is no more need of the Drapier."[177] When he later expanded in separate tracts the various themes of the *Letter to Both Houses of Parliament,* he did so anonymously and not under the Drapier's name.[178]

Even had Swift felt that a need for the Drapier still existed, he would have been unwilling to undertake the fairly extensive revisions in the seventh *Letter* that the withdrawal of the patent now required, for he was at the moment more seriously occupied with Lemuel Gulliver than with M. B., Drapier. He had interrupted the composition of Gulliver's Third Voyage to write *The Drapier's Letters.* During the summer of 1725, he was once again at work on *Gulliver's Travels,* and on August 14 he wrote to Ford, "I have finished my Travells, and I am now transcribing them."[179] Swift was premature in thinking that his work on the book was done, however, for although Wood's defeat made the Drapier's last *Letter* unnecessary, it afforded Swift the opportunity to add an episode to the Third Voyage. In a letter written on September 29, Swift informed Pope of his progress with the book: "I have employed my time . . . in finishing, correcting, amending, and transcribing my Travels, in four parts complete, newly augmented. . . ."[180] The newly augmented version contained, in the story of Gulliver's adventures in Laputa, an allegorical account of Ireland's successful resistance against Wood's halfpence. In his letter to Pope, Swift had hoped that the work would be published as soon as "a printer shall be found brave enough to venture his ears." A year later, he found a printer for the *Travels,* but Benjamin Motte valued his ears too highly to print the episode of the rebellion of Lindalino. The passage was omitted from every edition of *Gulliver's Travels* until 1896.[181]

The scope and intent of part III of *Gulliver's Travels* include

---

[177] *Corr,* III, 266.

[178] For a discussion of later pamphlets and poems which appeared under the Drapier's name (but for none of which Swift's authorship has been established), see *Drapier's Letters,* pp. 323-351, 384-387.

[179] *Letters to Ford,* p. xl.

[180] *Corr,* III, 276.

[181] The passage was discovered by G. A. Aitken in Charles Ford's interleaved copy of *Gulliver's Travels.* Aitken published it as an appendix to the Temple Classics edition of the *Travels* (London, 1896). It is reprinted in *Prose Works,* XI, 309-310.

much more than Ireland's struggle against English tyranny. As Swift wrote to the Abbé Desfontaines, the theme of his masterpiece is valueless if not universally applicable.[182] But the rebellion of Lindalino against the tyranny of the Flying Island is an appropriate illustration of a major theme of the Third Voyage: Swift's condemnation of the follies and corruptions of the Whig government in England. Under the protection of the court and the ministry, speculators, "projectors," and political charlatans flourished, and in Swift's eyes the follies of the new science were paralleled by the evils of new systems of politics and economics. To Swift, the Royal Society and Wood's patent were symptoms of the same sickness in the body politic.[183] Hence, it seemed to him altogether fitting to include in his attack on the English government the story of the Drapier's great cause.

[VII]

The defeat of Wood's patent was a personal triumph for Swift. While it is true that he could have done little had not the Irish executive stood firm in its determination to break the patent, it is also true that official action alone could not have welded the Irish into a unanimous front of resistance. *The Drapier's Letters,* more than any other single effort, achieved this miracle.

Swift succeeded in unifying the heretofore incompatible elements in the Irish nation despite the central flaw in his appeal: the injustice of demanding full responsibility from "the whole People of Ireland" without conceding them equal privileges. The glowing ardor of the passage "Were not the People of *Ireland* born as *Free* as those of *England?* How have they forfeited their Freedom? Is not their *Parliament* as fair a *Representative* of the *People* as that of *England?*"[184] is dampened with the realization that Protestant dissenters were not represented in the Irish Parliament and that Swift was tacitly following Molyneux's distinction between the descendants of "the *Antient Race* of the *Irish*" and their English

---

[182] *Corr,* III, 407.

[183] For a discussion of the "politico-sociological" satire in part III, see A. E. Case, *Four Essays on Gulliver's Travels* (Princeton, N.J., 1945), pp. 111-114. Marjorie Nicolson and Nora M. Mohler have noted the parallel between Gulliver's Third Voyage and *The Battle of the Books:* in Laputa the Ancients and Moderns were advocates of conflicting political and economic theories ("The Scientific Background of Swift's 'Voyage to Laputa,'" *Annals of Science,* II [1937], 317-318).

[184] *Drapier's Letters,* p. 40.

conquerors.[185] When Swift, in the fourth *Letter,* attempted to dissociate the Irish Catholics from the cause against the halfpence, he did so only to refute Wood's charge that the opposition was being managed by Papists and Jacobites.[186] The Drapier might appeal to the technically accurate fact that the Catholics "never once offered to stir in the Matter" (that is, as an organized group), but Swift knew that they were supporting the boycott of Wood's coin because they realized that they, like everyone else, would be ruined if the halfpence passed into general circulation. The brilliance of Swift's appeal to self-interest — and of his identification of self-interest with national interest — made its inequity unimportant in the immediate crisis. The people united; Wood gave up his patent; and never again did the English government grant an individual the right to coin money for Ireland.[187]

Ireland's triumph taught Walpole a valuable lesson, however. The controversy over Wood's halfpence had provoked a protest which endangered the very foundations of England's Irish policy, and he was determined to prevent the occurrence of any more such crises. A few months after Carteret's appointment as lord lieutenant, Dr. Hugh Boulter, formerly Dean of Christ Church, Oxford, arrived in Ireland as the new Archbishop of Armagh. He had received the appointment through his devotion to the Whig ministry and through the patronage of Viscount Townshend, Walpole's brother-in-law.[188] Boulter was not a callous adventurer of the Elizabethan or Cromwellian variety; he gained great and deserved renown in Ireland for his contributions to public charities.[189] His humanity, however, did not prevent him from accepting wholeheartedly the ministerial concept of Ireland as a depending colony, existing solely for England's advantage. As Primate of All Ireland, Boulter exercised a close control over Irish politics, and by his policy of filling all important vacancies in the church and the government with supporters of the English interest, he made certain that any organized opposition to the ministry's plans for Ireland would be impossible. So thoroughly did he carry out his program for keeping Ireland quiet that the halfpence controversy was the last great crisis in Anglo-Irish relations during the remainder of Swift's lifetime.

---

[185] Molyneux, p. 19.   [186] *Drapier's Letters,* pp. 67-68.
[187] O'Brien, p. 351.   [188] Mant, II, 415.   [189] Boulter, I, viii.

Boulter's appointment indicates the limited nature of Ireland's victory in 1725. The struggle between William Wood and M. B., Drapier, was only a version in miniature of the struggle between England and Ireland, and the outcome of the larger conflict had been long decided. Even Wood, though he lost the battle of the halfpence, salvaged something from the defeat. In compensation for the loss of his patent, he was given a pension of £24,000. The pension, negotiated with the utmost secrecy and issued to a fictitious "Thomas Uvedale, Esq.," was drawn from funds in the Irish establishment.[190]

Swift did not know of these arrangements, but he must have realized that his triumph was a limited one. He might also have realized that, for all its limitations, it was the only one he would ever achieve as the Irish Patriot. In the autumn of 1725 he was "the Darling of the populace; His Image and Superscription on a great many Sign-Posts" in Dublin and in towns throughout the country.[191] This popularity did not wane until years after his death, but Swift was never again able to achieve another victory comparable to the Drapier's. In the years to come, he was to labor as hard in Ireland's cause as he had in 1724-25, but he was to find only frustration, failure, and, in the end, despair.

---

[190] Coxe, II, 367.   [191] *Drapier's Letters,* p. lxvi.

CHAPTER V

The "Small Prolongation of Life"

[1]

From *The Injured Lady* to *The Drapier's Letters,* Swift's tracts on Anglo-Irish relations were based on Molyneux's thesis that Ireland was a kingdom and not a depending colony. This constitutional issue was as fundamental to an economic pamphlet like the 1720 *Proposal* or a church pamphlet like the *Letter Concerning the Sacramental Test* as it was to overtly political pieces like *The Injured Lady* or the fourth *Drapier's Letter.* So long as England refused to recognize the validity of this concept, so long would she continue to interfere in the "purely national" affairs — whether political, ecclesiastical, or economic — of Ireland. Nothing more clearly shows the limitations of Swift's achievements as Irish Patriot than the fact that at no time during the Protestant Ascendancy did England even consider treating Ireland as anything other than a colony: Swift's assertions of "independency" twice exposed his printers to the dangers of prosecution; the Sacramental Test Act survived the attempted repeal in 1708 only because of the demands of practical politics and not because of Swift's insistence that the issue lay outside England's legitimate sphere of interest; the Drapier defeated Wood, but he left Ireland's legislative status unchanged.

In 1726, Swift made yet another effort to persuade the ministry to adopt an Irish policy based on "the great *Law of Nature*."[1] Some six months after the Drapier's triumph, he was in England visiting with old friends and completing arrangements for the publication of *Gulliver's Travels*. While there, he presented Ireland's case, not in a pamphlet but orally — first to Princess Caroline and then to Walpole himself.

Ever since April, 1726 — when it "made a great noise" in England and Ireland — Swift's interview with Walpole has been subject to misunderstanding. At the time, it was rumored that Swift was making his peace with the chief minister for a price (according to one report, it was to be the bishopric of Cloyne) ; and more recently, a biographer has argued that Swift undertook his English journey mainly in the hope of obtaining "a snug English preferment" and that both Walpole and Swift were willing to try to find terms which Swift could accept with honor.[2] Walpole knew that Swift was being urged to join forces with the "Patriots," the antiministerial group led by the Whig Pulteney and the Tory Bolingbroke. Accordingly, when Swift's friend, the Earl of Peterborough, suggested a meeting, Walpole may have been especially inclined to agree. Or he may simply have been curious, like Princess Caroline, to see the "wild Dean from Ireland" who had recently opposed him so successfully.[3] For whatever reasons, in March he invited Swift to dinner, where for the most part the talk was general and inconsequential. The meeting that occasioned the "great noise" took place the following month, when Swift asked Peterborough to arrange for a private interview with Walpole.[4]

If Swift had hoped that Walpole would give him a snug English preferment, he chose an extremely curious way of asking for one. He met with the minister on April 27. The next day he sent Peterborough an account of what had taken place, and he was careful to explain his reasons for having requested the interview: "I had no other design in desiring to see Sir Robert Walpole, than to represent the affairs of Ireland to him in a true light, not only without any view to myself, but to any party whatsoever." This statement is true, and it is the whole truth; Swift was so sure his version of the meeting could not be contradicted that he asked

[1] *Prose Works*, IX, 19.   [2] *Corr*, III, 321 ; Murry, pp. 403-404.
[3] *Corr*, III, 304, n. 1 ; IV, 374.   [4] *Ibid.*, IV, 374; III, 321.

Peterborough to send his letter on to Walpole.[5] The only topic discussed was Ireland — and Ireland for Ireland's sake. To suppose that Swift demanded an English deanery for his services and an enlightened Irish policy for the sake of his honor in coming to terms with Walpole is to underestimate the intelligence of both men. Not only was Ireland the topic of discussion at the interviews with both Walpole and the Princess; but also Swift's letter to Peterborough suggests that Swift went to England hoping to argue Ireland's cause with some members of the government and had supplied himself with supporting facts and figures to do so. Further, it appears that he and Archbishop King either shared this data or received it from the same source; for King himself was in England in the summer of 1726, and he was in touch with Sir Peter King, the Lord Chancellor and Walpole's close friend and adviser on questions of constitutional law.[6] The archbishop sent the lord chancellor a paper on Irish taxation which he had compiled from 1716 to 1725, and this paper bears some striking resemblances to Swift's letter to Peterborough.[7]

The letter — a continuation in greater detail of Swift's discussion with Walpole — deals with the usual Irish complaints: the Anglo-Irish were "called and treated as Irishmen, although their fathers and grandfathers were born in England"; they were "denied the natural liberty of exporting their manufactures" without restraint; civil, political, and ecclesiastical appointments of any consequence were almost always given to English candidates. Swift also repeated a point he had briefly touched on in the seventh *Drapier's Letter:* in proportion to the wealth of the two countries, Ireland remitted more in taxes to the Crown than did England (it is this point which most strongly resembles King's treatise).

Like the earlier ones in print, this effort to persuade Walpole to mitigate his treatment of Ireland failed. "Sir Robert Walpole," Swift wrote to Peterborough, "was pleased to enlarge very much upon the subject of Ireland, in a manner so alien from what I conceived to be the rights and privileges of a subject of England, that I did not think proper to debate the matter with him so much as I otherwise might, because I found it would be in vain." What-

---

[5] *Ibid.,* III, 308-311.
[6] John Lord Campbell, *The Lives of the Lord Chancellors and Keepers of the Great Seal of England* (London, 1849), IV, 607.
[7] See appendix A.

ever hopes Swift now had rested on Princess Caroline's promise to "use all her credit" in Ireland's behalf when she became Queen. To remind her of their meeting and of this promise, Swift sent her some Irish plaid on his return to Dublin, with the hope that she would "descend to honour Ireland with receiving and wearing it."[8]

For a brief time in 1727, Swift may have hoped that Caroline would help both Ireland and himself. In June of that year George I died, and the new King — who had no love for his father's chief minister — intended replacing Walpole as lord treasurer. Swift was in England at the time. He had remained in Ireland throughout the winter of 1726-27, but as early as November — while English readers were acclaiming the memoirs of Lemuel Gulliver and the citizens of Dublin honored the Drapier by celebrating Swift's birthday with bonfires, bells, and other "unusual Demonstrations of Joy and Gladness" — he was making plans to return to England the following spring and go from there to France.[9] He arrived in England in April and was on the point of setting out for the Continent when news of George's death reached him. His informant was Bolingbroke, who urged him to postpone his journey so that he would be on hand to take advantage of any development, now that Walpole was out of power.[10] The prospect of securing an English living on his own terms appealed to Swift. With the exception of Stella, those whom he loved most in the world lived in England, and Stella was near death; with her gone, Ireland would seem more hateful to him than ever. He therefore resolved to delay the French journey. Before the end of June he had realized the futility of his expectations. Sir Spencer Compton, whom George II intended to make lord treasurer, was so manifestly incompetent that Walpole was asked to retain the office. He remained in power for ten more years; his most influential supporter was Queen Caroline.[11] As for the Queen's promise to alleviate Ireland's hardships, it was remembered no better than her promise

---

[8] *Corr*, IV, 266; III, 354.

[9] For the reaction in England to *Gulliver's Travels*, see *Corr*, III, 356-371, *passim*. The account of the birthday celebrations is in *The Dublin Intelligence*, Nov. 29–Dec. 3, 1726. A letter from Gay to Swift, dated November 17, 1726, shows that Swift's friends had already been apprised of his plans to revisit England (see *Corr*, III, 360).

[10] *Corr*, III, 396-397.

[11] Basil Williams, *The Whig Supremacy, 1714-1760* (Oxford, 1939), p. 193.

to give Swift a medal of herself in appreciation of the Irish plaid he had sent her.[12]

There was nothing for Swift to do now but return to Ireland. Whatever personal hopes he had allowed his friends to raise at the King's death were blasted, and letters from Sheridan warned that he must hurry to Ireland if he expected to find Stella alive.[13] On September 18, still suffering from an attack of vertigo and deafness that had struck him six weeks earlier,[14] he left London for Holyhead, where bad weather prevented his sailing for Ireland immediately. While he waited for clearing weather — sick and depressed, and lodged at an uncomfortable inn — he kept a journal of his discomforts, "to divert thinking." But all his complaints (of the food, the inn, the weather, the "dunce, puppy, and Lyar" who attended him) could not divert him from thinking of the tragedy that awaited him in Ireland. He made an attempt to treat his situation facetiously in a set of verses dated "Holyhead. Sept. 25. 1727":

> Lo here I sit at holy head
> With muddy ale and mouldy bread. . . .

He maintained this bantering tone for eighteen lines; then he could no longer keep from his consciousness the thought of Stella, dying — perhaps already dead — in Ireland:

> I never was in hast before
> To reach that slavish hateful shore
> Before, I always found the wind
> To me was most malicious kind
> But now the danger of a friend
> On whom my fears and hopes depend
> Absent from whom all Clymes are curst
> With whom I'm happy in the worst
> With rage impatient makes me wait
> A passage to the land I hate.[15]

"The land I hate" — with his hopes all behind him and only certain heartache ahead, Swift found the idea of further life in Ireland intolerable. As miserable as his surroundings were in Holy-

---

[12] *Corr*, IV, 176, 183.
[13] *The Correspondence of Alexander Pope*, ed. George Sherburn (Oxford, 1956), II, 445; *Corr*, III, 417, 418.
[14] *Ibid.*, III, 409-410, 419.
[15] *The Holyhead Journal* is reprinted in T. Scott, XI, 391-403. The verses only are also reprinted in *Poems*, II, 418-424.

head, he fancied that he could live there "with two or three friends, in a warm house, and good wine — much better than being a Slave in Ireld." His anxiety over Stella accounted perhaps for the intensity of his despair at returning to the land of slaves, but his contempt for Ireland was real enough, as is indicated by the next poem in his journal:

> Remove me from this land of slaves
> Where all are fools, and all are knaves
> Where every knave & fool is bought
> Yet kindly sells himself for nought
> Where Whig and Tory fiercely fight
> Who's in the wrong, who in the right
> And when their country lyse at stake
> They only fight for fighting sake,
> While English sharpers take the pay,
> And then stand by to see fair play,
> Mean time the whig is always winner
> And for his courage gets — a dinner.

About the only thing Swift found to be thankful for when he finally arrived in Dublin was that Stella was still alive (she was to live until January, 1728). Otherwise Ireland appeared as odious to him as he had expected. In November, a month after his arrival, he wrote to a friend in terms reminiscent of the letter of thirteen years earlier in which he vowed to take no part in Irish politics:

As to politics; in England it is hard to keep out of them, and here it is a shame to be in them, unless by way of laughter and ridicule, for both which my taste is gone. I suppose there will be as much mischief as interest, folly, ambition and faction can bring about. But let those who are younger than I look to the consequences. The public is an old tattered house, but may last as long as my lease in it, and therefore like a true Irish tenant I shall consider no further.[16]

He could, however, no more ignore Irish politics now than he could in 1720; as he later confessed to Bolingbroke, the itch to meddle in public affairs was incurable.[17] On March 19, 1728, Sarah Harding, widow of the Drapier's printer, issued an anonymous pamphlet entitled *A Short View of the State of Ireland*. The English journalist, Nathaniel Mist, noted its appearance in his *Weekly Journal* for March 30 and added that everyone knew the author of the pamphlet "by the bold Strokes in it."

The occasion for the *Short View* was not so dramatic as the crises

---

[16] *Corr*, III, 429-430.   [17] *Ibid.*, IV, 76.

which had provoked Swift's *Proposal* of 1720 and *The Drapier's Letters,* but it was no less serious. Because tillage in Ireland was practiced on so limited a scale, any marked decline in the production of grain caused the price of bread to rise beyond the reach of the Irish poor, who lived always perilously near a condition of famine.[18] In 1727 a bad harvest had brought starvation to hundreds of peasants and had driven thousands more from their homes to seek a living elsewhere. The following year the country was again threatened with famine. The scarcity of grain had forced small farmers to harvest their potatoes two months earlier than usual; when this supply was exhausted, there would be no food left. In February, a little less than a month before Swift published his *Short View,* Archbishop Boulter was predicting that the ensuing summer "must be more fatal to us than the last."[19] *A Short View of the State of Ireland* was written under the shadow of this imminent disaster.

Considering the circumstances, Swift's object in writing the *Short View* appears cruelly gratuitous. The express aim of the tract was to give proof of Ireland's poverty. Such proof was needed, Swift said, to contradict the false reports of Ireland's prosperity that were regularly carried to England either by uninformed English visitors just back from Ireland or by timeservers who made their court by assuring the ministry that reports of Ireland's sufferings were the work of disaffected persons. Swift did not invent this complaint to serve as the occasion for his pamphlet. One of his objects in talking with Walpole two years earlier had been "to represent the affairs of Ireland to him in a true light"; and Swift's friend Sheridan wrote a tract in 1728 (after the publication of *A Short View*) in which he expressed his "Indignation against those vile Betrayers and Insulters of . . . [Ireland], who insinuate themselves into Favour, by saying, it is a rich Nation."[20] Earlier, Archbishop King had written his treatise on Irish taxation in an effort to refute the "gen[rl] opinion in Great Britain . . . [which] passes current without Contradiction, that Ireland is in a flourishing condition"; and in his description of the nation's poverty, he had dismissed as incompetent witnesses those Englishmen or absentee Irishmen who "represent Ireland as the most plentiful Luxurious Country in Europe." King had estimated that there were no more

[18] O'Brien, p. 102.   [19] Boulter, I, 181, 178.
[20] *The Intelligencer* (London, 1730), No. 6, p. 53.

than a thousand families in all of Ireland "who live tolerably well [and] keep good tables." The stranger who had partaken of their lavish hospitality returned to England "full of the plenty and Luxurie of Ireland." In the *Short View*, Swift complained that "because there may be a Dozen Families in this Town, able to entertain their *English* Friends in a generous Manner at their Tables; their Guests, upon their Return to *England* . . . [report] that we wallow in Riches and Luxury."[21]

Very shortly before the publication of *A Short View*, there appeared in Dublin another example of the kind of false (or, in this instance, misleading) report that King, Swift, and Sheridan were anxious to set right. This was *Seasonable Remarks on Trade*, by Sir John Browne.[22] Browne was the Irish witness whom Walpole had coerced into appearing at the Privy Council's inquiry into Wood's halfpence. He had subsequently returned to Ireland and in 1728 began publishing a series of tracts on Irish affairs. He was genuinely concerned with the condition of Ireland, and in *Seasonable Remarks* he acknowledged that the nation lay "bleeding with many Wounds." Nevertheless he emphasized Ireland's potential wealth in a manner that seemed to Swift recklessly irresponsible. A stranger, Swift wrote in *A Short View*, might perhaps be excused for believing that Ireland was flourishing, but "a Native and Inhabitant of this Kingdom, who gives the same Verdict, must be either ignorant to Stupidity; or a Man-pleaser, at the Expence of all Honour, Conscience, and Truth."[23] Browne was no "Man-pleaser"; his intentions were good, as he later demonstrated when he asked Swift, both in a pamphlet and in a personal letter, to amend whatever faults were in *Seasonable Remarks* and another of his tracts.[24] But his view of the economic health of Ireland was altogether more optimistic than circumstances warranted:

[Ireland's] Situation for an extended Trade is more Advantagious than that of any other Nation in *Europe;* its Harbours are many and commodious, its Inhabitants numerous and hardy, inur'd to Want and Labour,

---

[21] King's treatise on Irish taxation (see appendix A), fols. 1, 44; *Prose Works*, XII, 12.

[22] See appendix B.

[23] *Prose Works*, XII, 12.

[24] Sir John Browne, *A Letter to the Author of the Short View of the State of Ireland* (Dublin, 1728); *Corr*, IV, 27. The other tract which Browne sent to Swift at this time was *An Essay on Trade in General; and, on that of Ireland in Particular* (Dublin, 1728).

easy to feed, and able upon poor Fare to run through a great deal of Work: All the Necessaries of Life are . . . at lower Prices than they are in any other [country] this Side the Globe; the People are incumbred with very few Taxes, and their Labour is cheaper than that of any of their Neighbours."[25]

Swift chose an unanswerable method of amending this account of Ireland's potentialities. The *Short View* enumerates "the true Causes of any Countries flourishing and growing rich" and then determines which of these causes are operative in Ireland. There were, Swift argued, fourteen essential conditions of national prosperity: fruitfulness of the soil; an industrious people; sufficient harbors; a merchant navy; unrestricted international trade; legislative independence; a stable agriculture to support a growing population; a resident administration; an influx of foreign traders or tourists; a civil service staffed by native employees; the expenditure of income within the country; the expenditure of revenue within the country; a public mint; thriving domestic manufacture. Of these indispensable prerequisites for a flourishing economy, Ireland could claim only two — a fertile soil and an abundance of excellent harbors. The widespread preference of grazing to tillage vitiated the first, and English trade restrictions made Ireland's harbors "of no more Use . . . than a beautiful Prospect to a Man shut up in a Dungeon." As for the remaining conditions that led to a nation's wealth, the industry of the people was thwarted by "a Million of Discouragements"; Ireland was totally dependent on English shipping; English law restricted trade and inhibited the Irish Parliament; Ireland was governed from England, and all important civil appointments were given to Englishmen; Ireland attracted no tourists, who would only find there "Scenes of Misery and Desolation"; revenues were sent to England; Ireland was forbidden a national mint; and finally the Irish themselves persisted in refusing to patronize domestic industry.[26] On the basis of his examination, Swift made the sardonic observation that if Ireland did flourish, "it must be against every Law of Nature and Reason; like the Thorn at *Glassenbury,* that blossoms in the Midst of Winter."[27]

The *Short View* next demonstrated not only that the *causes* of prosperity were lacking in Ireland, but also that what in other

---

[25] Sir John Browne, *Seasonable Remarks on Trade* (Dublin, 1728), pp. 36-37.
[26] *Prose Works,* XII, 5-9, *passim.*   [27] *Ibid.,* XII, 10.

countries would be sure *evidence* of wealth was in Ireland proof of the nation's poverty. In Ireland, the high cost of living was the result not of universal prosperity but of grasping landlords who systematically increased rents; to meet the higher rents, tenants raised the price of cattle and grain ("although themselves should live upon Chaff"), and the deceptive inflation spread to all phases of the national economy. The low interest on loans was the result of the great decline in trade ("there being no Trade to employ any Borrower"), and the sudden increase in the number of buildings in Dublin was a symptom of depression rather than prosperity, for "Workmen have nothing to do, but employ one another." Bankers, "a necessary Evil in a trading Country," flocked to Dublin not because the nation's business required them to but because there they could grow rich by selling Ireland's stock of gold and silver out of the country.[28]

Swift used this same kind of analysis of the state of Ireland's economy in another tract, *Maxims Controlled in Ireland*, which he probably wrote around the time of the *Short View*, but which was not published until 1765.[29] *Maxims Controlled*, like the *Short View*, showed that the generally accepted principles of economics, the maxims whose truth was obvious in every other civilized country in the world, were "controlled" — that is, invalidated — in Ireland. In both papers, Swift reached the same conclusion: "There is not one Argument used to prove the Riches of *Ireland*, which is not a logical Demonstration of its Poverty."[30] Only in Ireland did such a paradoxical situation exist. Only in Ireland were the "rules generally known, and never contradicted" inoperative. Hence the economic programs urged by "crude and short thinkers" were altogether without effect in Ireland because such programs were

---

[28] *Ibid.*, XII, 11.

[29] The earliest known printing of this tract is in vol. VIII of Deane Swift's edition of the *Works* (1765). Herbert Davis thinks it was probably written in 1729 or 1730, after Swift had written the *Proposal . . . [to] the Ladies* (see *Prose Works*, XII, xxii-xxiii). However, its close resemblance in theme to the *Short View* suggests that it was composed at about the same time as that tract. This suggestion is strengthened by the fact that Swift's notes for *Maxims Controlled* have been found among notes for his *Intelligencer* papers, which were all written in 1728 (see Irvin Ehrenpreis and James L. Clifford, "Swiftiana in Rylands English MS 659 and Related Documents," *Bulletin of the John Rylands Library*, XXXVII [1955], 378-380).

[30] *Prose Works*, XII, 11.

drawn from the examples of other nations which were at liberty to enjoy their natural advantages. To think, therefore, that schemes which were successful in England or on the Continent would be equally so in Ireland was to "reason upon general topics, without the least allowance for the most important circumstances, which quite alter the nature of the case."[31] In dealing with Ireland, one could not generalize; Ireland was unique.

In *A Short View* and *Maxims Controlled*, Swift first developed fully the theme of Ireland's uniqueness. And as he continued to brood on "the singular condition" of the country, he saw that if the maxims of other nations were "controlled" in Ireland, then by the same token of Ireland's grotesque uniqueness, proposals undreamed of in other nations would be both operative and appropriate for the country that was unlike any other *"that ever was, is, or . . . ever can be upon Earth."*[32]

But in 1728 Swift had not conceived of the projects which he would later describe in *A Modest Proposal* and *The Answer to the Craftsman*. He still clung — if with growing skepticism and despair — to the belief that the Irish could improve their situation despite England's repressive policies. The people could never flourish, but if they followed the simple and obvious steps which Swift and other writers were outlining for them, they could perhaps achieve at least "a small prolongation of life."[33] To help them do this, Swift wrote — in addition to *A Short View* and *Maxims Controlled* — seven other tracts in 1728-29: *An Answer to a Memorial* (1728); the nineteenth number of *The Intelligencer*, a paper managed by Swift and Sheridan in 1728; *A Letter to the Archbishop of Dublin, Concerning the Weavers* (1729); *Answer to Several Letters from Unknown Persons* (1729); *An Answer to Several Letters . . . from Unknown Hands* (1729); *A Letter on Maculla's Project About Half-pence* (1729); and *A Proposal that . . . the Ladies . . . of Ireland Should Appear Constantly in Irish Manufactures* (1729).

Most of these pieces, as their titles indicate, were written in answer to proposals offered by other writers on Irish affairs. Swift left the majority of them unpublished — either because the specific occasion which had prompted their composition had changed by the time he finished them (such was the case with *A Letter on Maculla's Project* and *A Proposal . . . [to] the Ladies*); or because,

---

[31] *Ibid.*, XII, 5, 23, 131.   [32] *Ibid.*, XII, 65, 116.   [33] *Ibid.*, XII, 123.

as he explained to Pope, "I write pamphlets and follies merely for amusement, and when they are finished, or I grow weary in the middle, I cast them into the fire, partly out of dislike, and chiefly because I know they will signify nothing."[34] It had been the same when Swift had waited the long week at Holyhead: "I have writt verses, and put down hints till I am weary," he had recorded in his journal. "What can I do but write every thing that comes into my head."[35]

But though they were occasional, written compulsively or "for amusement," these tracts of 1728-29 show that Swift was well informed on Ireland's economic problems, and they put his role as Irish Patriot in proper perspective. Swift had discussed economic problems — and the need and means of solving them — as early as 1720; and the seventh *Drapier's Letter* had touched on matters of Ireland's economy that were unrelated to Wood's halfpence. *The Proposal for the Universal Use of Irish Manufacture* and *The Drapier's Letters,* however, had been motivated altogether as much by political as by economic considerations, and they had urged resistance more than economic self-improvement. Furthermore, since they attempted to vindicate the rights of Ireland, they were concerned primarily with the Anglo-Irish. By 1728, Swift realized that nothing could be gained by urging the Irish to resist English oppression, whether legislative or economic; he had evidence in depressing abundance that Ireland was doomed to the status of a depending colony. "Our Trad[e] will never mend, the Navigation Act never be softned," he wrote in 1729.[36] One result of this realization was that the economic pamphlets of 1728-29 lack the incendiary appeal of the earlier retaliatory tracts. Their tone is at times angry or despairing, and some of them contain passages of great intensity, but on the whole, they are pale in comparison with the 1720 *Proposal* and *The Drapier's Letters.* Another — and a more important — result is that when Swift abandoned as hopeless of achievement the struggle for Ireland's legislative independence and turned to the broader problems of Ireland's economy, his aims necessarily reached beyond the narrow confines of the Irish interest. The economic tracts of the late 1720's are the conclusive answer to the charge that Swift used Ireland only as a convenient stick with which to beat England and the Whigs. They are proof that his awareness and his compassion included "the whole People of Ireland."

---

[34] *Corr,* IV, 194.   [35] T. Scott, XI, 398-399.   [36] *Prose Works,* XII, 66.

[II]

In the prescriptive tracts of 1728-29, Swift discussed four problems which the Irish were at liberty to do something about and which he felt they must do something about if they were to gain the small prolongation of life that was their remaining hope. These problems related to agriculture, domestic industry, coinage, and emigration.

As the famines of 1727-29 demonstrated, one of the two most serious of these problems was the declining state of agriculture. To Swift, the preference given in Ireland to grazing over tillage was utter folly, a practice "so sottish, that it wants a Name, in our Language, to express it by."[37] He believed that there was "not an older or more uncontroverted maxim in the politics of all wise nations, than that of encouraging agriculture";[38] yet this maxim was "controlled" by the Irish themselves. If she possessed little else, Ireland did have rich soil, but the ruinous practices of landowners and tenants made it of as little value as England's laws had made her excellent harbors. Swift first made the plea for greater and improved tillage in the 1720 *Proposal*. He was still urging it nine years later in the various tracts following *A Short View*, and he now considered such related agricultural problems as land reclamation, reforestation, and improved rural roads.[39] His most comprehensive study of the state of agriculture occurs in *An Answer to a Memorial*. In 1728, a few days after the publication of *A Short View*, an anonymous tract appeared in Dublin. It was entitled *The Memorial of the Poor Inhabitants, Tradesmen, and Labourers of the Kingdom of Ireland*, and it was addressed "To The R——D Dr. J——n S——t." It may have been written by Sir John Browne, author of *Seasonable Remarks* and *An Essay on Trade*.[40] The memorialist asked Swift's aid in recommending to the lord lieutenant and the Irish Parliament a plan to import one hundred thousand barrels of wheat to relieve the scarcity of grain. The wheat was to be imported by "merchants and others," and for this service they were to be given a premium of £10,000 by the Irish government. The funds for the premium were to be raised from taxes on imported luxuries.[41]

Swift wasted no time in replying publicly to the *Memorial*. His

---

[37] *Ibid.*, XII, 19.   [38] *Ibid.*, XII, 89.   [39] *Ibid.*, XII, 86-88.
[40] See appendix B.   [41] *Prose Works*, XII, 304-305.

Answer is dated March 25, 1728.[42] It is apparent from the opening sentence of the *Answer* that Swift disapproved of the importation scheme, but before examining it in detail, he first gave a "short
History" of the decline of tillage in Ireland. Actually, it is less a
history than a general indictment of everyone concerned with agriculture — landlords, graziers, and the tenants themselves. All were
guilty of practices which had led to the present languishing state
of tillage. Because they were irresponsible, tenants were turned out
at the expiration of their short leases; and they were irresponsible
because they knew they would be turned out. Swift did not attempt
to fix the initial blame for this vicious circle. Both parties were at
fault, and the result was the same: more and more land was given
over to "that abominable Race of Graziers"; the tenants were
forced off the land to beg for a living; grain had to be imported
from England; and the once-tillable land was turned into pastures
for sheep, for the benefit of the English woolen manufacturers.
"*Ajax* was mad," Swift wrote in the *Answer,* "when he mistook a
Flock of *Sheep* for his Enemies: but we shall never be sober, until
we have the same Way of Thinking."[43]

As for the memorialist's proposal, it was "liable to more Objections than there are Lines." The projector had been careful to show
where the premium of £10,000 could be found, but he had neg-
lected to explain where the "merchants and others" would get the
£100,000 which the grain would cost: "You are in Pain of two
Shillings *Præmium,* and forget the Twenty Shillings for the Price,"
Swift reminded him. "Find me out the latter, and I will engage
for the former." Nor was the scheme to provide funds for the
premium feasible, for increased taxes on imported goods would
result in fewer imports rather than greater revenues; and even if the
"prœternatural Sum" of £110,000 could be raised, it would take
time, and the Irish poor had little time left — "there is no dallying
with Hunger." Finally, even if the memorialist in some way did
contrive to overcome these difficulties, no one in Ireland would
have the money with which to purchase the grain, least of all the

---

[42] "Soon after . . . *The Short View,* etc. was published, came out another
intituled *A Memorial Address'd to the Reverend Dean S. . . .* In a few
Days after, a third Pamphlet was published, being an Answer to the said
Memorial" (*Mist's Weekly Journal,* April 23, 1728). In his issue for May
11, Mist printed an abstract of Swift's *Answer.*

[43] *Prose Works,* XII, 17-19, *passim.*

starving poor who needed it most. Insofar as his intentions appeared good, the memorialist was pardonable, but his proposal made it obvious that he was "either naturally or affectedly ignorant" of circumstances in Ireland.[44] In the place of his visionary scheme, Swift offered the practical — if admittedly limited — one of organizing a public charity to support the poor "in *Potatoes* and *Butter-milk*" until the new crop could be harvested. The long-range solution to the problem of recurring famine was equally simple and obvious: "Go and preach to your own Tenants," Swift advised the author of the *Memorial*, "to fall to the Plough as fast as they can; and prevail with your neighbouring 'Squires to do the same with theirs; or else die with the Guilt of having driven away half the Inhabitants, and starving the rest."[45]

The moribund state of Ireland's domestic industry affected the country almost as severely as did the decline of agriculture. One of the prerequisites for national prosperity that Swift had listed in *A Short View* was "a Disposition of the People . . . to wear their own Manufactures, and import as few Incitements to Luxury . . . as they possibly can live conveniently without."[46] As a general maxim, this was a condition essential to economic health for two reasons: the encouragement of industry provided employment for domestic workers; and flourishing native industries enabled a country to maintain a favorable balance of trade between its imports and exports. The second of these reasons was inapplicable to Ireland because of English restrictions on Ireland's export market. But if Ireland was not at liberty to export freely, she could still avoid excessive importation, especially of manufactured goods. Raw materials brought into the country at least afforded employment for Irish workmen; the importation of finished products not only handicapped local industry but also drained the nation of its supply of ready money. Hence Swift's reiterated insistence that the Irish use goods of their own manufacture as much as possible.

Because Ireland was overstocked with raw wool and because Swift knew at first hand the plight of the Dublin weavers ("The truth is, that the woollen manufacture of this kingdom sate always nearest my heart," he confessed in 1733[47]), the industry which received his special attention was the woolen manufacture. So well known was this preference that the Dublin weavers frequently

---

[44] *Ibid.*, XII, 20-22, *passim.*   [45] *Ibid.*, XII, 22.   [46] *Ibid.*, XII, 7.
[47] *Ibid.*, XIII, 90.

called at the deanery to ask Swift's help in forwarding the use of
Irish woolens.[48]   One such occasion was in April, 1729.   Swift
described his meeting with the weavers in *A Letter to the Archbishop of Dublin*.   In the *Letter*, he reminded King of their joint
efforts to encourage the wearing of Irish stuffs among the clergy,
and he attributed part of the failure of these efforts to the weavers
themselves, "the hottest and coldest generation of Men that I have
known."   As early as 1720, Swift had urged them to improve the
quality of their goods and to deal fairly with the public.   The
ignorance and greed of the northern linen weavers had lost them a
trade with Spain worth £300,000 a year, and the sharp practices
of woolen dealers made even patriots reluctant to buy their goods.
But the Dublin weavers had so far done nothing beyond assuring
Swift that they would institute standards of excellence and honesty
in the trade; they had not even shown him and Archbishop King
samples of the material they hoped would find favor among the
clergy, despite their promises to do so.[49]

The weavers were not altogether at fault, however.   In the 1720
Proposal, Swift had marveled at "the Biass among our People in
favour of *Things, Persons,* and *Wares* of all Kinds that come from
England."[50]   This bias was particularly hurtful to the Irish weavers,
who resorted to weaving a gold thread into their silks to pass them
off as goods of Indian manufacture, even though the Irish silk was
of better quality and workmanship.[51]   In the *Proposal that . . . the
Ladies . . . of Ireland Should Appear Constantly in Irish Manufactures,* Swift estimated that the Irish spent £150,000 annually
on foreign clothes and luxuries, a practice which appeared to him
"as prudent and necessary, as to see a man in an embroidered coat
begging out of Newgate in an old shoe."[52]   Both sexes were guilty
of this foppery, but the women were to Swift the principal offenders.   In the *Letter to the Archbishop of Dublin,* he condemned "the
cowardly slavish indulgence of the men to the intolerable pride,
arrogance, vanity and Luxury of the Women, who . . . seem to
employ their whole stock of Invention in contriving new arts of
profusion, faster than the most parsimonious husband can afford."[53]
Indeed, the subject of female vanity provoked more savage out-
bursts from Swift than any other topic he discussed in the economic

[48] *Ibid.,* XIII, 90.   [49] *Ibid.,* XII, 68-70, *passim.*   [50] *Ibid.,* IX, 19.
[51] *Ibid.,* XII, 9.   [52] *Ibid.,* XII, 126-127.   [53] *Ibid.,* XII, 67.

tracts of 1728-29. In the *Answer to Letters from Unknown Persons,* he abandoned all restraint in denouncing the women for their extravagance:

> Is it not the highest Indignity to human nature, that men should be such poltrons as to suffer the Kingdom and themselves to be undone, by the Vanity, the Folly, the Pride, and Wantonness of their Wives, who under their present Corruptions seem to be a kind of animal suffered for our sins to be sent into the world for the Destruction of Familyes, Societyes, and Kingdoms; and whose whole study seems directed to be as expensive as they possibly can in every useless article of living, who by long practice can reconcile the most pernicious forein Drugs to their health and pleasure, provided they are but expensive; as Starlings grow fat with henbane: who contract a Robustness by meer practice of Sloth and Luxury: who can play deep severall hours after midnight, sleep beyond noon, revel upon Indian poisons, and spend the revenue of a moderate family to adorn a nauseous unwholesom living Carcase.[54]

The thought and imagery here have led one critic to see in this passage an animus against women that was pathological.[55] Swift's attitude toward women may very well have been pathological, but it would be unwise to try to prove the point by reference to his Irish tracts. It was commonplace for writers on Irish affairs to complain about foreign imports and to single out women as notably guilty of folly and extravagance. Arthur Dobbs, in his *Essay on Trade,* noted that the women of Ireland were particularly responsible for the excessive importation of foreign luxuries, and he warned the nation "to put a stop to the disease, before it turns Epidemical."[56] The anonymous author who assumed the name of "M. B. Draper" in *A Letter to the People of Ireland* (1729) charged that the ladies of quality "think it Savage to be cloath'd in the Product of their own Country"; and in *The Tribune* in 1729, Swift's friend Patrick Delany referred to the deception Irish weavers were forced to play on their female customers, and he admitted his pleasure in hearing the ladies "display at once their Ignorance and their Eloquence, in Praise of a Piece of Silk, which they would never have worn with any Satisfaction, if they had known where it was made."[57] *The Dublin Intelligence* for January 14, 1729, reported that the journey-

---

[54] *Ibid.,* XII, 80.
[55] Murry, pp. 422-423.
[56] Arthur Dobbs, *An Essay on the Trade and Improvement of Ireland* (Dublin, 1729-31), [pt. I], pp. 43, 46; pt. II, p. 42.
[57] M. B. Draper, *A Letter to the People of Ireland* (Dublin, 1729), p. 8; *The Tribune* (London, 1729), p. 81.

men weavers were reduced to the utmost want ("no Work stirring, or Money to be had for Work") and added, "This is *known* mostly to be owing to the *Disuse* of our own *Manufactors,* by *those* who have it in their Power to Encourage Trade by their Example, (viz) our Women of Quality, who seldom Wear any of our own Goods, Except impos'd on them under the Name of Foreign Works." None of these authors matched Swift's intensity in denouncing idle women of fashion; but, for that matter, few authors matched his intensity in denouncing Presbyterians or Whig prime ministers. And at least one writer could attack female vanity with something of Swift's characteristic violence. Bishop Berkeley, certainly no misogynist, urged the need of sumptuary laws in England and condemned the extravagance of English women of quality as a grievous sin as well as an economic folly. He rounded off his attack by quoting, with evident satisfaction, Isaiah III:24: "And it shall come to pass that instead of a sweet smell there shall be a stink; and instead of a girdle a rent; and instead of well-set hair, baldness; and instead of a stomacher, a girding of sack-cloth; and burning instead of beauty."[58]

Of more relevance to Swift's views on Irish industry and Irish trade than the debatable question of his misogyny is one glaring inconsistency in his attack on needless foreign imports. Swift urged the proscription of foreign clothes from Ireland's import market, and he was willing to extend the ban to tea and coffee ("because they are unwholesome"[59]). He strenuously opposed, however, all efforts to increase the tax on French and Spanish wines. He had objected to this plan when it was proposed in the *Memorial of the Poor Inhabitants . . . of Ireland,* and when, in November, 1729, he learned that the Irish Parliament was considering laying an additional duty on imported wine, he wrote his *Proposal . . . [to] the Ladies* in protest.[60] The plan, he argued, was based on the fallacy that increased duties led to increased revenues, whereas in fact, they resulted in a decrease in revenue because people refused to pay the additional tax on the commodity. Moreover, if an added tax were put on wine, Ireland stood in danger of losing the few men of

---

[58] *The Works of George Berkeley,* eds. A. A. Luce and T. E. Jessop (London, 1953), VI, 75-76.

[59] *Prose Works,* XII, 20.

[60] *Ibid.,* XII, xxi. Because the tax was voted before Swift could get his tract into print, he did not publish it (see p. xxii).

fortune who lived there, the cheapness of foreign wine being the principal cause for their residence. In this tract Swift dismissed the sum spent on wine as "hardly tolerable," and in the *Letter to the Archbishop of Dublin,* he estimated that the annual expenditure for tea, coffee, and chocolate was five times that spent for wine.[61] He must have been aware of the inconsistency of his position. No matter how small a sum was spent on foreign wine, the expenditure meant that money was going out of Ireland, and as Swift and every other writer on Irish affairs had repeatedly shown, Ireland needed to keep within her borders every penny she could.[62] Swift clearly regarded wine — whether he knew he was rationalizing or not — as a necessity, one of the imported items which one could not live conveniently without. To him, it was "the liquor of the Gods"; when he was in London in 1710, he wrote to Stella that he missed the excellent, cheap wine to be had in Ireland; and years later, when he was old and sick, he wrote to a friend, "My disorders, with the help of years, make wine absolutely necessary to support me."[63] In only one of his tracts of 1728-29 did he include wines among Ireland's "detestable Extravagancies," and even then he blamed the extravagance on "the knavery of Merchants" who increased the price.[64] He had apparently persuaded himself to take seriously yet another reason for allowing Ireland to import wines with as little restraint as possible: "There is no nation yet known, in either hemisphere, where the people of all conditions are more in want of some cordial, to keep up their spirits, than in this of ours. I am not in jest; and, if the fact will not be allowed me, I shall not argue it."[65]

"The Directions for Ireland," Swift wrote in the *Answer to Several Letters from Unknown Persons,* "are very short and plain, to encourage agriculture and home consumption, and utterly discard all Importations which are not absolutely necessary for health or Life."[66] These were the basic prescriptions which Ireland had to follow or perish. All other problems were minor in comparison with the decline of tillage and domestic industry. There were, however,

---

[61] *Ibid.,* XII, 67-68, 125.
[62] Arthur Dobbs, for example, included imported wines among the items that contributed to Ireland's luxury (*Essay on Trade,* [Pt. I], pp. 43-44).
[63] *Corr,* I, 100; *Journal to Stella,* I, 190; *Corr,* V, 441.
[64] *Prose Works,* XII, 79.   [65] *Ibid.,* XII, 124; and cf. pp. 20, 68.
[66] *Ibid.,* XII, 79.

other problems, two of which caused Swift particular concern. These were the scarcity of small change and the rising trend in emigration.

Ireland suffered from a shortage of specie throughout the eighteenth century, but in the mid-1720's the problem became acute. Except for the debased copper issued under various private patents, Ireland's hard currency consisted of foreign gold and silver, the value of which had been set by a royal proclamation of 1725. The fixed rate was lower than the real value of gold and silver, with the result that speculators found a quick profit in selling Ireland's foreign specie on the international market.[67] Further, because the guinea was worth threepence more in Ireland than in England, Irish bankers and tradesmen paid for their English purchases in silver rather than guineas.[68] This practice led to so heavy a drain on Ireland's silver that the scarcity of small change was stifling the domestic commerce of the country. Landlords had difficulty in receiving their rents; employers had to wait until their laborers' earnings amounted to a fairly considerable sum before they could pay wages; shopkeepers lost sales because they could not make change; and money-changers charged as much as tenpence to change a thirty-shilling piece into small coins.[69]

The Dublin Intelligence for April 29, 1729, reprinted a petition of the inhabitants of County Armagh to be presented to Sir Arthur Acheson and other members of the grand jury of the county. The "Perishing Petitioners" noted the terrible conditions in the county — the scarcity of grain, wholesale unemployment, an increase in emigration — but their particular object was to implore a remedy for the lack of silver, halfpence, and farthings. Swift had been a guest at Acheson's home at Market Hill during the summer and winter of 1728, and while he was there he had written a paper on the scarcity of small change in the north of Ireland. This was the nineteenth number of *The Intelligencer*, the joint venture of Swift and Sheridan that ran to nineteen issues between May and December, 1728.[70]

---

[67] O'Brien, pp. 345-348.   [68] Goodwin, p. 651.

[69] *Prose Works*, XII, 54-55.

[70] A twentieth number appeared in May, 1729, and was reprinted in the second London edition of the periodical in 1730. *Intelligencer* Number XIX is the only new paper by Swift on Irish affairs. Number XV is a reprint of *A Short View of the State of Ireland*.

repeal the Test Act and to reprint his *Letter . . . Concerning the Sacramental Test,* written a quarter of a century earlier.[6] This unwavering intolerance of dissent — whether Protestant or Catholic — did not impair the effectiveness of Swift's efforts to help Ireland. English restraints and Irish apathy did that. If, however, Swift had had the enlightened view (rare in his time) to avoid associating Presbyterians with regicide and Catholics with Stuart absolutism, he would have been in fact the spokesman for "the whole People of Ireland."

During the years following *A Modest Proposal* and *The Answer to the Craftsman,* Swift took some interest in purely secular issues. In 1733 he published two tracts supporting his choice of candidates for the offices of recorder and member of Parliament of Dublin. In each election, his candidate won.[7] On the few occasions when he turned to the topics of his earlier Irish tracts, he repeated old phrases and attitudes. An unpublished paper on the subject of the Dublin woolen manufacturers (written in 1733) goes over the same ground Swift had covered in *A Letter to the Archbishop of Dublin, Concerning the Weavers* and echoes the theme of *A Short View of the State of Ireland* and *Maxims Controlled:* "Ireland is the poorest of all civilized countries in Europe, with every natural advantage to make it one of the richest."[8] In 1737 he published a prefatory letter recommending Alexander Macaulay's *Some Thoughts on the Tillage of Ireland* as a useful book, "if there were Virtue enough among us to follow the Author's Advice."[9] And his *Proposal for Giving Badges to Beggars in All the Parishes of Dublin* (1737) elaborates a plan he had first considered in 1726 and repeats his conviction that in Ireland people "are the Poverty and not the Riches of the Nation."[10]

---

[6] *The Advantages Proposed by Repealing the Sacramental Test* (1732); *Quaeries Wrote by Dr. J. Swift* (1732); *The Presbyterians Plea of Merit* (1733); *Reasons for Repealing the Sacramental Test in Favour of the Catholics* (1733); *Some Few Thoughts Concerning the Repeal of the Test* (1733). These pieces are in *Prose Works,* XII, 243-299. Swift's *Letter . . . Concerning the Sacramental Test* was advertised in various issues of Faulkner's *Dublin Journal* from April to October, 1732.

[7] *Prose Works,* XIII, xxiv-xxvi. Swift's tracts, *Some Considerations in the Choice of a Recorder* and *Advice to the Freemen of Dublin,* are on pp. 69-70, 79-85.

[8] *Observations Occasioned by Reading a Paper, Entitled, the Case of the Woollen Manufacturers of Dublin, &c., Prose Works,* XIII, 89-92.

[9] *Prose Works,* XIII, 143.

[10] *Ibid.,* XIII, xxxviii-xxxix, 135. Swift's tract, written in April, may

He was once more involved in the old question of coinage when, in 1736, Archbishop Boulter proposed to reduce the value of the guinea by threepence and at the same time to import a quantity of copper halfpence from England. Swift opposed both measures — the halfpence because of the "indignity" of their not being coined in Ireland; the reduction of the gold because he feared the devaluation would lower the price of commodities, to the sole benefit of government officials in Dublin and Irish absentees.[11] Although he made a speech against lowering the gold and "raised some ferment" about the halfpence, his opposition was unsuccessful. The copper was officially given currency in May, 1737, and the following August a proclamation by the lords justices and Privy Council set the new rate of the guinea.[12] Swift's objections to these measures were ill-founded. Boulter was both disinterested and correct in seeking to bring the rate of the guinea in Ireland closer to that which prevailed in England; and even if the English-minted halfpence were an "indignity" to Ireland, within a week of their being put into circulation, they were being "most greedily received."[13]

[II]

In 1734 Swift acknowledged the receipt of a pamphlet urging the development of English and Irish fisheries. He wrote a letter of thanks to the author, but he predicted that the proposal would be ignored, even in England — and compared with Ireland, England was "an Habitation of Saints." He used the occasion to review a number of old grievances against both countries, and he gave a succinct summary of his attitude toward Ireland and his part in her affairs: "As to my Native Country, (as you call it) I happened indeed by a perfect Accident to be born here, my Mother being left here from returning to her House at *Leicester,* and I was a Year old before I was sent to *England;* thus I am a *Teague,* or an *Irishman,* or what People please, although the best Part of my Life was in *England.* What I did for this Country was from perfect

have been partly responsible for the lord mayor's proclamation of October 7, 1737, requiring constables to arrest all beggars, "except those badged by the several Parishes" (see *The Dublin Gazette,* Oct. 8-11, 1737).

[11] *Corr,* V, 432; *The Rev. Dean Swift's Reasons Against Lowering the Gold and Silver Coin, Prose Works,* XIII, 119-120.

[12] Boulter, II, 162, 169; *The Dublin Gazette,* Aug. 30–Sept. 3, 1737.

[13] Boulter, II, 172.

Hatred of Tyranny and Oppression. . . ."[14] This statement makes Swift appear as something less than St. Patrick's successor, the title bestowed on him in a poem of 1726.[15]

The tribute, however, is typical of the veneration in which the people of Ireland held this patriot-in-spite-of-himself. When he walked through the streets of Dublin, he received "a thousand hats and blessings."[16] Once when he was ill for a period of two weeks, "many sorrowful Countenances were seen all over . . . [the] City"; and on hearing a rumor that he had died, "several Gentlemen, Tradesmen, and others, sent a Porter from a Tavern, to know the Truth." The report that Swift was alive "so much pleased the Company, that instead of putting the Messenger off with two Pence for his Trouble, they every one generously contributed, and gave him several Shillings to drink that worthy Patriots Health."[17] A few weeks earlier, when Swift had been threatened with physical violence by the victim of one of his satires, the inhabitants of the liberty of St. Patrick's had waited on the dean with a signed resolution to defend him.[18] Even after his death, pamphlets on various aspects of Irish affairs appeared under the name of the Drapier; and in 1750 John Browne, who had asked for and received Swift's pardon for the unwilling part he had taken in the struggle over Wood's halfpence, erected a monument at his home in County Mayo to the memory of "the greatest genius of our age, the late Dean of St. Patrick's."[19]

On May 27, 1730, Swift's services were officially recognized when the Dublin Corporation gave him, as a freeman of the city, a gold box, "the value thereof not to exceed twenty five pounds." The value of this gesture, like that of the box itself, was limited. Accord-

---

[14] *Prose Works,* XIII, 111-113, *passim.* For the details of this letter's subsequent publication, see pp. xxx-xxxiii.

[15] *Poem on the Dean of St. Patrick's Birth-Day, Nov. 30th Being St. Andrew's-Day* (Dublin, 1726). There is a copy of this poem in the National Library of Ireland.

[16] *Corr,* V, 415.

[17] Faulkner's *Dublin Journal,* Jan. 22-26, 1734.

[18] *Corr,* V, 54-56; Faulkner's *Dublin Journal,* Jan. 5-8 and 8-12, 1734. Faulkner printed a copy of the resolution, along with Swift's answer of thanks, in his paper for February 5-9, 1734. The man who threatened Swift was Richard Bettesworth, sergeant-at-law and member of the Irish Commons. He had been angered by Swift's attack in *"On the Words — Brother Protestants, and Fellow Christians . . . ,"* a poem written during the controversy over the tithe on flax (see *Poems,* III, 809-813).

[19] *Drapier's Letters,* pp. 384-387; *Corr,* IV, 463-464.

ing to Marmaduke Coghill, the corporation acted only after Swift had himself solicited the honor for three years; and when the gold box was presented, it contained no inscription, although Delany, at Swift's suggestion, had supplied the corporation with one![20] These facts are apparently accurate. What is lacking in Coghill's account of the episode is the more important fact that by 1730 Swift had become justifiably embittered by a succession of disappointments. His efforts to secure the First Fruits for his church had not been sufficiently acknowledged, and though his intervention in Irish politics had made him the hero of the people, it had cost him official favor and subjected him to the libels and insults of party scribes. It is understandable that when he received his gold box — the only tangible reward he ever got for his efforts on behalf of Ireland — he was disappointed that it did not bear an inscription "shewing some reason why the city thought fit to do him that honour."[21]

Swift had hoped that the corporation would inscribe on the trophy its acknowledgment of his "great zeal . . . in asserting the Rights [and] defending the liberties" of Ireland. The simple truth of the phrase outweighs Coghill's aversion to the "arrogant inscription." In a black period of the nation's history, Swift was one of the few men who asserted Ireland's rights. Other authors wrote economic and sociological tracts, but Swift based his whole program for Ireland on the thesis which Molyneux had stated in 1698. That "Ireland's rights" meant for Swift (as it did for Molyneux) the rights of the Anglo-Irish does not diminish the significance of his part in Ireland's slow progress toward legislative independence. In 1782 the act of 6 George I — the Declaratory Act — was repealed. The day the repeal was announced to the Irish Parliament, Grattan declared on the floor of the Commons, "Spirit of Swift! spirit of Molyneux! your genius has prevailed!"

---

[20] See *Notes & Queries,* CLVIII (1930), 416; *The Substance of What Was Said by the Dean on Receiving His Freedom, Prose Works,* XII, 145-148; and see my article, "Jonathan Swift, Freeman of Dublin," *Modern Language Notes,* LXXI (1956), 405-409.

[21] *Prose Works,* XII, 148.

APPENDIX A

King's treatise, "Some Observations on the Taxes Paid by Ireland to Support the Government," is in the Library at Trinity College, Dublin. For an account of two ms versions, see the article by R. Dudley Edwards in *Analecta Hibernica*, VIII (1938), 5-18. A brief abstract of the treatise is reprinted in Historical Manuscripts Commission, *Appendix to the Second Report* (1870-72), appendix XXX, pp. 256-257.

King wrote a first draft of his paper in 1716. He greatly expanded this version (from seventeen to sixty-eight folios) in 1721 and was still at work on it after the defeat of Wood's patent in 1725. The treatise was never published, but it was widely circulated in manuscript. In 1716 and 1720, King sent copies to Samuel Molyneux and Viscount Molesworth, respectively; in 1721 he wrote to Annesley that he had shown it to "several friends"; and there is a contemporary note that Thomas Prior made use of King's paper in writing his *List of the Absentees of Ireland*.[1]

Aside from a general similarity, there are several close resemblances between King's treatise and Swift's letter to Peterborough. Swift, for example, wrote to Peterborough that "whereas Sir Robert Walpole was pleased to take notice how little the King gets by Ireland, it ought, perhaps, to be considered, that the revenues and taxes, I think, amount to above four hundred thousand pounds a year; and reckoning the riches of Ireland, compared with England, to be as one to twelve, the King's revenues there would be equal to more than five millions here" (*Corr*, III, 310). King had taken the same proportional view of Irish taxation, and he had arrived at almost the same figures: "The hardships of the Taxes paid by subjects to support the government are not to be Estimated by the Quantity of the money given, but by the proportion it bears to the Substance of the Persons that give it. . . . If we compare the Riches of Ireland with those of Great Britain, we shall find, they do not beare the proportion of one to Thirteen. . . . [Ireland] has actually paid [annually] above £400,000. . . . When Ireland pays £400,000, Brittain ought in proportion to the riches thereof to have contributed 13 times as much, that is, £5,200,000" (fols. 2-5).

---

[1] See King Corr, to Molyneux, Jan. 24, 1715 [1716]; to Molesworth, Jan. 24 and Feb. 11, 1720; to Annesley, June 8, 1721; see also Gilbert Collection, MS No. 138, fols. 69-70. The DNB erroneously attributes the authorship of the paper to Thomas Molyneux because a copy was found among his papers after his death. This was obviously a copy which King sent to Thomas, or it was the one which he had sent to Thomas' nephew, Samuel.

In addition to this statistical resemblance, there are verbal parallels between King's treatise and Swift's letter. King believed that much of the prejudicial Irish legislation enacted in England was owing to false reports of Ireland's disloyalty: "The people of Ireland do find, that the greatest inconveniences which happen to the Kingdom, arise for the most part from the Misrepresentations of the State & Condition of it" (fol. 52). Swift wrote, "The people of Ireland, who are certainly the most loyal subjects in the world, cannot but conceive that most of these hardships have been the consequence of some unfortunate representations" (p. 310). King described the poverty of the Irish peasantry in the following terms: "One half of the people of Ireland wear neither Stockings or Shoes for one half of the year. . . . One half of the people of Ireland tast neither bread nor Flesh for one half of the year, but Live on buttermilk, potatoes and Boyled Cabbage & other plants . . ." (fol. 36). Swift's letter to Peterborough is quite brief, but it contains a description of the Irish poor that is reminiscent of the description given by King: "there is not one farmer in a hundred through the kingdom who can afford shoes or stockings to his children, or to eat flesh, or drink anything better than sour milk or water, twice a year" (p. 310).

Swift's interview with Walpole was in April, 1726. A little more than two months later, King wrote to Lord Chancellor King. The archbishop was at Bath from May through July, taking treatments for a severe attack of gout (see *A Great Archbishop*, p. 254, n. 4). His illness prevented him from seeing the lord chancellor. On July 2 he sent his regrets in a letter: "It would have been a satisfaction to me to have run over with your Lordship some Circumstances of the Irish affairs. . . . Since I can't hope to do myself the Honour or my Countrey such a Signal Service, I take leave to acquaint your Lordship that some years ago, I put together some particulars relating to the State and Condition of Ireland; if I thought them worth your perusal . . . I would order my Servt to coppy them and would send them to your Lordship." He repeated this offer on August 29; and on December 6, he sent the paper to the lord chancellor (see King Corr for July 2, Aug. 29, Dec. 6, 1726).

Finally, on his English visit in 1726, Swift saw Walpole and Princess Caroline. The same year — on his visit — King wrote to the lord chancellor, and after he returned to Dublin, he sent his compliments, by way of Swift, to the Princess (see *Corr*, III, 357). It would seem, therefore, that Swift and King had coöperated to plead the true case of Ireland with members of the English government.

APPENDIX B

It has not been previously noted that Browne's *Seasonable Remarks* preceded Swift's *Short View of the State of Ireland* and that Swift's tract was written in answer to it. According to its title page, *Seasonable Remarks* was written in England but first published in Dublin; and in his dedication to Lord Carteret, Browne said that the book was intended as "a Preface only to other Essays on the Manufactures and Trade of Ireland, which I have prepared for the Press, if this should meet with your Approbation." One of the "other Essays" was *An Essay on Trade in General; and, on that of Ireland in Particular. By the Author of Seasonable Remarks.* This tract was advertised in *The Dublin Intelligence* for March 23, 1728, as "just Publish'd." Since *A Short View of the State of Ireland* was published on March 19, 1728, it must have appeared after the publication of *Seasonable Remarks,* for Browne could hardly have seen through the press two pamphlets of seventy and one hundred and nineteen pages, respectively, between March 19 and March 23. Furthermore, the *Essay on Trade* indicates that *Seasonable Remarks* had preceded it sufficiently early to attract some attention. In the dedication to the *Essay,* Browne said that he had been encouraged to publish this second tract "by the Favourable Reception which my Seasonable Remarks have met with" (he was obviously not referring to the reaction it had provoked from Swift!).

Browne sent Swift copies of *Seasonable Remarks* and the *Essay on Trade* (*The Dublin Intelligence* advised that the two could be had "Bound together"), along with *A Letter to the Author of the Short View of the State of Ireland.* When he discovered that Swift knew his authorship (revealed by the man who delivered the tracts), he sent an anguished letter (dated April 4, 1728), asking that Swift keep his identity secret. He also gave an explanation of his conduct at Walpole's inquiry and requested that in subsequent editions of *The Drapier's Letters,* Swift delete the attacks on him. Swift obliged in the 1735 edition of the *Works,* by deleting the reference to Browne in the third *Letter* (see *Corr,* IV, 24-28; *Drapier's Letters,* p. 236).

Although the authorship of *The Memorial to the R —— d. J —— n S —— t, of the Poor Inhabitants, Tradesmen, and Labourers of the Kingdom of Ireland* has generally been assigned to Browne, there is no evidence for the attribution. Wagner was not able to find any proof of Browne's authorship (*Irish Economics,* p. 31), and there is some presumptive evidence against attributing the tract to Browne. For one thing, he never mentioned *The Memorial* in any of his subsequent tracts on Irish affairs. Nor is there a reference to it in his letter to Swift; there, he mentions "the little books," and he says that his authorship is known only by his printer, his bookseller, and the messenger who took the tracts to Swift. *Seasonable Remarks, An Essay on Trade, A Letter to the Author of the Short View,* and all of his other known tracts of 1728-29 were either printed and sold by S. Powell, or printed by S. Powell for George Ewing. *The Memorial* was printed by Thomas Walsh.

Browne's views in *Seasonable Remarks* and *An Essay on Trade* were attacked by others besides Swift. Shortly after their appearance, they were answered by *Considerations on Two Papers Lately Published, the First, Called Seasonable Remarks, etc. and the Other, an Essay on Trade in General, and on that of Ireland, in Particular* (Dublin, 1728). The author was probably Arthur Dobbs. For Browne's replies to *Considerations,* etc. and the answer that they in turn provoked, see Wagner (pp. 30-31).

APPENDIX C

———————

The following letter is without question the one from "Trueman and Layfield" to which Swift replied in his *Answer to Several Letters from Unknown Persons.* Its subject is Ulster emigration, and Swift's *Answer* specifically mentions several details which are in this letter — for example, the erroneous reference to "Sir" William Penn and the "decency" with which "Trueman and Layfield" treat the established clergy (*Prose Works,* XII, 76, 78). The letter was probably sent to Swift in late April, 1729, before he wrote *A Letter to the Archbishop of Dublin, Concerning the Weavers;* for in that tract (written in April), Swift said that he was "weary . . . of so many crude Proposals in letters sent . . . from unknown hands," and he added that he was "not in the least sorry to hear of the great Numbers going to America" (*Prose Works,* XII, 66). Swift must have received "Trueman and Layfield's" letter before May 8, because in his *Answer* he said, "That great Prelate, in whose cover you directed your Letter, sent it to me this morning, and I begin my answer to-night" (p. 75). The "great Prelate" was, of course, Archbishop King; and King died on May 8, 1729.

The Dublin Weekly Journal
Saturday, June 7th. 1729.
To the Publisher of the *Dublin Weekly Journal*
Sir,
   The following is from a Country Farmer, as you may observe by its plainness; its View seems intended as a Warning to remove the Cause of the Things complained of, which is heartily wished for by all true Lovers of their Country. Your inserting it in your Paper will be grateful to several, and in particular to

Your very humble Servant,
J.W.

A Letter from some Farmers in the Country to a Gentleman in Dublin, *shewing their Reasons for removing to the* British *Plantations in* America, *with other Remarks, &c.*
SIR,
   We receiv'd your Letter, wherein you desired to know the Cause why so many are grown fond of transporting themselves to *America:* In Obedience to your Commands we made Enquiry, and here send you as many of the Reasons as we could discover in the Country where we live, and hope you will pardon our Freedom, in expressing ourselves in the plain Terms and Language of the People.

About fifteen Years ago, many of our Friends and Acquaintance went with their Families to *Pensilvania,* from whom we have received many inviting Letters, which gave a fair Description of that Country, and much the same with a Book Entituled, *An Account of the British Empire in* America. Printed at *London* in the Year, 1708. These Letters fraught with Invitations and Encomiums on that happy Settlement, assure us of the abundance of all Necessaries, and Conveniences of Life, and that without the Dread of the *Racking Landlord,* and *Griping Tythmaster.* The Tenures of Land are to them and their Posterity for ever; so that there are no vexatious Covenants in Leases, *No: mina penas, Heriots, Duties,* or such base Impositions. no tedious Law Suits, nor exhorbitant Fees, and, but few Lawyers; their Laws are excellent, being carefully Collected by the judicious Sir *William Penn;* the Native Indians are said to be there very much civilized, and that the Conqueror's do not become Tyrants as in other Nations we have known; and there is great Care taken of the Poor.

Our Neighbour *William* has brought home the Maps of the whole World, where we find *Pensilvania* about the Centre of the *British* Settlements, and under the same Degree of Latitude with *Italy,* and the South of *France,* Countries always renowned for great Fertility.

Here, in the North of *Ireland,* we can easily observe the Country seems to be over peopled already, and that if the Number increases but Six or Eight Thousand Yearly, (which will be found to be a moderate Computation in the whole Kingdom) our Butter, Beef, and Leather, which used to bring us a little Mony, will scarce suffice the Inhabitants; and we may in time be obliged to send to *America* for such Things as we have formerly exported, as we do now for part of our Timber and Corn.

The Linen Trade, our chief Support, although under the best Regulation, is very much decayed.

Our Youth lye under great Discouragements, and Complain that few of them are preferred in the Church or Revenue, or admitted even to serve in the Army.

We are allowed but very little of the Benefit of Forreign Trade, nor are we even allowed a Mint for any sort of Coyn, a Priviledge seldom denied the meanest Principalities. 'Tis said, there is above five hundred thousand pounds carryed yearly, most part in Specie, out of this Kingdom, and most of that for things that might as well be wanted. What Money comes to us, is privately, or chiefly by Stealth, which is given for a Reason why Gold is so much more plenty than Silver, yet our Silver is not raised to make it equal to the Gold, nor any Method taken to keep our little Gold at home, or from going to those Places where it passes at a larger Value.

We, to supply the want of Change, would cut part of the forreign Gold and Silver into small Pieces, to be passed by Weight, but the Treasury will not receive them, although it would be both acceptable to the Army, and beneficial to all Degrees, by the present supply of Change.

But what we suffer from many of our Landlords is very intollerable, they seem Ambitious only of out doing one another in the Oppression of their Tenants, by exhorbitant Rents, Leases for short Terms of Years, filled with a Train of the hardest Covenants, the Lawyer's Wit can contrive; and after all, what Duties the Steward, the Lady, or the Cookmaid shall think needful: Thus must we spend our Lives and Fortunes in improving these Lands, which cost our Forefathers so much Time to Cultivate, and bring in from Woods and Boggs, which now from time to time are to be raised higher and higher, to supply some Prodigal, or gratify some covetous Landlord;

and in those calamitous Times, Landlords are unwilling to lessen their Rent Roll, by giving an abatement of Rent to their Needy Tenants, or to accept of a surrender of their dear Leases, so that many of the poor People, are under a Necessity of running away, either to *America,* or to some other part of the World; to shelter themselves from Imprisonment, for Debts and Arrears of Rent.

The Books of the *Judges* on their Circuits shew the vast Numbers of Civil Bills and Decrees for Debt against poor People, many of whom chuse rather to go any where than starve in Prison, and there are great Complaints that the Cost or Fees of every Decree, for the smallest uncontested Sum of Money (though fairly due by Bill or Bond) will be at least Nine Shillings; this and the unequal Tax called *Hearth Money,* is very heavy upon the Poor.

Some of the Reverend Clergy have been so far imposed upon, as to put their Tyths into the Hands of very ill Men, who do so overaw us by the Interest they pretend to have in the Courts, and by having a hank over us, for small Dues, or old Debts, that we are sometimes glad to please them with a seventh part of the Value, instead of a Tenth, and besides, they often threaten us with Law Suits for the Tyths of the little Gardens of Flax and Potatoes, and Christning, and Burial Money, by which Means the poorest People are great Sufferers.

The great Scarceity of Fewel puts us in mind, that the sinking of very deep Pits of fifty or sixty Fathom, (as in other Countries) in proper Places to discover Coals, or other Mines, which have appear'd almost above Ground in many parts of this Kingdom, to employ our Poor, and save a good part of our Money at home, is not practiced by our Great Men, or modern Projectors.

Instead of beneficial Projects, for the Good of the Nation, the Heads of our Men of Fortune run upon little else, but buying Estates, to be in a condition to Rack and Oppress the poor Tenants, who for want of Trade and Business, are bred for the most part to Husbandry alone, so that they eat up the Product of their little Farms.

Some of our Neighbours, who are but too superstitious, prognosticate strange Things, from these unusual Appearances in the Sky, and Lights in the North: And indeed all of us, when we observe the Sun's usual Heat, or Influence, so much abated, can't help thinking, it looks but too like the Frowns of Heaven; and when we see the Earth for these three Years past, refuse its former Encrease, though equally Tilled, we are apt to think our Land like that of *Canaan,* is cursed for the Sins of the People.

Now should a Famine, the forerunner of a Plague, or Pestilence afflict us, as there is now the most aparent Danger, we fear there would be as few *Joseph's* to provide for our Sustenance, as there are Drapers to take our Interests. It was a great Mortification to see our little Corn and Provision sold off publickly to other Countries, whilst our poor and honest Housekeepers are almost starving, in Countries where there are more Hands than Business, and more Mouths than Meat, its undoubtedly better, that considerable Numbers go Yearly Abroad, than be idle at Home, helping to starve their Neighbours.

The *Israleites* when oppressed by a Famine, removed to the Land of *Egypt.* Even Bees, are taught by Instinct, when crowded, to send off their Superfluous Numbers in Swarms; the people of the *Swiss Cantons* ramble to all Countries for Bread and Pay; and wou'd it not be prudent in us to withdraw upon these Accounts, and also avoid the threatening Arm of

Providence, which seems now Impending over our Nation, ready to punish its Pride, Vanity, Avarice, Infidelity, Oppression, and other Crimes.

Is it not very surprizing, to see many of our Great Men and Ladies, as if they were under an Infatuation, and insensible of the Miseries coming upon us, who, instead of laying out Money in Charity, or in contributing to the Importation of Corn; either hoarding up their Money, or passing it off in costly Apparel, fine Equipage, luxurious Danties, Gaming, or feeding up Stables of Horses, Kennels of Dogs, and useless Creatures, at a Time when thousands of poor People are ready to starve.

We must not omit the great Goodness and Charitable Endeavours of his Grace the Lord Primate of all *Ireland,* in relieving the Poor of the City of *Armagh,* and other Places last Year, with Money and Corn, nor those good Men, who have this Year, subscribed very large Sums of Money, in conjunction with his Grace, to be laid out in the Importation of Corn, to be distributed at a moderate price, for the Relief of the Poor in the Province of *Ulster.*

It is believed, that if all our Landlords were like those Good Men, many of the People that intend for *America,* would alter their Minds.

It is Reported, that the Landlords are drawing up Memorials, to prevent our going; in which they alledge, we carry off a great deal of the current Coin, but we beg of them to consider, that few but poor People are yet gone, who do not carry off even one tenth part of what they themselves *melt down* into Plate, or send abroad Yearly, for Wine, Tea, Spices, and foreign Cloaths, which at this Time, might be better spared.

And if it be true, that every Hand will earn in *America,* three Times as much Wages, as here, they will rather buy their Linen from us, where it is cheap, than to bestow their Time in making it there.

It was seldom known among our Forefathers, that they should be hindred of a Passage from any part of his Majestys Dominions to another, except when *Oliver Crommel* was stopped in his intended Voyage to *New England,* the consequence of which, any one that reads the History of those Times may find, besides, might it not be against the Interest of *Ireland* to make it a place of Confinement, or if it be so, we wish it was for the Rich, who carry or send away vast Sums of Money, to be spent in foreign Countries.

Some alledge, That the Protestants ought to be kept at home, as a Security for us against the Papists, least they should joyn our Enemies, or rise in Arms as they did in the Year, 1641. Now, in *Ulster,* the Number of Papists are not very considerable; and it is believed, if there was more Encouragement given to *Charity Schools,* and if the Clergy would spend a little Time in Conversing more freely with them, and treat them in a courteous and kind Manner, many of them would be brought over.

But if the Landlords fear any thing from that Quarter, why don't they give us better Bargains, to Encourage our Stay, for a Security to them, and their Estates.

It is observed, that when very great Tracts of Land are granted in Lease by the Nobility and Bishops, the Chief Tenants become Landlords, and there is no great care taken to secure the Poor Inhabitants that labour the Ground, from the Oppression of rack Rents, and severe Duties, even of unseasonable Days Work, and in the time of their Harvest.

Ireland was once covered with Wood, 'till cleared by the Industry of our Forefathers, whose Posterity are now, in like manner, for the Reasons aforesaid, inclined to clear their Way in forreign Countries; and since his Majesty's Plantations want Numbers of People to secure them against their

Enemies, our Removal seems no less for the Interest of the King, than of Us, besides, the Service that would be done to the Church and State, by the propagation of the Protestant Religion, and the *British* Interest, in that *Great Continent.*

Some of our Knights and Squires have courted our Interest, with pretended Love, and fair Promises of representing our Grievances in order to have them redressed, but no sooner have they gained their point, than they become Lazy, Heedless, or too Proud and Haughty, to mind us, or the Grievances of their afflicted Country, and consequently mute as Fish in moveing ought that may tend to its Benefit, and, in truth some of them seem as if they never thought of it, but preferment for themselves, or their Friends, or to be of some Party, or be skreend from Debts, seem to be some of their chiefest aims, whereas would they, with Spirit and Conduct, joyn heartily in a fair Representation of our Grievance to his sacred Majesty, there is no room to doubt of speedy Redress from so good a Sovereign.

It is observed, that Merchants, and Owners of Ships make such Advantage by the Fraught of Passengers to those Countries, that they frequently send Emisaries abroad to Entice and Ensnare the unwary People, who out of Hopes of becoming very Great, because some few, as in other Places, were successful there, they are often overperswaded to quit their Farmes, and comfortable Livings, for mere Uncertainties, to the hazard of their Lives, and the lives of their Wives and Children.

To conclude, if the Landlords, and others, who are unwilling to part with us, will in a proper Manner lay before his Majesty the National Grievances, so that by their Redress there may be Encouragement of Trade, and Employing of the Poor, who now, as an Instance of their Poverty, go yearly to *England* in Crowds, to look for a Day's Labour, and many of them die in the Fields by the Way; and in the Province of *Ulster,* there are great Numbers of Labouring Men and Women, going about the Country, in a starving Condition, Begging to get Meal alone for their Labour. Now if they will let us have fair Leases of our Land, at a moderate Rent, free from those barbarous Covenants and Impositions, and for such Terms of Years as our Children may reap some Benefit of our Improvements: And if the Clergy will be more moderate in their Dues, and not give them into the Hands of Racking Farmers, they may be well assured, we will not for the short Space that remains of our Lives, leave our Relations, our Friends, and our Native Soil, in search of distant Lands, to undergo all the various Toyles, Hardships and Dangers of the Seas, by Storms, Shipwracks, Turks and Pyrates, to be starved, or cast away by the Villany of Shipmasters, or when safe landed to be liable to many Troubles, and Disapointments; the Sickness and Seasonings of the Country, the fatigue of clearing Woods and Forrests, before we can sow our Corn, and the Incursions and Insurrection of the *Indians,* Civil Wars, or Invasions. We run upon these Hazards and Dangers (as we think) to avoid Landlords and other Afflictions. Tho' perhaps at length there may arise in those Countries Landlords, oppressors and devourers of Mankind, as in these; so that if we could be Easy at home, we should think it by much the best, to stay where we are, in hopes of better Times, and be buried with our Forefathers.

We are, SIR,
Your most obedient humble Servants,
Andrew Trueman,
Patrick Layfield.

Lisburn, May,
31st. 1729.

APPENDIX D

The struggle between Whitshed and the grand juries of 1724 had a fascinating, if ugly, parallel in the struggle between Whitshed and Swift. Whitshed's story is that of a good man led wrong by ambition and party zeal. The chief justice, who was of Irish birth, was an eminent jurist with a reputation for probity, "where party is out of the question" — the tribute and its qualification are Swift's (*Corr*, III, 116). For years Whitshed and Archbishop King had been close friends; and they had shared common views on the Annesley case (Ball, *The Judges in Ireland*, II, 96). When, however, Whitshed presided at the trial of Edward Waters, the printer of Swift's 1720 *Proposal*, his violent and arbitrary proceedings brought him into almost universal disfavor with the Irish people. He acted so intemperately in Waters' trial partly because of his Whiggish principles but more because of his ambition to become chancellor, the office held by Midleton. According to Swift, "the Chancellor, afraid of losing his office and the Chief Justice, desirous to come into it, were both vying who should show their zeal most to discountenance the pamphlet" (*Corr*, III, 65).

When Swift saw Whitshed behaving in 1724 exactly as he had done in 1720, he led an attack against the chief justice that for sheer personal cruelty surpassed even that against Wood. The *Extract* of the resolutions of the English Commons and the presentment which the grand jury delivered were measures designed to frustrate Whitshed's efforts, but they were nothing to the humiliating libels and lampoons that followed. In doggerel verse, Swift and his friends revived the story that Whitshed's grandfather had committed suicide in Christ Church Cathedral; questioned the judge's legitimacy; and treated with withering irony his family motto, *Libertas & Natale Solum* ("Fine Words; I wonder where you stole 'um," began one of Swift's poems [see *Poems*, I, 347-350, *passim*]). King tried to defend his friend by claiming that he had acted so violently only to provoke a heated reaction from the Irish that would cause England to withdraw Wood's patent (Ball, II, 105); but nothing could save the judge from public resentment — certainly not such an excuse as this. Among the attacks were the two *Letters from a Friend to the Right Honourable* ———, which "pinched Whitshed," according to Midleton, even more than Swift's *Extract* (*Corr*, IV, 227). Midleton may have been revealing a partiality to his son; for the author of the *Letters* seems to have been St. John Brodrick (see *Corr*, III, 229).

Whitshed's handling of the grand juries in 1724 effectively ended his ambitions and his career. In 1726, he requested to be transferred from the King's Bench to the Court of Common Pleas, because he found "the business of his present station very fatiguing" and desired "a place of less trouble." On August 26, 1727, he died; and it was the opinion of King and Boulter that his death had been hastened by the attacks he had suffered during the halfpence controversy (see Boulter, I, 89, 158-159; and Ball, II, 117-118). In a tract written seven months after Whitshed's death, Swift made a passing slur on the jurist's memory; and when he was criticized for this lack of respect for the dead, he answered that even though "such creatures" as Whitshed were immune to the corrective power of satire while they lived, it might be salutary to expose their characters after they were dead: "although their Memories will *rot,* there may be some Benefit for their Survivers, to smell it while it is *rotting*" (*Prose Works,* XII, 8, 25).

BIBLIOGRAPHY

EDITIONS OF SWIFT'S WORKS AND CORRESPONDENCE

The Works of J.S, D.D, D.S.P.D., ed. George Faulkner. Dublin, 1735. 4 vols.

The Prose Works of Jonathan Swift, ed. Temple Scott. London, 1897-1908. 12 vols.

The Correspondence of Jonathan Swift, ed. F. Elrington Ball. London, 1910-14. 6 vols.

The Drapier's Letters to the People of Ireland, ed. Herbert Davis. Oxford, 1935.

The Letters of Jonathan Swift to Charles Ford, ed. D. Nichol Smith. Oxford, 1935.

The Prose Works of Jonathan Swift, ed. Herbert Davis, Oxford, 1939——.

Journal to Stella, ed. Harold Williams. Oxford, 1948. 2 vols.

The Poems of Jonathan Swift, ed. Harold Williams. Second Edition. Oxford, 1958. 3 vols.

A Tale of a Tub, ed. A. C. Guthkelch and D. Nichol Smith. Second Edition. Oxford, 1958.

SECONDARY SOURCES AND BACKGROUND MATERIAL
FOR SWIFT'S IRISH WRITINGS

Manuscript Material

Correspondence of Archbishop William King at Trinity College, Dublin. Holograph, contemporary copies, and transcriptions (by T. Fisher).

[King, William]. "Some Observations on the Taxes Paid by Ireland to Support the Government." Manuscript in the Library at Trinity College, Dublin.

Correspondence of Edward Southwell in the British Museum.

Letters of Irish clergymen in the Gilbert Collection, Pearse Street Library, Dublin. Holographs and transcripts (MSS 27 and 28).

State Papers Domestic (Public Record Office, London).

Printed Material

[Anon.]. *An Account of the Journey-Men Weavers Grateful Congratula- tion of the Rev. Dr. Swift Dean of St. Patrick's Safe Arrival, with His Kind Answer, and Bounty to Their Corporation.* Dublin, 1726.

Ashton, John. *Chap-Books of the Eighteenth Century.* London, 1882.

Ball, F. Elrington. *The Judges in Ireland, 1221-1921.* London, 1926. 2 vols.

————. *Swift's Verse.* London, 1929.

Ball, J. T. *Historical Review of the Legislative Systems Operative in Ire- land, from the Invasion of Henry the Second to the Union.* London and Dublin, 1888.

Ballantyne, Archibald. *Lord Carteret.* London, 1887.

Beckett, J. C. *Protestant Dissent in Ireland, 1687-1780.* London, 1948.

Berkeley, George. *The Works of George Berkeley,* eds. A. A. Luce and T. E. Jessop. London, 1953. 6 vols.

[Boulter, Hugh]. *Letters Written by His Excellency Hugh Boulter, D.D.* Dublin, 1770. 2 vols.

Boyer, Abel. *The Political State of Great Britain.* London, 1711-40.

Boyle, John, Earl of Orrery. *Remarks on the Life and Writings of Dr. Jonathan Swift.* London, 1752.

[Browne, John]. *An Essay on Trade in General; and, on that of Ireland in Particular.* Dublin, 1728.

[Browne, John]. *A Letter to the Author of the Short View of the State of Ireland.* Dublin, 1728.

[Browne, John]. *Seasonable Remarks on Trade.* Dublin, 1728.

Burke, Edmund. *The Works of Edmund Burke.* Bohn's Standard Library. London, 1896. 8 vols.

Burnet, Thomas. *Essays Divine, Moral, and Political.* London, 1714.

Campbell, John, Lord. *The Lives of the Lord Chancellors and Keepers of the Great Seal of England.* London, 1848-50. 7 vols.

Case, A. E. *Four Essays on Gulliver's Travels.* Princeton, 1945.

————, ed. *Gulliver's Travels.* New York, 1938.

Coxe, William. *Memoirs of the Life and Administration of Sir Robert Walpole, Earl of Orford.* London, 1798. 2 vols.

Craik, Henry. *The Life of Jonathan Swift.* London and New York, 1894. 2 vols.

Curtis, Edmund. *A History of Ireland.* London, 1957.

Curtis, Edmund, and R. S. McDowell, eds. *Irish Historical Documents, 1172-1922.* London, 1943.

Davies, Godfrey. "Swift's *The Story of the Injured Lady,*" *Huntington Library Quarterly,* VI (1943), 473-489.

Davis, Herbert. "The Canon of Swift," *English Institute Annual, 1942.* New York, 1943.

[Anon.]. *A Defense of the Conduct of the People of Ireland, in Their Unanimous Refusal of Mr Wood's Copper-Money.* Dublin, 1724.

Delany, Patrick. *Observations upon Lord Orrery's Remarks on the Life and Writings of Dr. Jonathan Swift.* London, 1754.

——. *The Tribune.* London, 1729.

Dobbs, Arthur. *An Essay on the Trade and Improvement of Ireland.* Dublin, 1729-31.

Dunlop, Robert. *Ireland from the Earliest Times to the Present Day.* Oxford, 1922.

——. "Ireland in the Eighteenth Century," *The Cambridge Modern History* (Vol. VI). New York, 1925.

Ehrenpreis, Irvin, ed. *An Enquiry into the Behavior of the Queen's Last Ministry.* Bloomington, Ind., 1956.

Ehrenpreis, Irvin, and James L. Clifford. "Swiftiana in Rylands English MS. 659 and Related Documents," *Bulletin of the John Rylands Library,* XXXVII (1955), 368-392.

Ewald, William B. *The Masks of Jonathan Swift.* Cambridge, Mass., 1954.

Ferguson, Oliver W. "Jonathan Swift, Freeman of Dublin," *Modern Language Notes,* LXXI (1956), 405-409.

Forster, John. *The Life of Jonathan Swift.* London, 1875.

Froude, James A. *The English in Ireland in the Eighteenth Century.* London, 1906. 3 vols.

Goodwin, A. "Wood's Halfpence," *The English Historical Review,* LI (1936), 647-674.

Hall, F. G. *The Bank of Ireland, 1783-1946.* Dublin, 1949.

Hawkesworth, John, ed. *The Works of Jonathan Swift* (Vol. I). London, 1776-79.

Hely-Hutchinson, John. *The Commercial Restraints of Ireland.* Dublin, 1779.

[Anon.]. *Hibernia's Passive Obedience.* Dublin, 1720.

Irish Newspapers. Microfilms of Irish newspapers prior to 1750 in Dublin libraries. Prepared by the National Library of Ireland; released by University Microfilms, Ann Arbor, Mich., 1950.

Johnson, Maurice. "Swift and 'The Greatest Epitaph in History,'" *Publications of the Modern Language Association,* LXVIII (1953), 814-827.

The Journals of the House of Commons of the Kingdom of Ireland. Second Edition. Dublin, 1763.

Journals of the House of Lords of Ireland. Dublin, 1783.

Kearney, H. F. "The Political Background to English Mercantilism, 1695-1700," *The Economic History Review* (Second Series), XI (1959), 484-496.

Kendrick, Roger. *A Letter to the Reverend Dr. Swift Dean of St. Patrick's Dublin; Relating to the Present State of the Manufactures of Ireland.* Dublin, 1721.

King, Sir Charles Simeon, ed. *A Great Archbishop of Dublin.* London, New York, and Bombay, 1906.

Landa, Louis A. *"A Modest Proposal* and Populousness," *Modern Philology,* XL (1942), 161-170.

———. *Swift and the Church of Ireland.* Oxford, 1954.

———. "Swift's Economic Views and Mercantilism," *Journal of English Literary History,* X (1943), 310-335.

Lawlor, Hugh J. *The Fasti of St. Patrick's.* Dundalk, Ireland, 1930.

Lecky, W. E. H. *A History of Ireland in the Eighteenth Century.* London, 1892. 5 vols.

[Anon.]. *A Letter from a Member of the House of Commons of Ireland. To a Gentleman of the Long Robe in G-B: Containing an Answer to Some Objections Made Against the Judicatory Power of the Parliament of Ireland.* Dublin, 1720.

[Anon.]. *A Second Letter to a Gentleman of the Long Robe in G-B: Wherein Some of the Late Illegal Proceedings of the Barons of the Exchequer in the Kingdom of Ireland Are Set Forth.* Dublin, 1720.

[Anon.]. *A Letter to the Gentlemen of the Landed Interest in Ireland, Relating to a Bank.* Dublin, 1721.

[Locke, John]. *Some Familiar Letters Between Mr. Locke, and Several of His Friends.* London, 1708.

Longfield, M. "The Tenure of Land in Ireland," *Systems of Land Tenure in Various Countries,* ed. J. W. Probyn. London, 1881.

"M. B. Draper." *A Letter to the People of Ireland.* Dublin, 1729.

[Macaulay, Alexander]. *Some Thoughts on the Tillage of Ireland.* Dublin, 1738.

Maculla, James. *A Coinage or Mint, Proposed.* Dublin, 1728.

———. *Ireland's Consternation in the Loosing of Two Hundred Thousand Pound of their Gold and Silver for Brass Money.* Dublin, 1723.

———. *A New Scheme Proposed to the People of Ireland: For Increasing the Cash of this Kingdom, by Making Promissory Notes of Copper.* Dublin, 1728-29.

McCue, Daniel L., Jr. "A Newly Discovered Broadsheet of Swift's *Last Speech and Dying Words of Ebenezor Elliston,*" *Harvard Library Bulletin,* XIII (1959), 362-368.

McIlwain, Charles. *The American Revolution.* New York, 1923.

Mant, Richard. *History of the Church of Ireland.* Second Edition. London, 1841. 2 vols.

Mason, William Monck. *The History and Antiquities of the Collegiate and Cathedral Church of St. Patrick.* Dublin, 1820.

[Molesworth, Robert, Viscount]. *Some Considerations for the Promoting of Agriculture and Employing the Poor.* Dublin, 1723.

Molyneux, William. *The Case of Ireland's Being Bound by Acts of Parliament in England, Stated.* Dublin, 1698.

The Monthly Chronicle for the Year MDCCXXIX. London, 1730.

Murray, Alice E. *A History of the Commercial and Financial Relations Between England and Ireland from the Period of the Restoration.* London, 1903.

Murry, John Middleton. *Jonathan Swift.* London, 1954.

Neal, Daniel. *History of New-England.* London, 1720. 2 vols.

Newenham, Thomas. *A View of the Natural, Political, and Commercial Circumstances of Ireland.* London, 1809.

Nichols, John, ed. *Letters on Various Subjects, Literary, Political, and Ecclesiastical.* London, 1809.

Nicolson, Marjorie, and Nora M. Mohler. "The Scientific Background of Swift's 'Voyage to Laputa,'" *Annals of Science,* II (1937), 299-334.

O'Brien, George. *The Economic History of Ireland in the Eighteenth Century.* Dublin and London, 1918.

O'Flanagan, J. Roderick. *The Lives of the Lord Chancellors and Keepers of the Great Seal of Ireland.* London, 1870. 2 vols.

Petty, William. *The Economic Writings of Sir William Petty,* ed. Charles Henry Hull. Cambridge, 1899. 2 vols.

Plumb, J. H. *Sir Robert Walpole.* Cambridge, Mass., 1956-61. 2 vols.

[Anon.]. *Poem on the Dean of St. Patrick's Birth-Day, Nov. 30th Being St. Andrew's-Day.* Dublin, 1726.

Pons, Émile. *Swift: les années de jeunesse et le 'Conte du tonneau.'* Strasbourg, 1925.

Prior, Thomas. *A List of the Absentees of Ireland, and the Yearly Value of Their Estates and Incomes Spent Abroad. With Observations on the Present Trade and Condition of that Kingdom.* Dublin, 1729.

Robbins, Caroline. *The Eighteenth-Century Commonwealthman.* Cambridge, Mass., 1959.

The Rothschild Library: A Catalogue of the Collection of Eighteenth-Century Printed Books and Manuscripts Formed by Lord Rothschild. Privately Printed, Cambridge, 1954. 2 vols.

Rowley, Hercules. *An Answer to a Book, Intitl'd Reasons Offer'd for Erecting a Bank in Ireland.* Dublin, 1721.

[Anon.]. *Several Speeches in the House of Commons in England, For and Against the Bill for the Better Securing the Dependency of the Kingdom of Ireland, on the Crown of Great Britain.* Dublin, 1720.

Sherburn, George, ed. *The Correspondence of Alexander Pope.* Oxford, 1956. 5 vols.

Sheridan, Thomas. *The Life of the Rev. Dr. Jonathan Swift.* London, 1784.

[Sheridan, Thomas, and Jonathan Swift]. *The Intelligencer.* London, 1730.

Simms, J. G. *The Williamite Confiscation in Ireland, 1690-1703.* London, 1956.

Smedley, Jonathan. *Gulliveriana: Or a Fourth Volume of Miscellanies.* London, 1728.

The Statutes at Large (Great Britain). Cambridge, 1762-1807.

The Statutes at Large (Ireland). Dublin, 1765-82.

Stokes, G. T. *Some Worthies of the Irish Church,* ed. H. J. Lawlor. London, 1900.

Swift, Deane. *An Essay upon the Life, Writings, and Character of Dr. Jonathan Swift.* London, 1755.

Teerink, Herman. *A Bibliography of the Writings in Prose and Verse of Jonathan Swift, D.D.* The Hague, 1937.

Temple, Sir William. "An Essay upon the Advancement of Trade in Ireland," *Miscellanea.* Second Edition. London, 1681.

[Toland, John]. *An Act for the Better Securing the Dependency of Ireland. To Which Is Added, J[ohn] T[oland], Esq; His Reasons Why the Bill . . . Should Not Pass.* Dublin, 1720.

[Toland, John]. *A Collection of Several Pieces of Mr. John Toland. . . . With Some Memoirs of his Life and Writings.* London, 1726. 2 vols.

Trevelyan, G. M. *England Under Queen Anne.* London, 1936. 3 vols.

Wagner, H. R. *Irish Economics: 1700-1783. A Bibliography with Notes.* London, 1907.

Williams, Basil. *The Whig Supremacy, 1714-1760.* Oxford, 1939.

Williams, Harold. *Dean Swift's Library.* Cambridge, 1932.

————. *The Text of Gulliver's Travels.* Cambridge, 1952.

Wittkowsky, George. "Swift's *Modest Proposal:* The Biography of an Early Georgian Pamphlet," *Journal of the History of Ideas,* IV (1943), 75-104.

[Anon.]. *A Word or Two to the People of Ireland, Concerning the Brass Money that Is, and Shall Be Coin'd by Mr Woods, and Which He Is Endeavouring to Impose upon Us.* Dublin, [1724].